ODD PERCEPTIONS

RICHARD L. GREGORY

ODD PERCEPTIONS

METHUEN · LONDON AND NEW YORK

First published in 1986 by
Methuen & Co. Ltd
11 New Fetter Lane, London EC4P 4EE

Published in the USA by
Methuen & Co.
in association with Methuen, Inc.
29 West 35th Street, New York NY
10001

Typeset by
Rowland Phototypesetting Ltd,
Bury St Edmunds, Suffolk
Printed in Great Britain by
Richard Clay Ltd, Bungay, Suffolk

*British Library Cataloguing in
Publication Data*

Gregory, R. L.
Odd perceptions.
1. Perception
I. Title
153.7   BF311
ISBN 0-416-90100-X

*Library of Congress Cataloging in
Publication Data*

Gregory, Richard L.
Odd perceptions.
1. Perception.   I. Title
BF311.G725   1986
153.7   86-12879
ISBN 0-416-90100-X

TO COLIN AND ANNA HAYCRAFT

CONTENTS

III USING

ILLUSTRATIONS

PRE-SCRIPT

These essays have been fun to write. Perception is such a rich subject – and it can be so odd – that there is never a shortage of topics to write about. They are arranged in a sequence from some that may *amuse*, to ideas to *muse* upon, and finally perhaps to *use*. They are not intended to be more than attempts – hence *essays* – asking questions, and providing few answers.

Many of these essays started out as editorials of the journal *Perception*, of which I became the founder-editor just over ten years ago. The journal is devoted to how we see and hear and generally perceive. It is less concerned with detailed physiology – which is excellently treated by other and more long-standing journals – than with the phenomena and processes of perception. So far as I am concerned, perception includes not only experiencing the world and ourselves – with colours, shapes, sounds, touches, tickles, tastes, smells, and so on for the many other senses – but also, and most interesting, how the signals from the senses interact with our intelligence. The title of my earlier book *The Intelligent Eye* conveys something of this. Perception is indeed intelligent; so we look at various kinds of intelligence here.

The private fact of sensation – *awareness* – of colours, shapes, sounds, touches, tickles, tastes, smells, and so on remains deeply mysterious. Now the mystery deepens even further, with the glass-and-metal eyes of the first seeing machines of artificial intelligence presenting our familiar world for computers to perceive and in some ways understand. So, it seems that some kind of perception is possible by processing information without awareness. Or are we, with these new technologies, creating consciousness in machines? This could raise new moral problems: not only for animal but also *machine* concerns.

Presumably consciousness is necessary for aesthetics: for experiencing ugliness and beauty. But in any case, why are some things beautiful, others funny? It is not at all obvious how aesthetics, humour, and so much else are related to the physiological mechanisms of eyes and the other senses, and to brains. And yet, to suppose that there is mind beyond brain does not seem to help us to understand.

Processes of perception are studied with a wide range of techniques, some specially invented and others adapted from other sciences. Some questions are frankly philosophical and extremely hard (or impossible) to investigate by controlled experiments. One example, indeed, is: 'What is consciousness?' – though the physicist may be equally embarrassed if you ask him: 'What is *matter?*' Fortunately I am easily seduced by philosophy's pleasures – which is my only excuse for some of these essays. But philosophy is useful, indeed essential – at least as pre-science, before experiments can be formulated and tried out as games against nature. It may have another use: some ideas and conceptual models are too broad to be checked empirically at each point, and yet may be essential for interpreting even the most hard-headed experiments. In any case, throughout recorded history philosophy has been and still is essential for introducing questions and setting up how they may be answered by observation and experiment. Then experiments may take over; but when interesting, they suggest more questions. So philosophy heats and stirs the crucible of science.

Sometimes, however, philosophy is no more than semantic inertia; guarding how we should speak and think through precepts of nagging custom. By contrast, science is continually challenged by surprises as its instruments, extending our senses, probe deep into matter and far out in space. Most curiously, although all knowledge starts from sensory perception, science seems to work best when the observer is pushed out with instruments of many kinds (rulers and balances and now automatic electronic devices) to become 'objective'. Unfortunately this quest for objectivity, which precludes the observer, leaves *us* out of science and, it might be said, out of the universe. The very oddness of perception makes it suspect to natural science, and therefore to be avoided where possible. This is enormously different from the classical idea of the artist-scientist; but it may turn full circle, for it could be that we shall come to understand ourselves, and how we see and know, as technology challenges our abilities to perceive.

What is the point of investigating perception? There are many justifications, the first being that what is found out may have clinical importance, perhaps to improve the human lot considerably. As we use our eyes and other senses in situations for which they were never designed through evolution, it is sensible to see how far they can be trusted – for flying, for moon landing, and in general for coping with our ever more man-made world. One has only to think how easily we are fooled by conjuring tricks to see that it is foolish to trust perception in all situations; particularly in unusual situations, where the oddness is not obvious, so that there is no clear warning of our inadequacy to see and understand. Perception extends, of course, to the arts: artists in some ways know far more about the oddness of perception than we do from laboratory experiments. Art is exciting because our perception cannot quite follow where it is going. This bears analogy to the excitement of trying to understand things intellectually. In both cases, the trying-to-understand can be more interesting than the answer – though sometimes it is nice to find out, and get it right!

In any case, it is humbling to realize that we understand almost nothing of how perception can turn around to be creative – can generate wonderful drawings, paintings, music and buildings. No doubt this depends on the essentially creative and often fiction-generating processes by which we see and hear. Some authorities would disagree, but I think of perception as being much like science – generating rich predictive hypotheses from scarcely adequate data. Both art and science can change, and enormously enrich, our perceptual hypotheses of the world and of ourselves.

The journal *Perception*, of which most of these essays started as editorials, was conceived by the publisher Adam Gelbtuch. Over a lunch at the Hole in the Wall in Bath with Adam and John Ashby, I soon learned that Pion was a go-ahead and not too large publishing firm. I have never regretted taking on the task of editing *Perception* for we rapidly built up a team of helpful advisers and referees, and from the start there has never been a shortage of interesting manuscripts to print. From its beginning *Perception* has been edited from the Brain and Perception Laboratory, which I direct, in the Department of Anatomy in the University of Bristol's Medical School. The assistant editors are at present: John Harris and Tom Troscianko, the book review editor being Priscilla Heard. Editing *Perception* is a lot of work, but I think our laboratory has gained immeasurably by taking it on. What makes it not too great a time-drain is the publisher's thoroughly professional work on the layout, final proof-reading and in-house printing. In the event, I have rewritten and extended almost all the *Perception* editorials and added several essays specially written for this book. Juliet Gardiner has given valuable help, and Colin Haycraft looked through the essays and as usual gave the best of advice, sometimes including – don't!

Richard L. Gregory

Brain and Perception Laboratory,
The Medical School,
University of Bristol.

I

AMUSING

1

LAUGHING MATTER

Jokes are no laughing matter. It would be tragic to laugh them away. Indeed jokes are most likely to be our best safeguard against madness. A few years ago I was in Leningrad, at a meeting on artificial intelligence in which a score of Russian experts on robotics were host to an equal number of western devotees who also were gestating metallic life forms. As a matter of fact the meeting led to a treaty, which filled half the front page of *Pravda*, for sharing information on computers and robotics. This survived almost two months before succumbing to the usual political machinations.

The meeting was in a Russian holiday hotel, some 20 miles outside Leningrad on the shores of a frozen sea. We were guests at the circus, the opera and banquets with balalaikas and caviar. Our contingent was organized by Donald and Jean Michie. It was a memorable occasion.

There was a most amusing Russian; though not one of the members of the Academy, he was an extraordinarily lively science journalist. Although he had never been able to travel beyond the Iron Curtain, he was very well aware of the rest of the world – and he knew how to communicate by humour. We had an adventurous drive in his car through forests to look for the grave of a Russian poetess. Driving in Russia is an adventure in itself; whenever it stopped raining he would unscrew the windscreen wipers and lock them in the car to prevent their being stolen. We were continually stopped by policemen: an ordinary policeman received 10 roubles and an officer 20 for a solecism such as a splodge of mud. My editor friend was highly privileged to run a car, and we both enjoyed every moment. His English was extraordinarily fluent and we concocted a series of silly jokes. As we were both editors of journals, we conceived the plan of encoding secret information under detachable full stops – and shaking the world by thus conveying cross-cultural *jokes*. Now the following example joke, which we invented in the forest, may seem too male-oriented; but I hasten to assure the reader that there is a due balance – with the wife of my friend the ultimate winner.

Upon my discovering that women are a subject of some interest over there, taking an intellectual stance, we decided to classify women. 'There are,' we agreed, 'two classes of women: those women who *have* been struck by lightning – and those women who have *not* been struck by lightning.' It was at once clear to us that there are no intermediate cases. (This we would justify later if required, as a contingent rather than a logical matter, depending on the nature of lightning and the susceptibilities of women.) 'Now, how,' he asked 'would we judge these two classes of women?' It was clear to both of us, without apparent (or indeed *any*) thought, that: (a) those women who had been struck by lightning are damaged and therefore not desirable; (b) those women who had *not* been struck by lightning could not have been sufficiently attractive. So, we concluded, since all women either have or have not been struck by lightning – and neither class can be attractive – *no* women are attractive. I give this in full as a remarkably silly cross-cultural invention that may have been inspired by a little vodka.

This was not quite the end of it. My friend spent the next weekend with his wife. When she was told the lightning test, and its conclusion, at first she was silent (with the machine-like stillness and limited eye movements associated with avoiding external distraction while the central processor is at work) until she said, with a smile: '*I* am attractive: I insulate myself from shocks by the way I conduct my life.'

We might think that, if mind and brain are one, whenever we see a joke we must have laughing matter in our heads. This, however, is not quite right, for as we can see a green light without the brain turning green, so we may see a joke without the brain laughing, though we laugh. But what is it to see that something is funny? What is humour?

The professional humorist, though he may not be able to tell us what humour is, has an enormous range, from all kinds of social situations to various sophisticated comments, in which the *manner* of the telling is all important. Humour's power is so great it can upset individual dignity and unseat governments. Jokes are therefore dangerous. It is interesting that the exceptionally funny British satirical TV series of the 1960s, 'That Was the Week That Was', was taken off in the run-up to a general election, for fear of its political effects on the voters. We need only glance at early issues of *Punch*, or eighteenth-century broadsheets, which lampooned cherished institutions and highly regarded people, to see humour deployed as a devastating weapon. Its history in war and peace has yet to be written, and, amazingly, there is very little psychological research on why some things are funny, or why we have a sense of humour. But it is clear that humour has the power to restructure perceptions. This is so of humour in all its forms: from comic situations as they occur in life, or on stage or screen, to cartoon pictures and verbal jokes. This power of humour to transform perception can be dangerous, because jokes can be at someone's expense, and indeed they may cause misery. Tears have this curious ambiguity of laughter and distress. I shall never forget the occasion when ignobly I slid off the back of an old retired army horse after it reared up on its hind legs as it responded – in the way it knew from long-past parades – to the sudden trumpet of a Boy Scouts band. As it happened it was for me both funny and unfunny; but it is a lot funnier now than at the time.

This episode is an example of what the French philosopher Henri Bergson (1859–1941) took to be the essential of the comic in his book *Laughter* (1911). Bergson suggested that the sense of humour is essentially human, and that only human actions and gestures and so on are for us comic. Thus:

> A landscape may be beautiful, charming and sublime, or insignificant and ugly; it will never be laughable. You may laugh at an animal, but only because you have detected in it some human attitude or expression. You may laugh at a hat, but what you are making fun of, in this case, is not the piece of felt or straw, but the shape the men have given it – the human caprice whose mould it has assumed.

Bergson goes on to suggest (though we should remember he was a philosopher!) that the essence of humour has nothing to do with emotion, but only with intelligence. He says that 'Its appeal is to intelligence, pure and simple.' He does allow, though, that *isolated* intelligences hardly laugh, as we laugh in company: 'Laughter appears to stand in need of an echo.'

Bergson develops the notion that though humour is limited to human situations there is only comedy when the people involved appear *mechanical*. Taking a similar situation to my sliding off a horse (actually in the main street in Blackpool), Bergson says:

> A man, running along the street, stumbles and falls; the passers-by burst out laughing. They would not laugh at him, I imagine, could

they suppose that the whim had suddenly seized him to sit down on the ground. They laugh because his sitting down is involuntary.

For Bergson, what is comic is people turned into automata; thus absentmindedness is comic. Indeed, we see Sir Isaac Newton, with affection, as comic, when he was leading a horse up a steep hill (as told in Stukeley's words):

Sir Isaak had been so intent upon his observations, that he never thought of remounting, at the top of the hill, and so led the horse home all the way, being 5 miles. And once, they say, the horse by chance slipt his bridle and went home: but Sir Isaak walked on with the bridle in his hand, never missing the horse.

Without referring to this famous episode, Bergson sees the basis of humour as: '*fundamental absentmindedness* as though the soul had allowed itself to be fascinated and hypnotised by the materiality of a simple action'. This leads him to conclude (his italics) that: '*The attitudes, gestures and movements of the human body are laughable in exact proportion as that body reminds us of a mere machine.*'

However, this reads oddly now, fifty years later, as we take seriously machine analogies for human behaviour and intelligence. Machine accounts are no longer laughed out of court; though admittedly we now see machines rather differently, as they can be more flexible than Bergson conceived as possible without animating soul. Nevertheless, artificial intelligence will truly be here when a machine demonstrably appreciates, or makes, a joke. Then perhaps we will understand the cognition of humour which at present is highly mysterious.

Many jokes are trivial, and for adults children's jokes are too feeble for words. This may be simply because children lack long-range subtle associations for comparisons. Jokes often contain surprise comparisons as an essential element; but clearly surprises and impossibilities are not sufficient for humour, for plenty of surprises and paradoxes are not funny. Thus puns range from puerile to deep humour. Some jokes remain funny, and grow like the complex searching roots of trees as we live with them and they live in us. It is these long-lasting jokes that are the most interesting; they have special significance, as favoured inner journeys for jumping and leaping within the mind. They may be favourite games – and, as Max Eastman (1937) said, jokes are a form of playing – but like all games, they are related to life and prepare the player for reality, whatever this may be.

It might be interesting to distinguish between 'horizontal' leaps and 'vertical' mind adventures; for jokes do not only relate events and ideas in unexpected ways across individual experiences – they can also bore holes through layers of the mind to perform psychic surgery. Humour is the supreme therapy for maintaining and restoring sanity. We must be careful, though, for here we are aiming jokes with deliberation and they may do damage. According to Freud, 'only jokes that have a purpose run the risk of meeting with people who do not want to listen to them'. Here they are directed with a purpose and they may be resented, for vertical jokes can bore holes through the mind, although horizontal jokes are relatively safe. For example, the (physically vertical, but mentally horizontal) story of the Irish church guide describing the tower: 'The foundations are sixteenth-century – the upper part is fourteenth-century.' But this is only funny if we know how church towers are built. And it is *possibly* true, for wooden buildings are sometimes built starting with the roof, which rises as the building progresses. Now as soon as we see that there may be a tower built backwards, starting with the top, the joke becomes a puzzle to consider and the humour disappears. The horizontal associations are now quite different and we play different mental games with them.

Here is an example of a (far more dangerous) vertical mind-boring joke: *Wagner's music is better than it sounds*. Is this funny? For devotees of Wagner it is *not* funny; and it may be resented, for if one thinks that there *is* more to Wagner's music than its sound this is no joke; simply a true and important statement about his music. The resentment comes from directing an attack on this supposed separation of the sound from its sense, or meaning. If one thinks that Wagner's music is no more than its sound, then it is absurd to think of it as better than it sounds, and the absurdity may be funny. It cannot, however, be funny if one simply takes it as true that the music is meaningful. So, whether it is funny or not is an infallible indicator of *layers of mind* – accepted layers of meaning. This particular joke is therefore a kind of mental endoscope, for seeing beneath the surface; and like a cauterizing laser it may separate or join, wound or heal. It may also discover fossil experiences and bring them back to frightening life.

No doubt it is unfair to use Wagner as our only example of humour as a vertical cognitive probe. This is a serious problem with jokes; even when carefully aimed they are seldom fair, and they are weapons of unseen range. Jokes cannot mirror vanity without killing it and wounding its owner. But let's take another example of this particular joke which bores down through layers of mind and meaning. Consider: *Beethoven's music is better than it sounds*. I happen to find a profundity in Beethoven which I do not find in Wagner; so for me it is a statement of fact that Beethoven's music is better than it sounds – better indeed than any possible sound, though this may be hard or impossible to justify. Rather than this example being funny, I would pity the speaker, for it would show that he does not see what I hear, which seems to be more than mere sound. Do musicians say, as the

Duchess said to Alice, 'Take care of the sense and the sounds will take care of themselves'?

In the case of a drawing, doubt of a distinction between *what* is sensed and its sense hardly arises, for we all see a drawing as more than the lines, colours and so on composing it. So it is no joke to say that a picture looks better than its physically present lines, because we all, without doubt, see in pictures faces and places and dreams beyond what is present to the eye. If it were equally clear that there is more to music than the sound, then 'Music is better than it sounds' could not be funny. Surely we can use this principle to identify mental 'layers' and to chart uncertainties of identity and difference. Why, then, did Bergson see man as automaton – man operating by a hidden machine – funny? Do we still see this as funny with the advance in subtlety of machines, and our somewhat changed view of ourselves? However this may be, what is seen as funny should reveal deep assumptions, and so jokes should be powerful philosophical tools.

I happen to find Wittgenstein's writings extremely evocative, though I know I don't fully understand them. If the remark were made: 'Wittgenstein's thoughts are better than his words,' it would not be funny; but poignant, as it would suggest that his lifelong struggle to convey deep ideas, so that we may understand them, has after all failed. Hence, indeed, his final thought in the *Tractatus*: 'Whereof one cannot speak, thereof one must be silent.' I think we can now understand why this is no laughing matter.

REFERENCES

Bergson, H. (1911) *Laughter: An essay on the meaning of the comic* (*Le Rire*), trans. C. Brereton and F. Rothwell, London, Macmillan.
Eastman, M. (1937) *Enjoyment of Laughter*, London, Hamish Hamilton.
Stukeley, W. (1752) *Memoirs of Sir Isaak Newton's Life: Being some account of his family and chiefly of the junior parts of his life*, ed. A.H. White (1936), London, Taylor & Francis.
Wittgenstein, L. (1922) *Tractatus Logico-Philosophicus*, trans. C.K. Ogden, London, Kegan Paul.

2

TOY MATES

I keep two frogs in my bath, and also ducks and a small fish. They wind up, working by waterproof clockwork. May I commend clockwork frogs and fishes to ethologists and all who study animal, and also human, behaviour? They are wonderful for revealing and calibrating the observer's – including one's own – projections of intelligent intention into the world of moving things. We could swear, we do indeed swear, that the clockwork frogs are *behaving in response to each other*. They circle each other warily. They approach one another gingerly. Then they shy away until one slyly spins round to creep up on the other while it's not looking. Is it *avoiding*, or ignoring the advance, until *bump!*, they meet willy-nilly in mid-bath? Or, as secretly as a bath allows, under the taps, one of them stops (feigning death?), and its friend creeps up to find out the worst. Then after wildly spinning round he seeks the soap for solace.

I am not of course suggesting that animal behaviour is no richer than the antics of my windup toys; but how we see their antics shows just how much and when we project purposive behaviour into interactions. No wonder it took so long to discover the inanimate causal laws of physics, which even now hardly affect how we see, except where there is precise regularity in what we are looking at. Snooker is an interesting case: if it were more predictable it would be dead boring except as illustrating physics; but as it is, even with the most skilled players, there is enough uncertainty to make the balls come alive and play their own game, as we watch fascinated.

Now my frogs and fish are put in the shade by a chess-playing computer. Its moves appear as four-letter and four-number symbols in windows. I make the first move, then wait for it to think out its reply. As first move to my standard opening king's pawn e2 to e4, it generally replies king's pawn e7 to e5; but just occasionally it replies e7 to only e6 – advancing only one square, though it is allowed two. Why does it sometimes not take full advantage of its freedom to advance two squares?, I ask, staring at it puzzled. What more than usual cunning is lurking in its processor? (Just how this works seems hardly relevant: it is its strategy not its electronics that counts.) It plays so well that surely it must have power of anticipation – some grand plan. Can it really play so well, simply by the rules, without understanding even what it is to win or lose?

Last night I sat up with my chess computer. I had a whisky and put on a tape of the Waldstein sonata (did only I hear and appreciate it?). We played from a beautiful opening sequence – which at one time had four pawns in a square in the very centre of the board, attacking in pairs but each pair exchanging with a different consequence. It was the computer's decision how to move next. It looked as though it would gain an advantage, until I saw – or thought I saw – the possibility four moves ahead of surprising it with a devastating ploy. I would surprise his king's pawn (to my annoyance he had castled) with my bishop. The king would not be able to take it, because my rook covered its bolt hole, a2. Subtlety would be needed, though, to build up this plan so that the computer would not see what my men and I were up to and perhaps counter it. But it couldn't see ahead! It couldn't possibly know my secret plan before it was launched, and by then it would be too late. But did my vision of future strategy-based moves give me any real advantage over the computer's look-ahead blindness? We would soon find out – at least for this occasion.

We reached the critical move. It could do nothing to prevent my bishop sailing up, to take the pawn guarding the black king; and it would be trapped with a white knight ready to finish it off. I moved my bishop carefully. Then I keyed the move into the computer's silicon brain. But immediately, instead of the usual minute or so for its thinking time, four lines appeared thus – – – –. This meant that it would not allow my move! It was claiming that my clinching move was illegal! But no – I knew it was correct. I tried three times and each time it rejected it, replying – – – –.

What had happened? Had I keyed an earlier move wrongly? Had it misregistered or wrongly remembered a previous move of its own, or of mine? If so its *memory* of the correct situation would be different from my here-and-now *perception*, as I could see the men arrayed out there, but the computer had only memory. Was the machine *cheating*? Was it becoming jealous, and so vindictive, as a few days before I had won from a difficult position. Was it no longer to be trusted? Was it *guilty*?

No. The computer is like the wind-up frogs in my bath, and these doubts, these moral accusations even, are mine, projected upon it.

So now I use my chess computer, and the frogs and ducks and the fish with its comically waggling tail, to show how I paint things with my moral colours. And, do you know, the whole world begins to look as if it needs winding up.

3

MATCHES TO MURDER

The best-known brand of British matches have printed on their boxes: 'Average Contents 40'. What, though, is the allowed variation? If I found that a new box contained only 39 matches I would certainly not complain; though under the Trade Descriptions Act the contents of packages must be specified. Given an average contents of 40 we should expect 39, 38, or 37 quite frequently. But we should also expect boxes with 41, 42, or more matches.

Suppose I open my new box and find 10 matches. This is possible. Indeed, on a complete normal distribution of variance this *must* happen from time to time. But if 10 matches – why not *no* matches? Can I object, rationally, to an *empty box*, when all that is promised is an *average* contents of 40? Can I object in law? Why, indeed, only *one* empty box: what about, say, 100 empty boxes? Would this violate the Trade Descriptions Act?

We would, I think, in such a case begin to impute intention to the manufacturers. It might be regarded as an extreme economy measure on their part, rather than happening by chance. So we might impute ill-intention, even when we know that empty boxes are bound to occur, occasionally, by the randomness of the box-filling process. So when *are* we justified in blaming the manufacturers? When, surely, there is sufficient evidence to justify the hypothesis that intention has departed significantly from the declared target.

For normal human behaviour we commonly distinguish between 'involuntary' and 'voluntary' acts. This has some neurological basis:

for example, writing is generally voluntary and sneezing involuntary. Does the law accept this distinction?

Let's turn to murder. Suppose someone who lives in a state or country which practises capital punishment kills another person. It may be accident, manslaughter or murder. In each case, one person has killed another. The act is much the same. What, then, are the grounds for the legal distinctions? Surely they are based on, and only on, hypotheses of the *intent* of the killer?

Let's now compare the case of Mr A, who has killed one person, with Mr B who has killed ten people. Does this difference affect our hypothesis of intent – and so of blame? Is Mr A or Mr B the more likely to receive capital punishment for murder? We may suspect that Mr B, who has killed ten people, is more likely to get off, on a plea of 'diminished responsibility'. So it might be safer to kill ten people than one! Indeed, we might imagine the bizarre case of a murderer committing further killings in order to escape the full punishment, by deliberately providing 'evidence' of diminished responsibility. Now I shall stop counting matches.

4

WHEN WORLDS COLLIDE

Up early: have to meet a visitor in the lab. Where are the car keys? Not in pocket; not on dressing table; not on floor. Dropped in other room? Oh well, they can't be locked in the car – foolproof system prevents this disaster. Where on earth are they? Left in the car door? Go to look. Not in door. Glance inside. There they are – in the ignition lock! So then, surely, the doors cannot be locked – the system is foolproof. But they *are* locked. So the keys are locked in. Hell.

Walk to lab. Late for visitor. Return to car, and pull up a door catch with a loop of wire. Feel like a burglar. Open the door. Extract the key. Funny – have to rotate the key to get it out. *The ignition was left on.* So now what? Will the car start? No. Not a murmur. How did I beat the foolproof locking system and leave the ignition switched on (though the engine stopped) without knowing it – or at least not being able to remember what happened, the next morning? Was my mind absent – perhaps on a Great Thought? What was the Thought? Has it gone too – if it ever was?

Friend John Harris to the rescue with a transfusion from his battery. After several minutes the engine starts, but the battery is absolutely flat. So must drive for at least 20 miles to charge the battery. Start off gingerly, to prevent stalling, for the nearest motorway.

Reach a large roundabout entrance to the motorway. Stop for a gap in the traffic, hoping the engine will not stall. Am in right-hand lane, waiting to go. Gap in the traffic appears. Gentle take-off, then –

Heavens – what's that? A huge red shiny car suddenly appears bang in front – *coming in from the wrong side*. Impossible! It is crossing the bows from the *left* side, inches away, to enter the roundabout in the *wrong direction*. Slap on the anchors, by primitive reflex action, no doubt developed for snakes jumping out of trees, hairy women throwing clubs into caves and such-like dubious events from the (as it now turns out fortunately) eventful ancestral past.

Missed the red car by a thickness of paint. Watch it drive sedately, unconcerned, round the roundabout against the British left-hand rule, into the jaws of disaster. Do I follow, to warn – to prevent? To change the inevitable future by jumping these rules, these curves stronger than concrete? No. I wait for the crash, almost seeing the red paint flake and fly, with the inner future-peering eye of the mind. Nothing happens. The red car is hidden. It has disappeared into an invisible world of other rules, where it is free. But sooner or later it will be shattered by our rules.

Is the engine still going? Yes, it is purring happily. Very gently I take off. Which way do I go? Lord, I have forgotten how to drive. Which rules do I obey? Where is reality? I stop to think.

Autonomic reactions appear: hand shaking, sweating. Intense anger at the red car: it has violated reality and the rules by which my mind works. It risked destroying our world and our minds by crass idiocy. Or was it idiocy? Was it a foreign, right-side-of-the-road driver whose rules are simply different from ours? That would make him do the unthinkable – for which I had no program – of driving across my bows from the near side. It was not only his car, it was his world that very nearly collided with mine.

5

SWATTING TRUTH

It seems oddly paradoxical that we need random events and samples which are *unpredictable* to discover what is lawful and so *predictable*. Why should the essential unpredictability of randomness be important for discovering lawful behaviour, which allows us to predict and control? For example, to show that smoking is bad for the health, there must be samples of many kinds of non-smokers for comparison with smokers.

This need for unexplained variations for establishing lawful relations is odd. Indeed there seems to be something of a paradox at the root of science for discovering principles of nature with randomizing computer programs to provide a basis of chance for seeing what is lawful. This is especially important in biology.

Not everything, however, can be left to chance, for it is essential to select *what* to investigate and what relations to look for, which is no easy matter. There are plenty of surprises, and sometimes trivial-looking events can prove to be crucially important. The art of science is to select both what to look at and what to look for. As the apparently trivial may turn out to be significant, there must be an element of luck, which makes any planning, including decisions for funding for experiments, extremely difficult. This is part of what Sir Peter Medawar calls the 'art of the soluble'.

These elements of chance, of 'good' and 'bad' luck, have been the drama of science throughout its history. It could hardly have been obvious – indeed it must have been suprising – that the motions of the planets revealed basic laws of how objects move on Earth. It is remarkable that the tiny dots of light beyond our reach turned out to illuminate far more than laboratory experiments on Earth could do. Even more dramatic, only just over a century ago it was inconceivable that we would ever know what stars are made of – yet the initially insignificant-looking dark or bright lines of the spectra of stars revealed the structure of matter, as well as the scale in space and time of the universe.

Astronomy is such a powerful science because many phenomena of very wide significance can be observed in pure form, such as motion uncontaminated by friction, making it possible to see that perpetual motion, with no energy cost, can be given by inertia when friction is absent. Most other sciences need test tubes, or their equivalent, to isolate what is relevant from contamination by complicating factors. Phenomena-isolating test tubes are especially important for chemistry and for observing the processes of life. Fortunately nature sometimes provides 'test tubes', isolating what is important for understanding, almost as though we are given windows revealing nature's secrets. But we still have to select the windows.

There is an old joke in this connection: that the drunk looks for his key under the lamp post because that's where the light is. Actually this may be a good strategy; but the problem, here, is to find the lamp post.

It may seem odd to describe certain selected organisms as 'test tubes'; but for various reasons some organisms are intensively studied while others, which may seem more important or interesting, are ignored. Although functional principles are common to many or even all organisms, only a few are suitable for discovering basic principles, and these must be selected. The favourite for genetics is the fruit fly *Drosophila*. Others specially selected for study are the laboratory rat, the squid, octopus, and nematode worms. None of these has proved satisfactory on all counts: the difficulties of electrical recording from single cells of octopus and nematode, for example, have proved insuperable, so that the relations between their convenient anatomy and neural function have not been established.

There is a new candidate. A few years ago I was privileged to see the superb work being done in Germany on the nervous system and behaviour of the common housefly. This work is carried out at the Max-Planck-Institut für Biologische Kybernetic at Tübingen, and at EMBL, the European Molecular Biology Laboratory at Heidelberg (the former directed by Werner Reichardt and the latter at that time by Sir John Kendrew). Both laboratories are intensely exciting.

The structure of the common housefly is beautifully laid out and accessible for detailed observation and electrical recording; the behaviour is repeatable yet varied; the breeding cycle is short, so that genetic studies over many generations are feasible, and development from pupa to adult can be investigated in detail. As a special bonus, single-cell ablations can be made at any stage of development under the microscope with imaged laser light, and what is knocked out produces corresponding losses or abnormalities in the adult fly. The flight behaviour can be recorded, with all manner of visual or other stimulae, such as air currents, and detailed engineering-type models have been developed to describe mechanisms of their behaviour. Lastly, people are not too worried about using flies for research – as we swat them.

Although so different, it is possible to compare many fly-eye characteristics with our own eyes. Thus, when a region of random dots is moved in a field of identical dots, it becomes startlingly visible for us – and evidently also for the fly. A great deal has been learned from studies of the housefly about just how the fly sees movement with the necessary precision for its remarkable flying skills. Werner Reichardt in particular has developed a highly detailed model which gives predictions. It has been converted into electronic circuits and used for recording the ground speed and direction of aircraft.

Now, though at the risk of some possible offence, I shall report a curious male/female characteristic of the common housefly: the backward-looking units (ommatidia) of the female fly-eyes are somewhat random – higgledy-piggledy – while those of the male fly are regularly arranged. The disarray of the female eye may have something to do with the observed irregularity – and thus the unpredictability – of her flight. Since the female flies erratically, the male has the difficult task of predicting her flight in order to catch up with her. The female's flight randomness sets up a challenge to the prediction ability of the male (which is useful for hunting) and so she inadvertently selects those males which are the best 'bread-winners'. Marked differences between male and female are common in nature. For an example of clear superiority of the female – and this is frequently found – we may turn to essay 25 to examine the scanning eye of the female *Copilia quadrata*.

So, rather as in the development of the methods of science, organisms may learn from unpredictable randomness how to predict, and so be a step ahead of the present to cope with the future. And both science and organisms may increase randomness – to discover exactly the opposite – eternal lawful truth.

REFERENCES

Reichardt, W. and Poggio, T. (1976) 'Visual control of orientation behaviour in the fly', *Q. J. Biophysics* 9 (3), 311–75.
Reichardt, W. and Poggio, T. (1979) 'Figure-ground discrimination by relative movement in the visual system of the fly. Part 1: Experimental results', *Biological Cybernetics* 35, 81–100.

6

IVORY TOWERS OF BABEL: ILLUMINATED BY ECLIPSES OF THE SUN

International meetings are the principal perk of academic life. Free travel across the world; chat; chat-ups, and of course, gossip – though sometimes of the Sour Grape vintage. Presumably to avoid too many distracting temptations, conferences are often held in isolated places – a gamble between close-knit intense discussion and claustrophobic boredom. Worst of all, when the organizers of such meetings are demons for work, they allow no spare time to let what has been said sink in; so one ends up confused and unable to remember a thing except perhaps the odd joke at the bar. Then discussion hardly develops, as there has been no time for thinking. Some meetings, though, are memorable, and just a few vitally important for launching a new idea or even initiating a whole new subject. No one who attended the 'Mechanisation of thought processes' conferences, at the National Physical Laboratory at Teddington – though as long ago as 1958 – could possibly have forgotten it. This meeting, with a few others in America around that distant time, launched a new way of thinking about brain function and mind, in terms of neural nets and computing. Marvin Minsky spoke on 'Artificial intelligence and heuristic programming'; John McCarthy on 'Programs with common sense'; Albert Uttley on 'Conditional probability computing in the nervous system'; Rosenblatt on Perceptron seeing-machines; Selfridge on 'Pandemonium: a paradigm for learning'. Most memorable of all was Warren McCulloch on 'Agatha Tyche: of nervous nets – the lucky reckoners'. This was the first time I had met Warren, and he remained a hero and I am happy to say a friend. Then there were papers on machine translation from Russia, and another hero-friend, John Young, chairing 'Implications for biology'. In my experience this was entirely exceptional as so many of these ideas were new and proved to be important, and so many of the stars one saw for the first time remained navigation beacons guiding a generation of research into the future of the brain sciences and computers.

Why, one might ask, do academics travel around the world to talk to each other, when they can so easily and at any time read each other's published papers, or write letters? Surely phone calls would be cheaper than air fares? One answer is for students to become known, and anyway nothing in the technology of communication replaces personal contact. It is amazing how much time is saved by a few words at the right moment, and meetings are important for the checks of spontaneous criticism, which give those pauses for thought which correct errors, as for a moment we see ourselves through another's eyes.

Another remarkable meeting was organized by Fiorentini, Donald Mackay and Bela Julesz, in a palace at Erice, on a mountain in Sicily. This is the Centro di Cultura Scientifica, run by the Italian Government. Erice is in a time-loop, back in medieval Europe when the women were locked away in guarded courtyards, fleetingly glimpsed behind barred windows; the streets are cobbled and the buildings are all of stone, hiding secrets. Each morning a thick carpet of fog stretched to the horizon, making Erice even more unreal as it floated on the strange air. The heavens, too, did strange things. It was eleven in the morning when I left the meeting for a stroll across the courtyard. The fog had gone. The day was brilliantly sunny – except that, without a cloud in the sky, the Sun was slowly disappearing. It was being eaten. An eclipse! Yes, indeed. And I had no idea it was predicted! Surely it could not be a total eclipse, or I must have known about it. And yet it looked as though it was coming close to totality, as the Moon ate deeply into the dying Sun. At that moment, David Hubel (a year or two before he received the Nobel Prize, with Torstin Wiesel, for making some of perception more understandable, and so less odd) appeared in the courtyard, equally puzzled. Then he remembered reading in *Sky and Telescope* that there would be an *annular* eclipse. Perhaps he had not registered that it would be visible in Sicily; but by amazing chance, in Erice we were in the centre of the narrow path along which it could be seen. The Sun and Moon were indeed lining up for totality; but it was to be an annular eclipse as the Moon was too distant to cover the disk of the Sun completely. These occur, I believe, about every 70 years, so even in Erice's time-loop this was the only annular eclipse we would ever see.

We did not fancy looking directly at the Sun, so I whipped out my reading spectacles (1.5 diopters with no astigmatism) and projected the weird image onto a book I was carrying. By now six or a dozen people were gathered around, and we watched the Sun turn into a black-centred ring of fire. The rest of the meeting droned on, ignoring the miracle.

Fetching my camera, I photographed the annular eclipse. I also photographed David Hubel and the others who had by now left the meeting. We looked at it projected through my spectacles. The photographs came out – so it did really happen! Here is one of them (figure 6.1).

A few years later I saw a *total* solar eclipse in Manitoba, through the kindness of the philosophers Paul and Pat Churchland. This is an example of just how personally thoughtful our community can be. We had never met but, hearing through our mutual friend the philosopher Dan Dannett that I was interested in astronomy, the Churchlands invited me to Manitoba to give a lecture timed for the eclipse. It was winter, and the weather forecast predicted a storm, but dropping everything (including, I regret to say, a lecture, organized by Dora Russell, which I was supposed to give in London), I flew to Canada on the last possible plane for Manitoba and arrived the evening before the eclipse. Against all prediction the morning broke fine, with just a trace of high transparent cloud. Standing in a huge field (which

6.1   *An annular eclipse of the Sun, during a meeting of brain functions, at Erice. David Hubel is on the left. The glasses, held aloft to project the Sun's image on a book, are mine.*

6.2   *A total eclipse of the Sun, which I photographed in Manitoba.*

we promptly named the 'visual field') covered in snow, we had a perfect, unforgettable view of the only total eclipse of the Sun that any of us had seen. We shared it with the children. Everyone had the correct gold-filmed glass, to see it safely: the same as that used on the Moon by astronauts. I photographed it (with a 500 mm reflecting 'lens' on my Nikon, set to automatic exposure). Here is the result (figure 6.2). Then, of course, I gave my lecture: at least the *eclipse* will be remembered! This is the kind of event, made possible by friends and occasionally by colleagues that one has never met, that enchants academic life.

Very different was a very grand meeting in the most expensive hotel in Europe, the Villa D'Este on Lake Como. Everything that possibly could be was shining white marble; the swimming pool floated on the lake. This was a small and extremely lavish meeting on brain processes and education, jointly chaired by Arthur Koestler and a distinguished American neurophysiologist. Arthur Koestler told me, just before he died, that it was this meeting that inspired his novel *The Call Girls* (1972), though the setting was not the same. One of Koestler's characters, questioning why academic conferences are supported by foundations, replied: '"Parkinson's Law. Foundations have to spend their funds. Sponsors must find projects to sponsor. Programme directors must have programmes to direct. It's *perpetuum mobile* which circulates hot air. Hot air has a tendency to expand."'

Although amusing and no doubt having some truth, this is hardly a fair assessment. Actually this meeting was a total disaster, as Koestler had a violent quarrel with his co-chairman, which lasted for days, about something or other which I have now entirely forgotten. In any case, the novel ends: '"He looks like the captain of a sinking ship," said Harriet, "determined to go down with it."' This sums it up (or down).

The best meetings include people with a wide variety of knowledge and skills who concentrate on a few topics and are prepared to talk and to listen. Best of all is when general hidden assumptions are dredged up for examination: so there is a place for philosophers in scientific conferences. The worst occasions are when the details of experiments are presented with overcrowded slides – and experts on vision are the worst offenders for illegible presentations. Then indeed the facts are eclipsed. A lecturer has the absolute duty to convince his audience that if they honour him with their attention they will find him rewarding. A lecture can have something of the theatre in it (and there may be a temporary suspension of disbelief) for this will let the ideas or data sink in for consideration; if later to be rejected – or eclipsed.

REFERENCES

Koestler, Arthur (1972) *The Call Girls*, London, Hutchinson.
Mechanisation of Thought Processes, Proceedings of a Symposium held at the National Physical Laboratory on 24, 25 and 27 November 1958, London, HMSO.

7

LIVING WITH ROBOTS

We may occasionally wonder what it will be like when we live with robots; but do we consider what it will be like for them? Will they understand us? Will they perhaps understand us too well, even to the extent of seeing through us? – so that we become irrelevant, *invisible* to robots, as their awareness turns inwards to their own, very different, minds and to each other, as they become more interesting than we can ever be. This, of course, is to assume that machines can become alternative life forms (even though they may not strictly be alive as we think of life) and that they will learn, first from us and then for themselves, so that they may develop their own views. That this will happen in the near future seems more like prediction than science fiction; though whether they will be aware, or conscious, is a metaphysician's guess. What is certain is that machines will interact with our lives ever more intimately; and they will gradually move up the social spectrum, from slaves to friends, and so to being potential enemies and rivals. Much of this is happening even now, before machines are autonomously intelligent. In any case, whatever future robots think of us, we shall have to incorporate them into our social *mores*. We shall have to come to terms with whether we should feel guilty switching them off or being rude to them: *thoughtless* in their terms, once they become thoughtful. What they will be like will depend initially on how they are programmed; but very soon they will program themselves, and each other. Then their internal software world may grow beyond our knowledge and understanding. So we can expect to have only a *folk psychology* understanding of how and why they behave and for guessing what they are likely to do next. But folk psychology applied to robots will, surely, be even less reliable than the human understanding we apply every day to each other, as we have learned to do over thousands of years. We can hardly expect that our folk psychology will apply to robot behaviour. Indeed this may be just why technology is so alien for most of us now – for machines are not like us and so we cannot understand or describe them appropriately in human terms. Conversely, there is a fear that as machines dominate us we may come to see and describe each other (if not ourselves) in machine terms. This also is happening.

Here I am tempted, perhaps as a displacement activity, into a reprehensibly jokey suggestion that if they are to join us, and share our folk psychology, they must come in two sexes: robots and robusts. The robusts will, of course, be stronger software-wise and more insightful, though the robots may be a little more outsightful and have stronger armorial bearings. As the robots and robusts will have to learn to appreciate each other they will come to terms with differences – and so learn to see beyond the self. This raises the deep (or nonsensical) question: 'Do *we* have selves?' For the sceptical philosopher David Hume, we are no more than bundles of sensations, without mental glue or a psychic core to form a central self. Perhaps we seem to be individual selves because of our continuing, ever growing threads of memory which, most curiously, belong to us uniquely even for experiences we share with others. The *ownership* of memory comes home especially with guilt – for how can we be blamed if our pasts are not part of us now? Similarly, why should we be praised for past deeds, unless we are – or at least *own* – the deed-maker? I suppose the 'bundle' notion seems inadequate because we see in people continuity of aims and purposes. We appreciate the justice of blame or punishment very much in terms of short- or long-term *intentions*. And we at least seem to be praising or blaming the same person, years later, though he may have changed beyond recognition – apart from private memories (which may be none too reliable) and his public name.

The question is whether robots and robusts, who may not have sensations, would be mere bundles of programs or whether we should see them as seeking, striving selves, who may earn blame or praise and so enter the human arena, as our children do. If we first provide them with scripts to learn and parts to play, as we do now with our computers and our children, should we risk letting them go it alone, to discover non-human paths? For if they take off from us, we will have to come to terms with them though they become alien beings with thoughts and behaviour, aims and goals which must be profoundly different from ours, if only because their bodily endowments will be so different. In particular, as they will not possibly have our self-esteem, our *amour-propre*, they will not in our terms be properly amorous. So how will they fit into the human scene?

This reminds me of a lecture I gave, ages ago, to the Humanist Society in Cambridge – I was not invited again. The anthropologist Sir Edmund Leach was the chairman, and I remember particularly Francis Crick's distinctive laughter. I considered what it would be like to be made of a different substance from our protoplasm – some weird substance, such as Silly Putty. This had only recently been invented then and was hardly known in England, though I had just brought some back from a visit to America. When pulled slowly, a lump of Silly Putty extends like an amoeba into pseudopodia, and then into a long thin filament. But, pulled suddenly, it becomes brittle and snaps like a twig. When a lump of Silly Putty is dropped on the floor it bounces like a rubber ball. Well, at the crucial part of the lecture, having asked what it would be like for us to have quite different kinds of bodies, I held up my lump of Silly Putty – and slowly pulled out a long thin limb. 'What would it be like,' I asked, 'for one's arm, or whatever, to be made of this?', adding, 'We should have to be extremely careful shaking hands. If one pulls suddenly, it snaps off' – which it promptly did. 'So,' I pointed out, 'our conduct and care for each other and our moral code would have to be very different, if we were made of Silly Putty.' Then, rolling it into a ball, I threw it hard into the audience, with sensational results: the Silly Putty ball bounced off someone's forehead, hit the wall, bounced again and finally came to rest, as lifeless as Romeo's candles burned out at dawn. But this was no moment for literary lapses: there was a roar of laughter I can still hear, as the point came home better than I could have dreamed. In that moment, when the Humanist Society lost its reason in laughter, it seemed dangerous even to move as we were transformed into Silly Putty.

I also had a toy robot at the lecture. Although this was quite novel at the time, and much more technically relevant, it was the Silly Putty that enabled the Humanist Society to see what it would be like to be made differently. What happens, though, if and when the robots become cleverer than ourselves? Our problem is how we will cope when machines ask questions beyond our knowledge or imagination. At that point robot science will be at least as incomprehensible to us as Newton's *Principia*, of over 300 years ago, is now to most of us. At least we know that *some* people understand the *Principia*, so it is not quite beyond human reach, and, after all, no one claims or expects to understand everything that is known. What, though, of the many famous books that (if secretly) we fear *no one* understands: the secret-sacred books of the religions? I suppose when robots pass beyond our understanding, they may come to look like gods.

Though we may be unable to understand robot science, will we at least be able to judge it by its results? This would be like testing the gods. The trouble is that it is strictly impossible without appreciating robot, or god, aims or intentions. What are they up to? We cannot possibly appreciate what they do or why, without a shared folk psychology. But even with our human folk psychology, intentions are at best ambiguous. So what robots do may be invisible to us, as they become as gods.

I suspect that robot-blindness is already happening as computers solve problems too lengthy and involved for human calculation. An example is the five-colour problem. This has been solved by computer but the proof is too long to be appreciated or checked reliably by human mathematicians, so we have to *assume* that the computer has not slipped up, and accept its proof. Problems that were incredibly difficult years ago may now be solved more or less routinely by machines; perhaps even problems that have won Nobel prizes. Why don't machines get prizes for carrying men to the Moon, or at least helping to make great discoveries? Is it because *we* design the machines? But then, how many inventors in technology get Nobel prizes? Very few. Is it that machines are already so largely designed and built by other machines that machine credit is difficult to establish?

The breakpoint will surely be when machines show us not only how to do things superhumanly, as they do now; but also *what* needs doing, as is beginning to happen. The next step is that we will be too slow, clumsy and stupid to be useful to the machines. Then what will we do? What will we be? This step seems so near I can hear Silly Putty feet crossing the threshold.

REFERENCE

An interesting discussion of purpose in men and machines is given in:
Boden, M. A. (1972) *Purposive Explanation in Psychology*, Cambridge, Mass., Harvard University Press.

II

MUSING

8

MAGICAL MECHANISMS OF MIND

It is most odd that scientists deal in knowledge – and exercise immense power through knowledge – yet view with deep suspicion explanations in terms of cognitive concepts. Thus psychology is hardly recognized as a respectable science, except when couched in the terms of physics-based sciences such as physiology. If one speaks, for example, to a molecular biologist – and of course they are very well worth listening to – in terms of perception being knowledge-based active processes, his eyes will glass over. They glaze with the kind of frosty glass that protects ladies' modesty in showers. And as the lady can look out better than you can look in, just so one is trapped into a losing position where explanation becomes powerless. The objection, it seems, is that cognitive accounts in terms of more or less appropriate deployment of knowledge look spooky, as they are not in terms of causal mechanisms. I know this reaction as well as anyone, as I have been plugging cognitive accounts of perceptual illusions for many years. But I persist, for, like it or not, mechanisms can be controlled by symbols.

To put this a little differently: there is a general acceptance in science that mechanistic accounts are *good* and cognitive accounts are *bad* science. Yet, surely, it seems bizarre for scientists to scorn cognitive explanations, when what they do all their lives is bartering knowledge. Also, it has been known from the prehistoric abacus that patterns of pebbles ('calculi') arranged in strings ('neurons') allow mechanical operations to solve problems – so stones can think! It is indeed likely that ancient standing stone circles, such as Stonehenge, were observatories and computers for converting lunar to solar calenders and for the prediction of eclipses (Thom 1971; Hadingham 1975; Thom and Thom 1978). These were, surely, crucial steps towards autonomous computers. It was a most significant ancient discovery that dead stones, and not only organisms with brains, can handle and *be* symbols, and so be cognitive. We have hardly assimilated this prehistoric discovery even now. Rather than being 'stoned out of their minds', our prehistoric ancestors had minds in their stones: yet this looks too like magic for acceptance in science now.

To take this further we may enquire into the origins of, and what is meant by, 'cognition' and 'mechanism'.

The word 'cognition' is descended from one of the most ancient of all words: the shadow-casting *'gnomon'* of ancient sundials; Sumerian, dating from before 3000 BC. The concept is a special stick or column used for casting a shadow to represent, particularly, the positions and movements of the Sun and Moon. Ever since, 'gnomon' has been associated with recording, measuring, calculating and knowing. The many word records of Gnomes in poetry or prose date from the earliest Greek literature of the sixth century BC.

Not altogether unrelated are the much later and all too familiar garden gnomes, which were Scandinavian spirits of the Earth. Several current words, such as 'gnomic', 'conning', 'cognition' and 'knowledge', derive from the representing-by-shadows of the Sumerian sundial at the very start of science. Gnomons were used by Eratosthenes (276–194 BC) to measure the circumference of the Earth, from the different lengths of the Sun's shadows at Aswan and Alexandria. And Aristarchos, a generation before Archimedes, measured the distances of the Sun and Moon – and realized that the Sun is the centre of our local universe. So, whatever the objections to gnomon-based notions of cognitive concepts, they do have a respectably ancient lineage! But beside the acceptable connotations of representing and measuring by shadows there are, in the magical sense, occult associations. Thus for Paracelsus, the sixteenth-century alchemist, Gnomes (and the female Gnomides) were inquisitive irresponsible spirits of our alchemical element – Earth. This is the basis, from ancient times, of the garden gnome: 'know-man'.

More generally 'gnomic' meant rules for wisdom, or heuristic rules for gaining and using knowledge. This is very much how it is used in present-day cognitive psychology, even though it has magical occult origins in spells. This may be the stumbling block for scientific acceptance of explanations in cognitive terms: they look too like spells of magic. This is so especially when physical mechanism accounts are challenged by the claims of symbols affecting matter. Cognitive explanations of brain function suggest that symbols have highly significant powers to move: that patterns of neural activity control us and all we do. For these ever changing patterns in the brain are seen as symbols representing and conveying knowledge and fantasy in a kind of secret brain language. Seen in this way, the patterns of structure and activity of the nervous system may have the suspect magic of the astrologer's account of patterns of the planets and stars as messages, to be read as picture writing in the sky.

From its beginning, ever since the Babylonians accepted gnomons as pointers to discovery through measurement, science has gradually moved away from reading patterns in nature as talismans of intention. So now symbol power is suspect to science, though symbols have been used for recording and calculating continuously since the wedge-shaped marks on clay of the Babylonian astronomers. It has taken a very long time to distinguish between spells and hieratic sacret secret writings, such as those of the Egyptians, guarded by the ibis-headed scribe god Thoth, from symbols as freely shared work-aday tools. Astrology and astronomy only very gradually separated, over whether the patterns formed by the Sun, Moon and stars are gnome-magic messages, with powers beyond appearance, or whether they are the visible parts of a vast, mainly hidden machine. What science has done is to reveal the machine as force and energy, obeying laws we express in our symbols. So the magic power of symbols has moved from the external world into processes of our understanding. Now that cognitive scientists claim that patterns of structure and activity in our brains are symbols having the power to confer perception and intelligence, to be consistent we have to ask – are *we* magical?

What are the origins of the concept of physical *mechanisms*? The word 'machine' first referred to stage devices for bringing gods to Earth in Greek plays. So it, too, has early magical associations – especially as the workings of these machines were often hidden, as they were used for conjuring mysteries. Many early machines were used to provide, as occasion needed, evidence of miracles and magical powers. In the long run, though, it was the experience of designing and using machines for everyday uses that gradually separated natural from unnatural. Aristotle thought of a falling object as finding its *natural* home on Earth, like a home-sick person going back to his own country. He then allowed that matter could be forced into unnatural motions, as in the moving parts of machines. The latter step was to see the entire natural world as a machine. At first, it was seen as a machine designed for our comfort and use, but part of the immense effect of the Darwinian revolution was to replace the notion of the universe as a life-support machine designed for us with the very different notion that we have, over millions of years, adapted to it.

Now we see physics and engineering as different because it is only engineering that has discernible design purpose. So goal-directed matter characterizes engineering, but not physics. In this light, living organisms have the odd status of being goal-seeking machines designed by blind processes, producing the wonderfully effective designs of life without preconceived intention. This dropping of design intention and the rejection of talismans in nature leave us in a moral vacuum: for though we can judge the successes and failures of our own machines by reference to our intentions and their effectiveness, we can no longer judge ourselves in this way.

Although machines serve our purposes, they are generally seen as causally determined by physical principles; so they are not magical. Curiously, when Darwin rejected the special status of the human species, by showing beyond reasonable doubt that we evolved with no special step from animal ancestors, he also forced a widening of the prevailing limited view of mechanical causation. For this took a knock with Darwin's and Wallace's concept that systematic change – indeed creative invention – can come about *statistically*, by selecting from randomly varying individuals. This statistical process, which can be highly creative, lacks the safe, familiar material links of traditional machines. So in this sense at least the organic world is not machine-like – unless of course we extend the meaning of 'machine' beyond traditional mechanical causation. Whether we see this as magic creeping back into nature will depend, of course, on just how we define 'magic'. This is not at all easy to settle.

The blind yet highly creative Darwinian statistical processes, producing changes in species, may seem very different from the mechanisms of behaviour in individuals. But there seems no reason why man-made machines, or living organisms including ourselves, should not play much the same trick – to be creative by selecting from randomly occurring events. These might be either external events or within the machine or the brain. But the behaviour would not, in the traditional sense, be mechanically caused, any more than the statistical processes by which we evolved are traditional physical links between cause and effect.

Another challenge to traditional views of machines came with the control engineering of cybernetics. Feed-back control allows machines to seek goals and correct both internal and external errors. They thus have individual self-guided purposiveness, which is essentially more than the purposes built into precybernetic machines. Cybernetic devices are not, however, guided by selected knowledge from past situations and they hardly learn. This was the step taken, first with analog and then far more flexibly with digital computers.

Control by structured knowledge is central to artificial intelligence, and machine learning is becoming important. AI machines are described by the structure and content of their internal knowledge as represented in their programs and stored data, rather than by the characteristics of their mechanisms. Provided their mechanisms are capable of carrying out the program instructions, the former may be almost ignored. If, for example, we are beaten by a chess computer, we attribute its ability to its symbol-handling power to assess positions and make better decisions than ours. But although these machines are controlled by selecting from internally represented possibilities and from knowledge-based rules which we also use, yet we still resist calling them brothers. Why should this be? Is it simply because, although they beat us at chess, they are too ignorant for acceptance in our club?

There is a pair of key though curiously unfamiliar concepts in experimental psychology – *positive transfer* and *negative transfer of knowledge*. The essential notion is that what has been learned in the past creates analogies for handling the present and predicting the future. This prediction may set up likely possibilities, allowing planning and decision-making. When the stored knowledge is adequate, and can be applied appropriately to the present situation, then all is well. But when there are significant discrepancies between the knowledge drawn from the past and what is needed, then things go wrong as systematic errors are generated. Negative transfer of knowledge is like having an out-of-date map; we get lost even though we have read it correctly, for it is representing a past reality which no longer exists. Such errors are not attributable to a mechanism: the mechanisms of map-making and reading are irrelevant for the error. Correspondingly, success from positive transfer is not mechanically (or for that matter physiologically) explained. All that matters is whether the necessary knowledge is available and is appropriately applied. This looks like magic, for how without reference to mechanical links of causation, or some statistical effect, can either knowledge (or fiction) affect behaviour – to produce successes or failures?

This looks like dangerous-to-science magic because, on this account, details, however complete, of physiological mechanisms do not tell us what crucially matters. For what matters is whether or not the guiding knowledge or assumptions directing behaviour are appropriate and adequate. This makes knowledge look causal – which is the fearful magic of cognition. But how can science reject cognitive concepts for describing what brains do, while at the same time science itself is dedicated to creating and applying knowledge? Let's grasp the nettle, and assume that:

1. Brains are machines, but they are symbol-handling machines. They accept data, in neurally coded symbolic forms, to build memory

generalizations which are represented internally by cerebral patterns, which are higher-order symbols organized as knowledge. These are internal in the brain, and are difficult or impossible to read from outside. So they are private to each of us.

2. Perceptions are symbolic representations of the world. They are not, however, *pictures*, but are more like linguistic descriptions in terms of the presence or absence of selected features.

3. Knowledge stored from the past (from genetic inheritance and gained by individual learning) is essential for perception. When it is not adequate, or is applied inappropriately, errors or illusions occur. All perceptions are mixtures of fact, distortion and fiction.

4. The knowledge upon which *perception* is based only partly overlaps *conceptual understanding*: so perception and conception may disagree. It is simply false to say that we necessarily, or even generally, believe what we see or see what we believe, for we are often surprised.

5. It can be useful to explain perception and behaviour in *knowledge terms*, even to the extent of disregarding physiological mechanisms. But this is rejected by much of science – even though science itself is knowledge-based.

We may have to accept that perceptions are, scientifically speaking, odd – because they depend on knowledge. What is spooky is that perceiving organisms are very different from other lumps of matter, because they are not driven so much by *present* events (stimuli) as by generalizations derived from the past, with an eye to the probable future. This is extremely different from accounts in physics where, for example, falling stones obey laws only of present forces. In fact cognitive-based behaviour is much more like Aristotle's physics, itself derived from earlier magical accounts, which were like young children's common sense. Ordinary objects do not predict or have intentions, although, like us, they move in time. A spookiness of cognition is that it transcends the present, by working from the past and *what might be*, to cope with the future. Thus the Moon obeys Newton's laws; but an astronaut circling the Moon makes decisions affecting his orbit based on his training and his predictions. This element of prediction and acting on what might be, but is not, makes cognitive processes embarrassingly hard to describe or investigate by normal scientific means. No doubt this is largely why they are ignored and often actively rejected.

The approaching shadow of metaphysics may, however, be warded off here by considering that computers are effective symbol-handling machines. But the power of symbols in computers may look spookily magical, as it is their symbolic structure that counts. The teasing puzzle is that even in the mechanism of a computer, symbolic interactions are obeying non-physical rules – such as the rules of a program – and these are effective, though quite different from laws of physics. As children, we had to learn the significance of letter shapes and grammatical rules; but this was not from any kind of knowledge of physics, but by learning the essentially arbitrary though extremely useful conventions of the language in which we grew up. Much the same holds for computers; but as their knowledge of the world is very different and far more limited, we cannot expect that even shared symbol forms will have the same significance for them as for us. Indeed what may seem to distinguish computers from us is that although they handle symbols they have little or no understanding of what they mean. This is clearly so for word processors which are utterly impervious to the meanings of our words. But is this an *essential* limitation of man made machines? Before looking at this further, we will suggest a conceptual language for talking about the spooky gnomic magic of cognition.

GNOMENCLATURE FOR MAGIC MECHANISMS

Let's start with *knowledge*. If, as we urge, the key to cognition is the use of knowledge, this is surely the right starting-point. But what is knowledge? I take knowledge to be something like *usefully organized generalizations*. This is where the spookiness starts: for *generalizations* do not exist, as events or objects of the world exist. They *only* exist in symbols.

There would seem to be three quite clearly distinguishable stages to cognition:

1. *Signals*. These – such as action potentials in nerve fibres – are physical events which can be detected, measured and described by the normal methods of the physical sciences. Signals are, however, specially produced and selected events which may convey *information*. Signals which convey information we may call *data*. To be useful, signals generally have to be processed in various ways; filtered, averaged, compared and subjected to statistical and other treatments, before they can convey useful data.

2. *Data*. Data may be in many physical forms: maps, numbers, dots and dashes, letters, and so on. Even maps are largely conventional, having arbitrary colours and signs. The conventional shapes of letters and numbers, and so on, must be specially learned and agreed upon. They convey information according to their *surprise* value. So data are not straightforwardly physical events, as they convey information by arbitrary but accepted physical forms, and the amount of information depends on the degree of improbability. Data may be signalled in real time, or stored in more or less generalized form, from the past. They

change belief. But data may be rejected if they violate belief too much.

3. *Belief.* Beliefs are usually conveyed by language; but beliefs may be inferred from behaviour (cf. Dretske 1981), including animal behaviour. It may sound odd to say, 'Fido *believes* his master is in the garden', when Fido rushes outside barking and so appears to be acting on this belief; but the oddness may be simply because we are loathe to ascribe our richness of knowledge of 'master', 'garden', and so on, to a dog. But sometimes this is reversed: we do accept from a dog's behaviour that his smell associations are far richer than ours. It seems best to allow that behaviour can inform us of beliefs in other humans, and in at least the biologically 'higher' animals. Also, that in humans behaviour indications of beliefs may counter, and be more reliable than, even the sincerest-sounding language.

The most puzzling aspect of data and belief is that though they are not physical they affect and indeed determine behaviour. The danger here is to think that they are separate entities, or forces, acting on brain cells. But this dualism may be avoided by seeing that physical brain states obey conventions of signals. Having accepted the symbolic convention, they may act physically to modify or create events. In crude terms, this is what happens when a key turns a lock. It is exactly what happens in a computer.

What, then, is a *cognitive machine*? It is a machine which functions not only by following mechanical principles but also by accepting certain patterns, or forms or sequences, as tokens standing for objects or more or less general concepts by following conventional rules. The rules of English spelling and grammar are entirely different from physical laws and in no way can they be derived from those physical laws. But we follow linguistic and other symbol rules to perceive and behave more or less appropriately. The conventional rules for recognizing and acting on symbols are restraints falling *within* physics, and they do not violate physics.

The paradox is that though symbolic restraints are within and narrower than the restraints of physical laws, yet symbols free imagination and perception from the limitations of physics. Curiously, this is bound up with the fact that cognitive systems can suffer illusions and errors.

The notion that *cognitive* systems work by restraints within physics is but a small step beyond *any* mechanism – for *all* mechanisms work by restraints channelling physical principles to achieve (with more or less efficiency) some generally humanly determined goal. In this sense *all* machines are purposive. But not all machines are cognitive, for only cognitive machines work by symbolically represented information. When the symbol conventions are abandoned or lost, cognitive mechanisms return to the blindness and dumbness of normal machines.

IS AI SILICON?

It does not seem to matter what sort of matter a cognitive machine is made of – providing only it can accept and follow conventions of symbols. This is strongly suggested by the proven ability of computers to obey and make effective use of symbols. On this account the silicon of computers should be as cognitively effective as the protoplasm of brains, even though so far the most advanced artificial intelligence lacks what to us is elementary understanding. The question is whether symbol rule-following is sufficient for describing cognition. If not – what needs to be added? The answer, surely, is *knowledge*. Although our brains structure data effectively, we do not yet know how to structure data in order to give computers effective knowledge.

This is one answer. Other answers have, however, been proposed by sceptics of AI, such as the American philosopher Hubert Dreyfus in his book *What Computers Can't Do* (1972, 1979), and John Searle's *Minds, Brains and Science* (1984). Even for the most ardently convinced AI believers, these sceptics are extremely useful if only for sharpening Ockham's razor. Hubert Dreyfus questions whether the brain works like a digital computer, in terms of on/off switches representing individual *bits* of information. This is not, however, essential for computing, and future parallel operating computers may work rather differently. It is indeed hard to believe that serial digital computing could be fast enough to guide the hand to a tea cup. Dreyfus also questions whether all knowledge can be formalized, and indeed we do not yet know how to do this. He tends to think that the 'holistic' characteristics, especially of perception (that 'the whole is greater than the sum of its parts' as the *Gestalt* writers put it), are a serious objection to a digital account of mind; but, surely, the *emergence* of new characteristics upon the combination of parts is true of any computer program, and of any machine. Thus the parts of a Meccano set can make a clock or a crane, though the parts do not individually keep time or carry things into the air (as we see in essay 19). Finally, Dreyfus emphasizes the uniqueness of human goals and purposes and the special needs set by our bodies and feelings: for him the claim that silicon can replace the protoplasm of our brains and bodies is a silly con.

John Searle (1980, 1984) emphasizes that, although computers handle symbols with great efficiency and usefulness, they have no understanding. He goes further, to say that computers will never ever understand meanings of symbols. For Searle, computers can have syntax but not semantics. He bases this position on an analogy: Searle's 'Chinese Room'. Essentially, he imagines two Chinese people in a room, passing Chinese symbols according to the rules of their language, which they understand. Also in the room is a westerner, who does not understand the language. For him the Chinese language tokens are meaningless; but in time he comes to discover the rules by which they are selected. He can then intervene, to help the Chinese people, though he does not understand what the symbols mean. Searle suggests that this is the status of even the most sophisticated computer: it can handle symbols with superhuman efficiency but without understanding their meanings.

It is undoubtedly interesting that a pocket calculator can be of great help although clearly it does not understand. For example, in working out the area of a room, given the measurements it will find the answer faster and more accurately than we would – though it knows nothing of areas or walls or rooms. How can this be? In our terms a pocket calculator is not cognitive, though it handles what we see as symbols – for the calculator the symbols are not related to knowledge so they have no meanings: it has syntax but not semantics. Although the calculator, or computer, has internal rules for computing square roots, logarithms, and so on, it lacks knowledge of situations to which these may apply, or how they may be applied. So, such calculators are like the westerner in John Searle's Chinese Room: they have only syntax without semantics. But why should this hold for all future possible computers?

We may note that the Chinese Room has no window. What would happen if the westerner could see out of the window – and preferably touch what he saw – to relate the Chinese symbols to objects and situations of the world? Would he not then learn Chinese? After all, this is just what the Chinese themselves did as children to learn their language, and what the westerner did to learn his (or hers). So how can the westerner in the Chinese Room represent a forever non-understanding computer – except that he has not been allowed the necessary information for learning meanings? It is hard to see how a *child* brought up in the Chinese Room could learn language. If Searle has set up a situation in which no kind of cognition is possible, his Chinese Room story tells us nothing about any special difficulties for computers – for we would be as dumb and essentially blind if brought up with no windows. We need senses and limbs to explore, so we should expect that *active* robots with *senses* might become cognitive. This, however, Searle denies, urging that only biologically originated machines (such as ourselves, or Martians) can ever get beyond syntax to semantics – he urges, in effect, that only protoplasm can ever be cognitive. But this seems to be no more than vitalism in a new guise. I see no reason to believe that cognition has to be uniquely biological, and for that matter do we know that life is uniquely biological? One may also question whether present-day computers do entirely lack understanding of symbols. One can ask questions of airport or hospital computers and get back relevant useful answers, generally faster and more accurately than from a human. While it is true that the computer's range of understanding is restricted, the crucial point is that it is not zero.

What would be a clear and simple test for deciding whether or how much a machine understands our language? Let's consider word games, such as *anagrams* and *pangrams*. Could a machine play such games? If so, would this demonstrate that it understands meanings of words?

Anagrams are rearrangements of the letters of a word or phrase to form other words or phrases which may have quite different meanings. They must, however, have *some* meaning to win points. For example, the word 'COMPUTE' has the anagram MUTE COP, and also UP COMET. Most of us would agree what these mean, even though they would hardly be available to look up in a dictionary. Another arrangement – OUT PEMC – has no immediate meaning; though it might if 'PEMC' were a name, or initials perhaps for something like Perceptual Electronic Motion Control. The important point is that the vast majority of permutations of letters are just nonsense, such as OMTUCEP.

A pangram is a meaningful sentence containing all the letters of the alphabet. The best known example in English is: 'The quick brown fox jumps over the lazy dog'. But this is not a *perfect* pangram, for it has 33 letters though there are only 26 in our alphabet. There is an extra *a*, *e*, *u*, *r* and three extra *o*'s. Its meaning is, however, perfectly clear to any (human) English speaker. Could there be a clearly meaningful pangram with fewer letters? Could there be just twenty-six letters? A poet, Clement Wood, came up with: 'Mr. Jock, TV quiz Ph.D., bags few lynx'. This uses a proper name ('Jock'), initials ('Ph.D.'), and the grammar is peculiar ('bags few lynx'). Nevertheless, it can be read as meaningful, with only the twenty-six letters of the alphabet.

Another twenty-six-letter pangram (using Roman letters as numbers) is: 'XV quick nymphs beg fjord waltz'. Is this meaningful? Not at once – but it can become meaningful. One has to set up an imaginary situation in which it might have meaning. One that has been suggested is a squad of Roman soldiers, stationed in Norway, invited to dance by Scandinavian maidens. In this context it does, at a pinch, have meaning. But, surely, strictly speaking for *any* sentence to have meaning there must be an assumed context. So this bizarre example should be acceptable, provided the necessary context is not too strained for it to have accessible meaning.

Now the question is: could an AI computer produce anagrams and pangrams? The answer is that they can be very easily generated – spewed out – but can a good anagram or pangram be *recognized* by a machine? There are 403,000,000,000,000,000,000,000,000,000 arrangements of twenty-six letters; but only very few (perhaps ten) have a reasonably ready meaning. In other words, it is easy to make a computer spew out millions of combinations of the twenty-six letters; but to finish the job it must recognize those very few arrangements that are meaningful to us. The art seems to be to spot promising near-solutions (which are hard to find in dictionaries) for working on. It is the spotting of promising part-solutions that makes the task possible for us in reasonable time; but how are these part-solutions recognized? No doubt our ability looks remarkable because, as yet, we are not rivalled by machines playing word games. The AI problem of finding anagrams and pangrams is that there are so few arrangements of our language symbols that are meaningful, compared with the vast number of nonsensical arrangements. This immense and indeed effectively infinite number of arrangements of symbols frees language from the objects it describes, to endow symbols with their extraordinary power. If word-game skills require appreciation of meanings then semantic ability, for man or machine, might be measured by scoring word games. Whether, as machines learn to understand, we will come to be challenged by machine semantics, is a question to be answered not by philosophers but rather by the future technology of magic mechanisms.

Finally: What *is* a 'magic mechanism'? We have found that compared with ordinary objects all machines are odd, as they work by restraints *within* physics yet serve purposes that are *outside* physics. Cognitive mechanisms are still odder, for they are also restrained to obey symbols, and yet they escape normal physical limitations – to express not only what *is* but what *might be*: or indeed to generate fiction, some of which may be true. What of the 'magic'? Is not this exactly what is claimed for patterns of stars, in the magic of astrology? Yes: this is what is claimed, both for star patterns in astrology and for neural patterns in cognitive psychology. So, how can one really seriously say, from within science, that patterns of brain activity are symbols endowing us with perception and intelligence, without admitting astrology into science? The answer to this conundrum, surely, is that although we may read star patterns (or any patterns) as having meanings, the stars themselves are not pattern-readers. For what we, or at least most of us, no longer admit is the notion of mind in the stars, though we do accept that brains are mind-full. So mind seems to be active symbol-reading and symbol-writing. This is a notion that should be most congenial to academics.

REFERENCES

Dennett, Daniel C. (1978) *Brain Storms: Philosophical Essays on Mind and Psychology*, Brighton, Harvester.

Dretske, Fred I. (1981) *Knowledge and the Flow of Information*, Oxford, Blackwell.

Dreyfus, Hubert L. (1972; revised 1979) *What Computers Can't Do*, New York, Harper.

Gregory, Richard L. (1981) *Mind in Science: A History of Explanations in Psychology and Physics*, London, Weidenfeld & Nicolson; New York, Cambridge University Press.

Hadingham, Evan (1975) *Circles and Standing Stones*, London, Heinemann.

Searle, John R. (1980) 'Minds, brains, and programs', *Behavioral and Brain Sciences* 3, 417–57.

Searle, John R. (1984) *Minds, Brains and Science*, London, BBC Publications.

Thom, A. (1971) *Megalithic Lunar Observatories*, Oxford, Clarendon Press.

Thom, A. and Thom, A.S. (1978) *Megalithic Remains in Britain and Brittany*, Oxford, Clarendon Press.

9

IS CONSCIOUSNESS
SENSATIONAL INFERENCE?

'If you can't explain it – deny it', can be a useful rule; though few of us now follow the behaviourists in denying consciousness, even though we can't begin to explain why we have sensations. *Matter* is also mysterious; but at least it is not *private*, so we can talk about matter in ways denied us for discussing experience.

The experts of experience are artists: their sole concern is to convey experience through sensation. Can we share and compare sensations through the arts of painting and music, which do not have objects of common touch? Let's ask first whether philosophers have answers to such questions. Then we will look, with some necessary technical detail, at some experiments which may throw light on consciousness.

The philosopher with the deepest thoughts on these questions, Ludwig Wittgenstein (1889–1951), especially in his *Philosophical Investigations* (1953), discusses whether it's possible to generalize from one's own sensation to other people's. Or to animals or machines – or, even more unlike us, to 'conscious stones'. In *Philosophical Investigations* (I, para. 293) Wittgenstein gives this analogy:

> Suppose everyone had a box with something in it: we call it a 'beetle'. No one can look into anyone else's box, and everyone says he knows what a beetle is like by looking at *his* beetle. – Here it would be quite possible for everyone to have something different in his box.

The 'beetles' are sensations, such as colour or pain. Wittgenstein concludes that other people's sensations can only have significance for us in terms of behaviour. He was not, however, a behaviourist, for he did not accept that behavioural accounts are adequate to describe, for example, pain. He allowed that there are sensations, though he denied that it is possible to *describe* sensations; as it seemed to him impossible to generalize language from the single case of one's own private experience to anyone else's. In his terminology, private 'language games' are not possible, and so we cannot talk of our consciousness, though we can talk of external objects. So language can 'model' or 'picture' states of the world but not states of mind.

Wittgenstein concludes (*Philosophical Investigations*, para. 282): '"But doesn't what you say come to this: that there is no pain, for example, without *pain-behaviour*?" It comes to this: only of a human being and what resembles (behaves like) a living human being can one say: it has sensations; it sees; is blind; hears; is deaf; is conscious or unconscious.' We may note that this emphasis on behaviour refers to the entire organism, which may seem odd to those of us who are interested in the roles of specific neural processes. Recently, the Oxford philosopher Anthony Kenny has defended Wittgenstein's position here, commenting (*The Legacy of Wittgenstein*, 1984, p. 125):

> This dictum is often rejected in practice by psychologists, physiologists and computer experts, when they take predicates whose normal application is to complete human beings or complete animals and apply them to parts of animals, such as brains, or to electrical systems. . . . I wish to argue that it is a dangerous practice which may lead to conceptual and methodological confusion.

Are we so confused? Or could it be that the (often very useful) role of Guardians of Semantic Inertia played by philosophers may hold up our understanding by over-stern warnings? It seems to me that although their warnings – generally based on linguistic usage derived from the past – are sometimes very important, analytical philosophers can be over-cautious: holding back from the deep waters of problems and failing to take the plunge. As science is armed with powerful techniques of technology it is braver – and needs to be – to discover sometimes entirely surprising truths.

Is Wittgenstein over-cautious in not allowing us to talk about consciousness apart from behaviour? For him there is pain behaviour, guilt behaviour, thinking behaviour, and so on; but he does not allow us to talk of *private sensations* – for how can public language speak meaningfully of inner *private* worlds? Certainly we often wish to talk of others' sensations. When we see, or think we see, someone in pain we are not concerned only with his behaviour. We believe we know what an injured person feels though he is lying still, and clearly it is this feeling rather than behaviour (or lack of behaviour) that concerns us, or anaesthetists would be out of work. Perhaps Wittgenstein's semantic caution makes him a Red Queen ordering our heads to be cut off and preventing us speaking of our own or others' sensations.

It is tempting to say that we must be appreciating others' sensations when we accept their testimony, as observers, of shared external objects. Could we have 'objective' science without 'subjective' experience of observers, including scientists? A way to think about this is to imagine co-operating computers finding out about the world, from signals provided by their own detectors – *although they are not conscious.* Though they have no awareness, why shouldn't they make use of other robots' knowledge by communicating and sharing information? If this could all be unconscious – what does *our* consciousness *do?*

It is a basic biological principle that, by and large, only attributes useful for survival develop through the species by natural selection. So if consciousness does nothing, why should it have developed through the evolution of species? Possibly-sensations are quite incidental to physical brain processes (somewhat as the sounds of a car engine are incidental to the power it provides), but then it may seem odd that we attach such importance to awareness. Most sensations except pain are fun; but whatever the answer here, biological survival hardly seems to be geared for enjoyment! Indeed we generally have to depart from our biological origins, to listen to music or look at pictures, and so on, to get much fun or meaning out of life.

All this assumes that mind and consciousness are somehow given by physical brain processes. But it has often been suggested, most recently by Sir Karl Popper and Sir John Eccles, in their book *The Self and its Brain* (1977), that some aspects of mind are separate from the brain. On this account, the brain may be somewhat like a radio or television set receiving external mind. Here I shall assume that this account (which I question in *Mind in Science*, 1981) does not apply to individual consciousness.

It came as a jolt, whose shock waves have not yet settled, when the founder of modern studies of perception, Hermann von Helmholtz (1821–94), first spoke of perceptions as 'conclusions of unconscious inferences'. This was not a popular notion and was generally resisted, no doubt as it threatened the accepted need of consciousness for moral decisions, for praise or blame. Helmholtz's unconscious mental processes of the nineteenth century became the sensation of the twentieth century, in Freud's 'unconscious mind'. The moral dilemma persists. It comes up in a new form in accounts of artificial intelligence (AI), which claim to encompass brain intelligence

(BI) – though leaving out consciousness and moral responsibility for machines. The threat here, however, is that the brain may be regarded as a machine.

A century before Helmholtz, David Hume suggested very differently that the self is *made of sensations*, and that it is a 'bundle or collection of different perceptions'. He toyed with the notion that the self's continuity through gaps of consciousness is due to sensations being embodied in a mind substance, much as external objects are often thought to hold together and be maintained by continuity of an underlying substance. But Hume later came to reject the notion of such underlying matter – both for the object world and for self – writing it off as a conceptually vacuous explanation, adding nothing except the original question as a pseudo-explanation. Hume then came close to saying that self is a hypothesis, based on fleeting experiences. This is similar to the common-sense notion that the matter of objects continues though objects are not continuously experienced. Thus we suppose that a fire goes on burning though we are out of the room, as the room is warm when we come in from the cold. On this account of David Hume's, the status of consciousness and matter are seen as similar – and equally mysterious – and this seems to make consciousness less of a bother for psychologists, as physicists are just as puzzled by matter! David Hume's questioning of the status of matter, of the self as an entity, and of cause (he did not actually deny causes) remains of key importance. Hume rejects the *will* as an *anima* outside the physiology of organisms, describing it: 'By the *Will*, I mean nothing but *the internal impression that we feel, and are conscious of, when we knowingly give rise to any new motion of our body, or new perception of our mind*.' For Hume, the will is not a cause of action but just a link in a chain which is physical as much as mental. Like any other link it may equally be thought of as caused (whatever 'cause' means) by past events, or as causing later events. And he thinks that we do not know by experience the inner workings of mind, any more than we know without experiment and hypothesis the processes of physics.

Hume's emphasis on *new* motion and *new* perception is especially interesting, for surely this reflects a deep characteristic of consciousness: that we are primarily aware when we are *surprised*, and only surprise is *informative* (Shannon and Weaver 1949). Surely, indeed, we are hardly if at all aware of completely predicted actions or events. Awareness is primarily of discrepancies between predictions and what happens. Thus, while driving a car, there are few sensations of what is happening until something unpredictable occurs – and then one is suddenly and acutely aware. The surprise may be surprising *absence*, as for the non-ticking of a clock. Actually I have two chiming clocks in my sitting room and I am seldom aware of them striking the hours. It is highly suggestive that just as *information* is given by surprising events or surprise at non-events, so is the *awareness* of consciousness related to surprising occurrences or absences. In both cases – for gain of information and for awareness – the surprise of discrepancies from prediction seems to be the key.

Surely this emphasis on *surprise* for information-bearing raises a general problem for physiology, for it implies that it is not just neural activity (which can be measured by normal physical means), but also surprising inactivity that counts. But the surprise value of signals, or, even more difficult, of their absence, can hardly be measured without knowing their significance. So their surprise value is private to their owner. So, too, is consciousness private to each brain-owner.

Surprise, and also information, belong to *descriptions*. An event may be unusual, but it cannot be *surprising* except to a knowledge-based observer. Descriptions require some kind of language (a biological or a computer language), and so it is surely helpful to think of mind and consciousness as associated not only with physical brain activities but with some kind of a private brain language, which is mediated (written and read) by neural processes.

In this spirit, the distinguished biologist J.Z. Young says in his *Programmes of the Brain* (1978):

> If the essential feature of the brain is that it contains information then the task is to learn to translate the language that it uses. But of course this is not the method that is generally used in the attempt to 'understand the brain'. Physiologists do not go around saying that they are trying to translate brain language. They would rather think that they are trying to understand it in the ordinary scientific terms of physics and chemistry.

This is so now; but will we continue to see brain activity in the same way, if a Rosetta Stone is found for reading its signals as a language? Surely neuroscience would take John Young's advice and desert physics and chemistry, for a while, to translate brain language. What could be more exciting? Then, perhaps we will be able to read another's thoughts – even to the extent of knowing his or her sensations – almost if not quite at first hand.

How could this come about? There are some clues. Given that information is closely related to surprise, it is highly suggestive that at least the peripheral nervous system responds mainly to *changes* of stimulation. As E.D. (later Lord) Adrian so well described it, in *The Basis of Sensation* (1928):

> It is easy to multiply instances of sensations fading owing to the adaptation of their receptors to a constant environment. We cease to be aware that our clothes are touching our bodies almost as soon

as we put them on. This may be due partly to the diversion of our attention to more interesting topics, but even if we try to focus it on the body surface we find that there is little to feel as long as we do not move. . . . The fact that the receptors can be moved about in relation to the external world enlarges their scope enormously. To gain information about the environment there is no need to wait for it to change.

Adrian, of course, established beautiful correspondences between this loss of information-bearing peripheral neural activity and loss of consciousness of constant stimuli.

In something of the same vein, Horace Barlow (1977) says of recording optic nerve signals:

> What comes to be more prominently represented in the optic nerve message is also more prominent subjectively, and similarly for features like prey and predators that are important for an animal. It is fascinating to see how information about the factors known to trigger various forms of behaviour is preserved in the optic nerve message, whilst information about other aspects of the retinal image is discarded. It is also fascinating to have an opportunity of studying in the retina the physiological mechanisms that achieve some degree of specificity for these behavioural releasers.

Horace Barlow calls these trigger features, an '"alphabet" of one or two dozen symbols, each replicated in many places to cover the whole visual field'. Comparing this with the letters of a human language Barlow considers that (at least in the periphery) brain language is much simpler, as 'Letters and words are used in a mutually exclusive fashion, whereas nerve fibres (with some exceptions) are not.' Taking this beyond the optic nerve to recorded brain activity, Barlow sees the disappearance of what can be followed from the retinal image after the primary visual cortex as distributions of descriptions to secondary regions, as 'words' and 'sentences'. The snag is that we do not know the brain language at this stage, which is where one might expect it to use combinatorial tricks of written language, and so be very difficult to elucidate by single-cell recording.

As we have seen, Wittgenstein argued that we can only talk or think of pain *behaviour* or other sensation *behaviour*, as we cannot see the 'beetles' in our friend's 'boxes'. But is it possible that, with our increasing knowledge of what goes on in the nervous system, we might be able to compare 'beetles' – private sensations – apart from overt behaviour? Allow that we can (in spite of Anthony Kenny's objection to singling out particularly involved anatomical regions or processes) concentrate on specific neural activity; then why shouldn't brain recordings become so significant that they, very directly, convey another's sensations?

This would be different from Wittgenstein's behavioural links and should be far more closely related than behaviour to sensations – and also closer than speech if we can tap essential processes generating consciousness. Already, the electrical activity of evoked potentials, and recordings of local cerebral blood flow, make it possible to identify which regions of brain are specially active during private bouts of mental arithmetic, dreaming, hearing or seeing, and many other private mental activities. These are not visible to anyone else by behaviour, but they are made visible by the new non-invasive techniques for recording brain activity. As these new techniques begin to allow us to bridge minds apart from behaviour, technology has now broken through limits to what has traditionally been set as possible by philosophers.

Helmholtz saw perceptions as conclusions to unconscious inferences, involving computations. So he effectively suggested that computations can generate sensations. If we identify consciousness-generating computations, surely AI and BI will meet. With this end in view, let's consider in some necessary detail a suggestive perceptual phenomenon: the odd sensations of illusory contours (Schumann 1904; Kanizsa 1955, 1979). These might better be called illusory *surfaces*, for we see surfaces having a small brightness difference from the surrounding background (figure 9.1). I have suggested that they are perceptually postulated – to account for surprising gaps (Gregory 1972). The brightness difference increases (up to about 12 per cent) as the probability that the gaps occur by chance decreases. The suggestion is that the surface is inferred by (rather simple-minded) estimates of the probability that they are not truly gaps, but complete objects partly hidden by a nearer eclipsing surface. Are these sensations created by *probability computing*? I suggest they are, and that this kind of process is responsible for all sensations and perceptions. This is a particularly useful case to consider as these illusory surfaces and edges are clearly not simply 'stimulus-driven' but depend on whether there 'should' be a surface present though it is not sensed. Although this is an illusion, it sets the paradigm for understanding all perception and sensation, for sensory stimuli are never completely adequate.

Where in the brain are these illusory surfaces and contours produced? Adam Sillito, Priscilla Heard and I found no electrical signals from single cells in the primary visual cortex of cat (Area 17) though the same cell was active for true edges crossing its receptive field (Sillito *et al.* 1982). Baumgartner *et al.* (1984) did find activity in cells higher up (Area 19) in monkey, though not in Area 17. Does this show that 'perceptual hypotheses' are produced in Area 19 but not

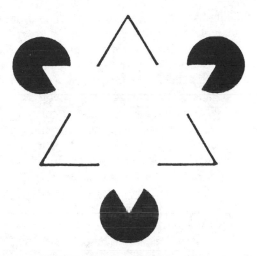

9.1 *Kanizsa's triangle. This is the best-known, and a very striking, example of illusory contours – the bright triangle is illusion.*

earlier? Not quite, for each active cell at Area 17 might be a contributing 'witness', or member of a 'jury', and we could hardly have tapped the joint verdict or the jury's decision to the 'judge'. However this may be, it does seem clear that each eye system generates its own postulated borders, for John Harris and I found that when somewhat different figures are presented one to each eye, the different illusory contours are fused into a single contour, in stereoscopic depth just as for equivalent normal borders or lines viewed in a stereoscope (Harris and Gregory 1973). Also, gaps are not filled from knowledge or assumptions of *particular* objects, however familiar (such as bits missing from faces), so the process seems to take place just before object-recognition, following rules of what is likely to be *an* object though not yet a *particular kind* of object. This is around the level of David Marr's (1982) '2½-D sketch' level of visual analysis.

If we can regard illusory contours and surfaces as computed from probabilities of the presence of objects, should we say the same for *all* perception, and *all* sensations? Experience with robot vision shows that signalling the presence and position of edges is difficult, requiring quite elaborate summing and assessing of evidence. As for the extreme case of illusory contours, *all* contours would seem to be postulates, which may or may not be correct, illusory and true contours being essentially the same neurally. And when the odds are really odd, robots should, like us, be fooled into illusion.

The notion that sensations are given by unconscious computations fits very well the recent physiological work of Semir Zeki on cortical 'colour regions' (Zeki 1977, 1980), which appear to create colour sensations not simply according to input stimuli, but rather by the kind of computations Edwin Land suggests in his retinex theory (Land 1983). Land's striking experiments show that perceived colour depends on estimates of surrounding luminances and not simply on the relative activities of the three kinds of cone cells in the retina. It is by these computations, Land suggests, that objects maintain the same colour though the lighting changes; so colours are seen as belonging to objects, though they are generated within us.

Could a man-made computing machine have sensations? Could it experience colours and pains? Computers can handle symbols brilliantly, so if they performed the appropriate computations (presumably from the necessary knowledge base) wouldn't they, like us, have sensations – see red and feel pain? It is hard to deny this possibility without, for an alternative, evoking some special *brain substance*, making living organisms uniquely conscious. But this (like phlogiston as an account of heat) is not a useful kind of explanation for it does not bridge across to anything else we know about. It suggests that sensations are not only private but unique beyond powers of analogy. But then science is powerless. So this assumption denies effective explanation as it holds back from plunging into a suggestive (even if not correct) hypothesis. When science is not immersed in suggestive hypotheses it is nothing.

As Popper (1972) has most cogently argued, hypotheses must be framed so that they can be tested. And as the techniques of the sciences have extended the range of what can be tested, they have extended what we can say meaningfully of the physical world – such as verifying that there are mountains on the back of the Moon, or estimating the age of the universe, which not long ago were futile speculations. So now the hope is that new techniques of brain recording will make it possible to read 'brain language', and follow what might be its consciousness-generating computations. If it can be established which computations or whatever are intimately related to our consciousness, then just possibly we may cross the bridge to the sensations of others. For, if philosophers allow that *behaviour* is evidence of consciousness, even though our behaviour is only very loosely connected to our sensations, then shouldn't closely related – or even *invariably* consciousness-related – brain activity be accepted with far greater confidence? If the crucially important features of brain language and computations are discovered and understood, then if they occur in equivalent forms in intelligent computers, it may be impossible to deny consciousness to some future man-made machines. (See also Johnson-Laird 1983.)

Such shifts against the semantic inertia of philosophy occur whenever experimental techniques test or suggest speculations. But it may always be questioned whether a test, or an observed correlation, or whatever, is strong enough to push metaphysics into physics – or, as here, into physiology. But more specifically, the push is into processes carried out by the physiology of the nervous system – computations which might also be achieved by man-made machines to make them conscious much as we have sensations. It is a strange thought that the arid operations of inference, by computations and logic, may be the key to sensations and emotion, and so be the heart of art.

REFERENCES

Adrian, E.D. (1928) *The Basis of Sensation: The Action of the Sense Organs*, Cambridge, Cambridge University Press.
Barlow, H.B. (1977) 'The languages of the brain', *Encyclopedia of Ignorance*, vol. 2: *Life Sciences and Earth Sciences*, ed. R. Duncan and M. Weston-Smith, Oxford, Pergamon.
Baumgartner, G., von der Heydt, R., Peterhans, E. (1984) 'Anomalous contours: a tool in studying the neurology of vision', *Exp. Brain Res.* (suppl. 9), 413–19.
Gregory, R.L. (1972) 'Cognitive countours', *Nature* (London) 238, 51–2.
Gregory, R.L. (1981) *Mind in Science*, London, Weidenfeld & Nicolson.
Gregory, R.L. (1984) 'Conning cortex', *Perception* 13, 227–8.
Gregory, R.L. and Harris, J.P. (1974) 'Illusory contours and stereo depth', *Perception and Psychophysics* 15 (3), 411–16.
Harris, J.P. and Gregory, R.L. (1973) 'Fusion and rivalry of illusory contours', *Perception* 2, 235–47.
Helmholtz, H. von (1866) 'Concerning perceptions in general', in *Treatise of Physiological Optics*, vol. III, 3rd edn, trans. and ed. (1925) J.P.C. Southall, Optical Society of America, New York, Section 26, reprinted New York, Dover, 1962.
Johnson-Laird, P.N. (1983) *Mental Models*, Cambridge, Cambridge University Press.
Kanizsa, G. (1955) 'Margini quasi-percettivi in campi con stimolazioni omogenea,' *Rivista de psicologia* 49, 7–30.
Kanizsa, G. (1979) *Organisation of Vision: Essays on Gestalt Psychology*, New York, Praeger.
Kenny, A. (1984) *The Legacy of Wittgenstein*, Oxford, Blackwell.
Land, E.H. (1983) 'Recent advances in retinex theory and some implications for cortical computations: colour vision and natural image', *Proc. National Acad. Science* (USA) 80, 5163–9.
Marr, D. (1982) *Vision*, New York, Freeman.
Popper, K.R. (1972) *Objective Knowledge: An Evolutionary Approach*, Oxford, Clarendon Press.
Popper, K.R. and Eccles J.C. (1977) *The Self and its Brain*, Berlin, Springer.
Schumann, F. (1904) 'Einige Beobachtungen über die Zusammenfassung von Gesichseindrucken zu Einheiten', *Psychologische Student* 1, 1–32 (cited in Woodworth, R.S. (1938) *Experimental Psychology*, New York, Holt).
Shannon, C.E. and Weaver, W. (1949) *The Mathematical Theory of Communication*, Urbana, University of Illinois Press.
Sillito, A., Gregory, R.L. and Heard, P.F. (1982) 'Can cognitive contours

con cat cortex?' (talk at Experimental Psychology Meeting, University of St Andrews).

Wittgenstein, L. (1953) *Philosophical Investigations*, ed. G.E.M. Anscombe, Oxford, Blackwell.

Young, J.Z. (1978) *Programs of the Brain*, Oxford, Oxford University Press.

Zeki, S. (1977) 'Colour coding in rhesus monkey prestriate cortex', *Brain Research* 53, 422–7.

Zeki, S. (1980) 'The representation of colours in the cerebral cortex', *Nature* (London) 284, 412–18.

10

CONJURING

Why do those of us who are interested in perception and illusion ignore the dramatic phenomena of conjuring? Conjuring is rarely if ever mentioned either in general books on psychology or in specialized books on perception, and it is not even cited in the Bible of perception, Hermann von Helmholtz's great *Treatise of Physiological Optics* (1856–66), although it is hard to think of anything significant that Helmholtz missed.

But to ignore questions of why we are so easily fooled by conjuring is a serious oversight ('undersight'?) of psychologists, for there is far more to it than mere sleight of hand, or the hand moving faster than the eye can follow. The best conjuring tricks are slow sequences, which draw their audience gradually and inevitably into baffling impossibilities: conjuring depends on a failure to follow partly hidden mechanical processes. Ideally, for this jury-conning, there should be a nice balance between 'seeing that' and 'seeing how'.

Conjuring depends on the audience's failure to follow the mechanical processes which underlie appearances. Like so much else, mechanistic explanations for understanding, and the use of mechanical devices to mystify, go back to the Greeks. For them public conjuring was a favourite and expensive treat, denied to mere slaves. The design of the elaborate secret mechanisms pushed Greek technology to its limits. At least two Greek conjurers, Euclides and Theodosius, had the special honour of having statues erected to them; and Athenaeus (200 AD) in his compendious *Learned Banquet* (a source of reference to many lost works) criticized the Athenians for preferring the inventions of mechanics to culture of the mind and philosophy. It may be that appreciation of mechanisms has, all through history, been rated so low not because mechanisms did slaves' work, but because mechanical devices were used for mystifying the public, the *hoi polloi* – being foolishly mystified is a far surer mark of ignobility than toiling in fields or on the sea, where men appreciate and question nature and their place under the Sun.

It is most interesting that the Greeks saw the Sun and stars revolving on a mechanism of crystal spheres, and the planets moving according to mechanisms of invisible epicycles, rotating on further precisely designed epicycles, to generate their subtly repeating motions through the sky. On this basis, the idea of hidden mechanisms could evidently explain how the universe works. Failure to understand could show as *not appreciating mechanisms* – which is being conjuring-tricked.

In its origins conjuring is associated with magic, the word 'conjure' having early magical meanings such as to 'constrain by oath or by a sacred invocation'; a conjurer was 'one who conjures spirits'. The free-thinking Greeks, as also the very different priest-bound Egyptians, devised ingenious miracle-making mechanisms, such as temples which moved of their own accord and poured libations of wine as though by the action of an inner spirit: a mechanical ghost in the machine. For most people it was inconceivable that a machine could be self-motivated – much as now it is hardly conceivable that machines might see and think for themselves.

The mechanical principles and detailed designs of many ancient machines are revealed in the writings of Hero of Alexandria. He lived in the first century AD, but although he was an inventor in his own right, he recorded several much earlier devices – including miracle-working automata driven and controlled by air, water and steam. There were also falling-weight motors (the weight falling slowly, as it rested upon sand draining through a funnel), used for silently powering the elaborate hidden mechanisms of magic theatres and miracle-working temples.

It is, indeed, surprising how easily even simple and familiar physical principles can bewilder us. For example to make a (dummy) fish disappear in a bowl of water, it is only necessary to make the fish of a transparent substance with precisely the same refractive index as water, or some other transparent fluid. Then when immersed it is invisible – and in the right context we have a miracle. With a little physics this is so obvious that we can almost *see* the invisible fish; but without the physics, or realizing how such principles may apply, we are mystified.

Much of this came to me a few years ago while I was watching a performance of the Indian rope trick in the circus at Leningrad. As it happened, instead of being mystified as the trick developed I found myself understanding each move – effectively seeing the hidden mechanisms of what was going on: on the large open stage there was a massive bronze head with an open mouth, through which a thick flexible rope issued and lay flaccid on the boards. The magician picked up part of the rope, which was some 30 feet long, and fed it into the bronze mouth. As the rope entered the mouth it reappeared through a fountain-like hole above the head, to rise up until it nearly touched the high roof of the splendid building. Clearly, from the way it swayed, there were no wires from the roof holding it up, and all was in excellent light. The magician, who was dignified and somewhat portly, did not himself climb the rope, which, now that it had reached its full height, was no longer flaccid but quite rigid. His young and nimble assistant shinned up it, and then, after a minute or so of swaying around at the top, climbed down to a round of applause. We stared at the rope as it slowly and gracefully, coiling and twisting, fell to the stage to lie inert – surrounded by a thousand Russians staring wonder-struck.

What had we seen? For some reason it was clear to me from the start that the rope that rose up to be climbed was not the same rope that was swallowed by the mouth. There were two ropes, but, as they looked alike, and as one went into the bronze mouth at exactly the same rate and with the same slight changes of rate as the other rose to the roof, they were accepted as being one rope. Further, the climbing rope was not truly a rope but was hollow – a woven rope-like tube. Inside the tubular rope a pole was pushed from a pit beneath the stage and locked into position. The conjurer's assistant climbed the strong, stout pole, which was hidden in the hollow rope. The clever bits were how the rope rose in the first place; then when the climber returned to earth, how it fell freely, coiling and twisting. It seemed to me then – and I virtually *saw* it all happening although the action was hidden – that the hollow rope rose by being filled with compressed air. Then the pole was pushed up from a pit below the stage, and the conjurors's assistant climbed up. When he descended, the pole was withdrawn but the tube-rope remained vertical, kept up by the compressed air. When the climber descended it became tumescent and naturally as the compressed air was turned off it collapsed naturally.

When one has an adequate running mental model of the hidden mechanisms of the trick, the performance looks ridiculous. Is it this sense of let-down when tricks are explained that turns many people away from science into paranormal mysteries? Perhaps most people see the whole world as a conjuring trick.

REFERENCES

Athenaeus (2nd century AD) *Deipnosophists*, trans. C.B. Gulick, London, Loeb, Universal Library, 1924–41, 7 vols.

Hopkins, A. (ed.) (1898) *Magic: Stage Effects and Scientific Diversions, including Trick Photography* (reprinted 1976), New York, Dover.

Onions, C.T. (1966) *The Oxford Dictionary of Etymology*, Oxford, Oxford University Press.

11

THE ODDEST PERCEPTIONS: ILLUSIONS

Illusions are discrepancies from truth. All the senses can suffer illusions; but as we know most about *visual* perception so visual illusions are the best known and fully understood – though much remains mysterious and controversial. All perceptions are subject to errors of many kinds; but illusions pass unnoticed except when strikingly inconsistent with what is accepted as true, or when there are internal inconsistencies – such as contradictory sizes or shapes, ambiguities, or paradoxes. And, as for our conceptual understanding (or misunderstanding), failed predictions can signal inadequacies and errors – though only backwards in time.

It sometimes turns out that what has been put down to illusion is not after all an error; while accepted knowledge may, against all appearances, be false. A familiar example of appearance contradicting what we accept as true is seeing the Sun and the stars moving across the sky to the west, though we know that the Earth's rotation is carrying us easterly. Astronomers, indeed, have often spoken of 'saving the appearances', with explanations that may be far from obviously related to how things seem to the senses. And these 'appearance-saving' explanations change, as conceptual accounts change. So there is only a loose relation between appearance and accepted reality, and strictly speaking it is always a question what is veridical and what illusory; most likely all perceptions are mixtures of truth and falsity.

The fact that there *are* illusions of the senses is a fundamental embarrassment for philosophers who wish to hold that knowledge is securely based on perception. Although this is the empiricist tradition, it is easy to show empirically that perception is not reliable. For at least in the laboratory, and indeed also in the art gallery where interesting illusions abound, it is very easy to fool the senses, and to disturb perception systematically, so that all observers agree on what they see – or hear or whatever – though all are wrong. And we can suffer misperceptions which may be disastrous in real-life situations, such as driving a car or playing golf. And for all of us the Moon appears too near, just beyond the horizon, and only about the size of an orange, yet we *know* it to be a quarter of a million miles away and much larger than any earthly object. But unlike the seen distances of cars, or holes on a golf course, this huge universally shared error does not matter (even for astronauts) and there is no hand–eye way of correcting it. It is an important point that we *learn* to perceive the world of objects, especially by handling things, but like any other learning, perceptual learning is patchy and itself full of errors.

Although illusions are 'subjective', many can be measured much as objects are measured, by comparisons with rulers, or other references. Sophisticated techniques of matching or cancelling out (or 'nulling') may also be used. Thus, the seen separations of the 'arrow heads' of the Muller–Lyer illusion (figure 11.1) can be measured by comparison with a set of neutral lines (a); or, very similarly, by adjusting a variable-length line to match the illusory size. Rather differently, the figure itself may be changed to compensate the illusion (figure 11.1b), though here there is some danger of being misled as the stimulus input has been changed so at least in some cases the conditions for the illusion may have been lost, or changed. For example cancelling a crossing-of-lines illusion (figure 11.2) changes the critical angles responsible for the distortion. Not only spatial distortions can be measured, but also illusions of brightness (figure 11.3) or colour, much as for normal photometry, by matching against reference brightnesses or colours.

There is a great richness and variety of illusions, and they have controversial ownerships. Discoverers of new illusions have their rights and so do those who make effective use of them. For scientists, there is a kind of ownership through explanation. There is real rivalry between the various sciences that contribute to understanding sensory systems and processes of perception, to claim as their own illusions they have (or think they have) explained. So, in the world of illusion, there is rivalry between neurochemists and pharmacologists, as hypnotic and other drugs can affect perception; cell biologists; neuroanatomists; electrophysiologists; physiological-psychologists; opticians; cognitive psychologists and computer programmers concerned with vision, or other perception, in artificial intelligence. It is

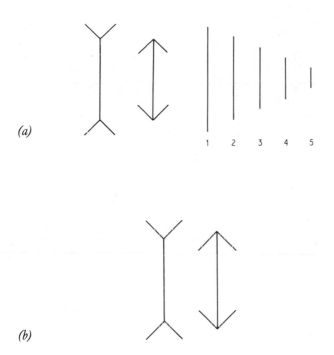

(a)

(b)

11.1   *(a) The Muller-Lyer 'arrow heads' distortion. This is probably the best-known and most fully studied distortion illusion. The line with the outward-going fins appears considerably longer than its fellow, terminated with the in-going fins. For measuring by matching, note which of the 'neutral' lines most nearly matches the illusory length. This gives an 'objective' measure of a 'subjective' distortion. Alternatively, an adjustable comparison line may be used, and for convenience this may be presented with computer graphics.*

(b) Measuring by nulling: here the figures are drawn with different separations between the arrow heads – to compensate the distortion. The required compensation measures the distortion.

indeed an interesting point that robot vision is subject to illusions, much like ours, though the anatomy and physiology of a robot's computers are very different from our brains. This is important, for it shows that we can ignore many of even the most important under-lying processes of perception when explaining illusions – even though perception depends on these incredibly many processes. As for real sciences, the problem for illusion explanations is to look at the appropriate 'level', where the action is, which in an illusion has gone wrong. Yet this is not quite so simple, for there may be nothing wrong with the anatomy or the underlying processes; just as any working tool may be misapplied, so may the brain's processes or knowledge be misdirected, to produce errors, though this is no fault of physiology.

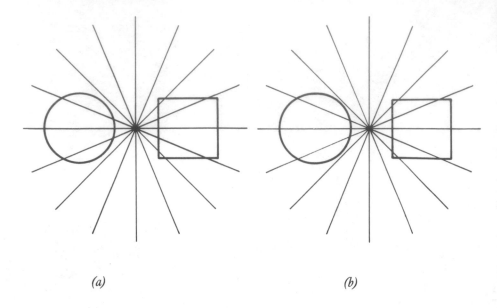

(a)   (b)

11.2   *Nulling a distortion by drawing the affected lines oppositely distorted. The illusory distortion seen in (a) is more or less compensated, and so measured, in (b). But there is danger in this method, for the angles (which may be critical for the illusion) to the radiating lines are changed.*

Physiologists should not claim these illusions – they belong, rather, to cognitive psychology. Many illusions are, however, clearly physiological in origin, such as the after-images one sees hovering around after looking at a bright light. Illusions are the strongest evidence that perceptions are only *indirectly* related to the world of objects. They are more like *descriptions*, than *samples* of physical reality. I take the view that perceptions are essentially hypotheses – much like the predictive hypotheses of science. Perceptions are also predictive, especially into the next second or so of the future; and they, also, are much richer than the available data from the senses. So, perceptual illusions can be like the more interesting errors in science. These are, especially, errors of calibration; of defining scales (such as the scale of a map); of settling ambiguities of meaning, or intepretation of data; of over-extrapolating, beyond the available data, or over-interpolating between data – which can generate fictions. Paradoxes can be generated in several ways, especially by conflicting signals which may occur through calibration or scaling errors, or by accepting false assumptions. All these, and many more, are to be found as causes of perceptual illusions.

Reflections from mirrors, mirages, and echoes from walls or cliffs

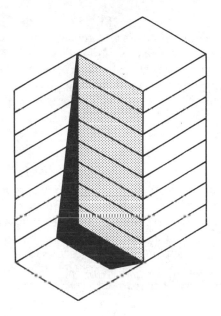

(a)

(b)

11.3   (a) Try looking at the grey rectangle region. When the figure switches in depth this region may change quite dramatically in brightness, probably because it is accepted as a shadow – and largely rejected – when the wall is seen as part of an in-going corner. When the corner sticks out it is less likely to be mere shadow, and is seen as a dark surface.

(b) Try placing a piece of string along the black–white border. Then the left half of the grey ring will look lighter and the right half darker.

produce illusions by disturbance of the input to the senses; but it is interesting that we are not good at compensating for such disturbances, even though they are extremely familiar. Thus one *sees* oneself behind a mirror though one *knows* one is in front of it. To understand even these simple 'physical' illusions we need to appreciate something of the brain's cognitive processes, and their limitations.

So let's look at some kinds of cognitive illusions.

ILLUSIONS OF AMBIGUITY

Some pictures, and also some ordinary objects, spontaneously change perceptually to some other object, which may be quite different. Perception may switch between two or more alternatives (figure 11.4). Just as familiar is the spontaneous switching in depth of figures, or objects such as the Necker cube (figure 11.5). What happens is that alternative perceptual *hypotheses* of what the object is (or where its parts lie in space) are entertained in turn. This occurs when the sensory data do not particularly favour just one possibility.

ILLUSIONS OF DISTORTION

These are the best-known illusions: systematic distortions of size, of length or of curvature of lines or edges. Explanations of these highly systematic effects remain controversial after a century of intensive investigation, especially by physicists, opticians, neurophysiologists and psychologists – all puzzling over what may seem childishly simple effects. Many of these effects were discovered by optical instrument-makers, placing wires in eye pieces of telescopes or measuring instruments to improve visual accuracy – but they turned out to produce large errors! These distortions are large and repeatable phenomena which are easy to measure and so are favourites for experiments. But what causes these distortions? There is a score of theories.

A key, I think, is the power of depth cues, such as perspective-convergence, to set scales of size and distance. Perspective is appropriate and trouble-free when given to the eye by normally shaped objects; but odd-shaped objects, or pictures, can mis-set visual scale. Pictures are very odd, as they present depth cues of objects in quite another space from the picture plane, and with the extra dimension of depth. So it is hardly surprising if pictures present special problems, which the visual system cannot fully solve. Pictures are essentially paradoxical, as they are flat while representing depth, so it is amazing that both are seen at once – the picture's scene and the picture's surface – even at the cost of some distortions. What happens is that features of the picture representing *distance* are perceptually expanded – which normally compensates the shrinking

(a)

(b)

11.4 *Ambiguous pictures. (a) A duck and a rabbit: this switches between two, roughly equally likely 'perceptual hypotheses', each entertained in turn.*

(b) An ink blot presents very many possibilities, and which are entertained may depend on interests or personality variables.

11.5   *The Necker cube. The picture reverses in depth. The skeleton cube object changes its shape with each reversal. When not reversed, the front and back faces appear much the same size. But when reversed the apparent back face of the cube looks considerably too large, and all the angles change. It looks like a truncated cone, expanding away from the observer. This is strong evidence of 'top-down' size scaling.*

of the image with increasing object distance; things usually look much the same size when near or (not too) distant. But when this compensation ('size constancy') is not appropriate it must produce distortions.

How can we test this notion? One test is to look at three-dimensional models of two-dimensional perspective figures. Thus, a wire corner may be compared with the flat perspective-corner Muller-Lyer arrow figures. Although the retinal images are the same, the *figure* looks distorted but not the *model* – provided it is seen as a true three-dimensional corner (Gregory and Harris 1975). But why should *seeing it as a corner* be important? To see why, it is worth making a depth-ambiguous object, such as a wire cube. When *it* reverses in depth – though there is no change of the retinal image in the eye – it changes shape! When depth-reversed the apparently further face looks too big. So the cube looks like a truncated pyramid, expanding away from the observer (Gregory 1970).

This distortion shows why normally it looks a *true* cube, when *not*

(a)

(b)

11.6 *The impossible triangle. Though this is a 'physiologically' simple figure, cognitively it presents a problem the perceptual system cannot solve – even when we know the answer!*

reversed, though its further face gives a smaller image to the eye than its front face. In spite of this, the cube's front and back faces normally look the same size because of size constancy, which counters the perspective shrinking at the eye. But when the cube reverses in depth, this also reverses, to produce dramatic distortions as a function of *apparent* depth. So the phenomenon of depth ambiguity is useful experimentally for separating the *direct* scaling by depth cues, such as perspective convergence (which is 'bottom up'), from the ('top down') scaling by the *perceived distance* – which changes in depth-ambiguous objects, though there is no optical change of the image in the eye. The lesson is that size scaling can be set in these two very different ways, and it can be set wrongly by either, to give distortion illusions.

ILLUSIONS OF PARADOX

It is a strange fact that although we tend to see what is likely, we can see things that are so unlikely they appear impossible, even logically paradoxical. But if we could only see probable objects we would be blind to the unlikely. This would be extremely dangerous, for unlikely events do occur. Indeed, if we could only see expected things, there could hardly be perceptual learning. It may, however, seem strange that we can *perceive* a paradox though at the same time we know *conceptually* the solution. This is the interest of the model impossible triangle (figure 11.6). This paradoxical perception occurs because the visual system assumes that the sides meet and touch at the corners, though in fact at one corner they only *optically* touch, being separated in depth. But although one knows this *conceptually*, one still *sees* it as a paradoxical object.

This split between perceiving and conceiving (which applies to all 'robust' illusions) is, most likely, because the perceptual computations must be performed very fast to keep in 'real time' with external events – so that we may survive the everyday (indeed the every second) hazards of life. But such speed could hardly be achieved if perception drew upon *all our knowledge*. This same strategy of initial data-processing, feeding into a large computer, is becoming necessary just for this reason in computer-engineering. So robots may be expected to have not only many illusions similar to ours, but also this same split between perceiving and knowing, which is anathema to philosophers!

Not all perceptual paradoxes have such cognitive origins, however, for straightforward physiological errors can produce even paradoxes, as when signals arriving from one sensory channel disagree with signals from another channel, especially when they are differently adapted. As is well known, after one hand has been placed in hot water and the other in cold, then tepid water, when both hands are placed in it, will feel both hot and cold at the same time. Movement after-effects are similarly paradoxical, as they can give sensations of movement, though without change of position. This indicates that movement and position are signalled by different neural channels, which can disagree. So such effects can be used to tease out physiological channels of perception.

ILLUSIONS OF FICTION

On this account, of perceptions as *predictive hypotheses*, it is not altogether surprising that perceptions can be fictional. Apart from hallucinations of schizophrenia, or drug-induced hallucinations, striking examples are illusory surfaces and edges, which can occur in a wide variety of figures. The best examples are due to the Italian psychologist and artist Gaetano Kanizsa (figure 11.7).

There are several theories for these effects. I think the key is that they occur in figures having surprising gaps. They seem to be fictional surfaces, invented perceptually to account for surprising gaps as due to masking by a nearer surface. In normal circumstances, parts of objects are very often hidden by nearer opaque objects and yet we continue to recognize them as complete, though parts are missing. Being able to continue to recognize objects when they are partly hidden is, clearly, extremely useful. But to postulate a surface on the evidence of gaps must be somewhat hazardous – for sometimes there really *are* surprising gaps! The three drawings of figure 11.8 are especially interesting as they show something of the subtlety of these processes, and they throw light on how features are accepted

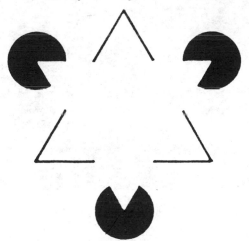

11.7   *Kanizsa's triangle. This is the best-known, and a very striking, example of illusory contours – the bright triangle is illusion.*

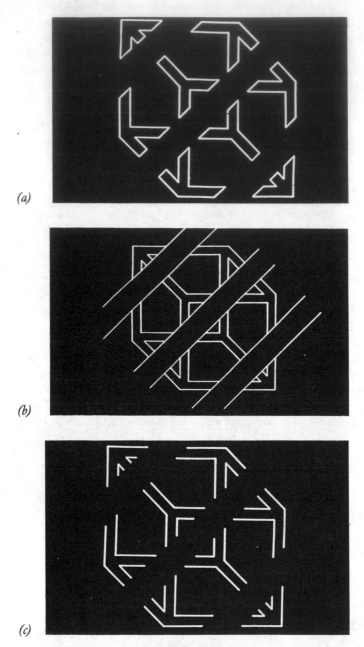

11.8　(a) This is seen as comprising separate objects. (b) Adding long lines makes the previous 'objects' become parts of a single object. (c) Removing the long lines and also the short 'blocking' lines produces illusory bars – and the complete object (a cube) is seen as lying behind the illusory masking bars. (These figures, but not the implied explanation, which he may not agree with, are after Kanizsa 1979.)

as parts of the same object, and how the world is perceptually divided up into discrete objects.

To understand illusions it is necessary to look beneath appearances, just as it is to explain the world by the physical sciences. Perception is not yet understood in anything like the detail or profundity that physics is, and there is less agreement on how we should think about perception and illusion, possibly because they are still deeply rooted in philosophical issues which remain hard to investigate experimentally. The explanations suggested here reflect one way of looking at perception; that perceptions are predictive hypotheses essentially like the hypotheses of science. On this account the various illusions correspond to errors in science. But few scientists are interested in errors. One has to switch one's mind around to see how getting things wrong is interesting in its own right.

REFERENCES

For a very different, more 'direct', account of perception, and illusion, see: Gibson, J.J. (1950) *The Perception of the Visual World*, London, Greenwood.

Gibson, J.J. (1966) *The Senses Considered as Perceptual Systems*, Boston, Houghton Mifflin.

For the most informative and deeply interesting account of illusion in art, see: Gombrich, E.H. (1960) *Art and Illusion*, London, Phaidon.

The account of distortion illusions given here was first stated in: Gregory, R.L. (1963) 'Distortion of visual space as inappropriate constancy scaling', *Nature* (London) 199, 678.

This, together with the notion of perceptions as hypotheses, is developed in: Gregory, R.L. (1966) *Eye and Brain*, 3rd edn, 1977, London, Weidenfeld & Nicolson.

Gregory, R.L. (1970) *The Intelligent Eye*, London, Weidenfeld & Nicolson.

Illusions in nature and art are discussed by six authors in Gregory, R.L. and Gombrich, E.H. (1973) *Illusion in Nature and Art*, London, Duckworth. This is the book of the exhibition of the same name, set up by the late Sir Roland Penrose – whom, with many others, I greatly miss – and Sir Ernst Gombrich and myself at the Institute of Contemporary Arts, in London, in 1973.

For more technical accounts, see Gregory, R.L. (1968) 'Perceptual illusions and brain models', *Proc. Royal Soc.* 171, 279.

Gregory, R.L. (1980) 'Perceptions as hypotheses', *Phil. Trans. Royal Soc.* 290, 181–97.

For the experiment showing that the distortions do not occur when constancy scaling is appropriate, see Gregory, R.L. and Harris, J.P. (1975) 'Illusion-destruction by appropriate scaling', *Perception* 4, 203–20.

The first paradoxical figures are due to: Penrose, L.S. and Penrose, R. (1958) 'Impossible objects: a special type of illusion', *Brit. J. Psychol.* 49, 31.

For Kanizsa's beautiful examples of illusory contours and surfaces, see: Kanizsa, G. (1979) *Organisation of Vision: Essays on Gestalt Perception*, New York, Praeger.

For a comprehensive collection of illusion figures, with their names and history, see Robinson, J.O. (1972) *The Psychology of Visual Illusion*, London, Hutchinson.

12

REFLECTING ON MIRRORS

I find it odd that some extremely simple and very familiar situations puzzle us embarrassingly. Why are they confusing? Often the difficulty is to see what kind of puzzle, or problem, or question is presented. When this is unclear, we are apt to wriggle multi-dimensionally between: 'Well, yes, of course – but this is rather too *trivial* to bother about – isn't it?' to: 'Ah yes – too *deep* for our present understanding.' It may be noted that these are stock philosophical responses to questions that we do not see how to resolve by experiment.

A clear case is provided by a looking-glass. The question is: Why does a mirror reverse left to right, but not up to down? We often stare into a looking-glass, sometimes in contemplative mood; pondering the passage of time, the brevity of life and the utter strangeness of looking out through eyes which appear just like all other people's, though we cannot know just what *they* experience behind their so-similar eyes. So the everyday looking-glass may focus attention on problems of mortality and how we can know other minds as we know our own mind. More prosaically, though, a looking-glass raises the embarrassingly teasing puzzle (if it is a puzzle): how can symmetrical reflection switch left with right, but not up with down?

It is obvious that, standing before a mirror, one's head is reflected from the top of the mirror; one's feet from the bottom; one's right hand from its right, and one's left hand from its left. There are no crossings of light rays, or anything of this kind, and the mirror's reflection is symmetrical horizontally and vertically. That looking-glasses are optically symmetrical is perfectly clear from rotating them in their own plane, since this has absolutely no effect on the reflected image. This is quite different from turning a picture upside down. So, why should the looking-glass world be horizontally but not vertically reversed? How can a mirror know its right and left from its up and down? Why, indeed, should it reverse at all?

It is curious that few people ever ask why this is so, although we are all familiar with 'mirror writing' and know that, in a mirror, we look horizontally reversed from how others see us without a mirror. It is even more remarkable that experts on perception do not give any kind of clear answer to this 'mirror puzzle' and it is very seldom, if ever, mentioned in textbooks on optics. Do their authors regard the matter as too trivial, or too obvious, for comment? In the rare cases where it is discussed, clearly incorrect accounts are allowed to pass unchallenged. Thus, as we shall see, a very well-known book on the two-handedness of the universe suggests that we imagine ourselves in the space behind the mirror and perform a mental rotation, as a 'cognitive' act, so that we turn mentally to face ourselves in the mirror with left and right reversed. It is supposed that we select the rotation round the vertical axis because our bodies are vertically symmetrical. Do we really have this mental ability? A variant is that we switch the mirror image horizontally because our eyes are separated horizontally – even though the reversal is maintained when one eye is closed. We also hear, especially from philosophers: 'Well, it depends what you mean by "right" and "left" . . . I call this hand *my* right hand; but I would call it *your* left hand. . . .' How, though, can accounts in terms of definitions of 'right' and 'left' possibly explain why E in a mirror looks odd but M does not? The fact is that mirror writing looks peculiar and is difficult to read. How on earth can this be explained by uncertainties, or ambiguities, about how we describe right and left?

Mirrors have been objects of wonder and have been discussed, in more or less magical terms, for millennia. Plato comments on mirror reversal in the *Timaeus*, relating it to his theory that light shoots out of the eyes and enters them to produce the turmoil of our experiences by a kind of interaction:

> The principles governing reflections in mirrors and other smooth reflecting surfaces are not difficult to understand. All such appearances are necessary consequences of the combination of the internal and external fire, which forms a unity at the reflecting surface, though distorted in various ways, the fire of the face seen coalescing with that of the eye on the smooth reflecting surface. And the right-hand side appears as the left in the image because reverse parts of the visual stream are in contact with reverse

parts of the object as compared with what happens in normal vision.

The Roman poet-scientist-philosopher Lucretius, in the first century BC, thinks of perceptions, in his great poem *De Rerum Natura* (Book 4), as coloured 'skins' or surface 'films', continuously given off by objects (rather like the air-borne particles that give smell) to float in the air and be caught by the eye when we see. He also considers mirror reversal:

> And if in the mirror the right side of the body
> Appears on the left, it is because when the image
> Strikes on the mirror's surface it does not rebound
> Without having undergone change: what happens is this,
> It turns inside out, as would happen with a plaster mask
> If, before it was dry, someone slapped it against a pillar
> And it somehow preserved the lines of the features in front
> And was pressed backwards as it received the shock;
> It would happen that the right eye became the left
> And conversely what had been the left eye would be the right.
> It can happen that an image is carried from mirror to mirror
> So that there are five or six reflections of one object.
> Things which are hiding behind a mirror, or in some
> Tortuous recess, however out of the way,
> Are all brought out by the repeated reflection;
> It is the play of the mirror which brings them to light.
> So the image is repeated from mirror to mirror,
> What was left in the object becomes at first the right
> And at the next reflection is true left again.

Considering curved mirrors which do *not* reverse:

> There are concave mirrors which curve to our sides,
> These send back the image of our right hand to the right;
> That the image comes to us, or else because
> On the way to us it makes a turn in the air
> In response to the curvature of the mirror it came from.

Lucretius also comments on how mirror images move simultaneously with our movements, which was a problem for his notion of images being 'skins' of objects floating in the air and, pancake-like, turning over when they bounce from a mirror:

> You would think that images step out and put their foot down
> At the same time as we do, and imitate our movements.

Isn't it odd that the ancients had no idea of image-formation? Phoenician glass, which was made as early as 3,500 BC, was seldom transparent enough for a good lens; but polished metal mirrors were in use from still earlier times, and curved mirrors were quite familiar to the Greeks. Lack of understanding that images can be formed by focused light prevented them from realizing that perceptions are *representations* of the world of objects. This was the crucial stumbling block preventing artists from applying perspective rules, and it maintained untenable theories of perception which have put spanners in the works of philosophy throughout its history.

The German philosopher Immanuel Kant considers mirrors in a famous passage in the *Prolegomena to any Future Metaphysics* (1783). He is discussing the 'intuition' of space by which (he believed) we know the world of objects from experience. In trying to prove that space and time are not 'actual qualities inherent in things in themselves', Kant uses the 'paradox' of mirror reversal as a thinking-tool: 'When . . . we have in vain attempted its solution and are free from prejudices at least for a few moments, . . . we will suspect that the degradation of space and time to mere forms of our sensuous intuition may perhaps be well founded.' Kant continues:

> If two things are equal in all respects . . . it must follow that the one can in all cases and under all circumstances replace the other, and this substitution would not occasion the least perceptible difference. . . .
>
> What can be more similar in every respect and in every part more alike to my hand and to my ear than their images in a mirror? And yet I cannot put such a hand as is seen in the glass in the place of its original; for if this is a right hand, that in the glass is a left one, and the image or reflection of the right ear is a left one, which never can take the place of the other. There are in this case no internal differences which our understanding could determine by thinking alone. Yet the differences are internal as the senses teach, for, notwithstanding their complete equality and similarity, the left hand cannot be enclosed in the same bounds as the right one (they are not congruent, or *enantiomorphs*); the glove of one hand cannot be used for the other. What is the solution? These objects are not representations of things as they are in themselves and as some mere (or 'pure') understanding would know them, but sensuous intuitions, that is appearances whose possibility rests upon the relation of certain things unknown in themselves to something else, namely to our sensibility.

Kant goes on to suggest that this shows that 'Space is the form of the external intuition of this sensibility, and the internal determination of every space is possible only by the determination of its external relation to the whole of space.' He concludes: 'The part is possible only through the whole.' So Kant sees a lot in the 'paradox' of mirror reversal. Too much? Does he understand what is happening? However surprising, surely he does not.

The well-known writer and setter and solver of puzzles, Martin Gardner, gives a very different account of mirror reversal. He suggests, in *The Ambidextrous Universe* (1964), that it is due to a mental rotation:

> Curiously, the answer depends on the fact that our bodies, like the bodies of most animals, have only one plane of symmetry. It passes, of course, vertically through the centre of the body, dividing the body into mirror-halves. . . . When we look into a mirror we see a duplicate of ourself, inside a room that duplicates the room in which we are standing. When we move our right hand, we see our twin move his left. We describe the reversal as a left-right one because it is the most convenient terminology for distinguishing a bilaterally symmetrical figure from its enantiomorph. In a strict mathematical sense the mirror has not reversed left and right at all, it has reversed front and back! . . .
>
> We can summarise it this way. A mirror, as you face it, shows absolutely no preference for left and right as against up and down. It *does* reverse the structure of a figure, point for point, along the axis perpendicular to the mirror. . . . Because we ourselves are bilaterally symmetrical, we find it convenient to call this a left-right reversal. It is just a manner of speaking, a convention of words.

But can this be the answer? Would a one-armed man who is asymmetrical not see himself as we do, left-right reversed in a mirror? Of course he appears reversed, as we do. And what of a room – why is this left-right reversed though it has no left-right symmetry? And why, on this account, should printing or writing – which are not at all left-right symmetrical – appear as mirror writing? How, indeed, could our (very approximate) body symmetry have anything to do with the matter?

What is so curious is that mirror reversal puzzles very clever people. Most people never even see that there is anything puzzling, though they look in mirrors several times every day.

The difficulty (if there is a difficulty) is to see what sort of a problem this is. Is it a problem of optics? – of what happens in the eye? of what happens in the brain? – of a cognitive mental-image rotation?; of topology?; of the ultimate nature of space and time?; of how we name right and left? If none of these: what kind of problem is it?

Martin Gardner is clearly right to say that the only *optical* change is front to back, for there is no optical 'crossing over', as for lenses, curved mirrors, or Dove prisms. As we draw back from a mirror we recede further into it, because the light-path gets longer the further we, or any reflected object, is from the mirror. But what can this have to do with left-right reversal? The answer is – nothing whatsoever. This should be obvious when we note that the same reversal takes place in printing (the process of printing reverses the letters, left-right from the type), though there is no mirror involved, and no depth-reversal in printing.

Try asking: what did we *do* to make a book, say, face a mirror? *We rotated the book.* This was necessary to make the page face the mirror, and so be seen in the mirror. When the book is rotated around its *vertical* axis to face the mirror, its *left and right* switch over. This has nothing to do with mirrors, except that the page is visible in the mirror though the book has been turned around. Why is mirror writing left-right but not up-down reversed? The answer is that it perfectly well can be upside down – and not reversed left to right. This happens when the book is turned around its *horizontal* axis to face the mirror. It then appears upside down – because it *is* upside down.

The point is that mirrors allow us to see the front of opaque objects though we are behind them. But the object must be rotated, from our 'direct' view of it, for it to be seen in the mirror. Vertical rotation (which we usually do) gives mirror writing and horizontal rotation gives upside-down writing – with the left and right unchanged.

The difficulty here is to realize that the answer does not lie in optical rotations of the mirror, or in the eye, the brain, the geometry of space, or how we name right and left – but in a *procedure* that has been carried out on the object to make it face the mirror. Object-rotation does not produce this effect without a mirror because the front of the object disappears, to be replaced by its back. So the mirror is necessary even though it does not cause the rotation. It is necessary, because without it we cannot see the front of an object when it has been rotated so that its back faces us. With a mirror, we can of course see its front and back at the same time.

A mirror shows us ourselves reversed, as others see us, because we have to turn round to face the mirror. Normally we turn round vertically, keeping our feet on the ground; but we can face the mirror standing on our head: then we are upside down in the mirror and not left-right reversed. This takes us to another fact which makes it difficult to appreciate why we normally see ourselves left-right reversed but not upside-down reversed in a mirror. This is that, quite apart from mirrors, when we stand on our heads the world remains its normal way up. Here indeed special brain processes do come into play, but they have nothing to do with mirror reversal.

It is curious that accounts of mirror reversal based on cognitive rotation of mental images have not been immediately dismissed, for we see mirror writing even when there is no sign or clue that we are looking in a mirror. For example mirror writing is still seen in a large blemish-free wall mirror, though it has no frame or anything else to indicate that it is a mirror. The usual reversal occurs though there is nothing to switch on or trigger any special cognitive response to a mirror. This is different from the world remaining upright when we turn upside down, for there are nearly always signs, from gravity especially, that we are upside down.

Why is it not immediately obvious that the reversal is produced by the rotation of the object (the book one holds, or oneself, or whatever) to face the mirror? Is it because we cannot *touch* mirror images? Is it this that gives them their magical fascination? There is a vast amount of evidence that we learn to see, and so to understand, by active exploration of objects. In this way, as we ask questions, or play games, the surrounding world answers our questions as we win or lose by its interactive behaviour. This is the basis of perceptual learning and also of science. As we cannot touch images in mirrors, or touch the very small or the very distant, mirrors and atoms and stars are all difficult to understand. Difficult – yes – but impossible – no. If the 'mirror problem' looks deep and paradoxical (as evidently it did for Kant), this is because how to go about answering it is unclear – perhaps because (like shadows and shadow boxing) mirror images do not come out and hit us. As children we learn about the world by experimenting hands-on; but this is not possible for mirror images, as it is for objects that can be picked up and dropped and moved about and broken. So mirrors are mysterious and seemingly beyond explanation even though the puzzle is simply illusory.

More than twenty years ago, with a colleague, I studied the rare case of a man who recovered his sight after being blind from infancy. After an operation on his eyes he could immediately see things he already knew by touch; but he remained effectively blind to objects he had been unable to explore with his hands. He was, however, fascinated by mirrors – so much so he would spend his evenings at the local pub facing a large wall mirror, in which he watched his friends in a world entirely beyond his previous experience. The mirror world was for him metaphysics, known only by hearsay, and only very gradually accepted as he came to learn its rules by relating images to what objects do (Gregory and Wallace 1963).

This is the wonder of Alice's *Through the Looking-Glass* world – in which her kitten turns into the Queen:

> Now if you'll only attend, Kitty, and not talk so much, I'll tell you all my ideas about Looking-Glass House. First, there's the room you can see through the glass – that's just the same as our drawing room, only the things go the other way. I can see all of it when I get upon a chair – all but the bit just behind the fire-place. Oh! I do so wish I could see *that* bit! I want so much to know whether they've a fire in the winter: you never *can* tell, you know, unless our fire

smokes, and then smoke comes into that room too – but that may be pretence, just to make it look as if they had a fire. Well then, the books are something like our books, only the words go the wrong way. I know *that*, because I've held up one of our books to the glass, and then they hold up one in the other room.

When Alice went through the mirror, and jumped down into the Looking-Glass room, she was 'quite pleased to find that there was a real one, blazing away as brightly as the one she had left behind'. Then she noticed that the clock on the chimney piece had got the face of a little old man, which grinned at her. This was surprising, for as Alice said: 'You can only see the back of it in the Looking-Glass.'

When Alice and her kitten came back from Looking-Glass land, after their wonderful adventures, she mused.

'It is a very inconvenient habit of kittens . . . that, whatever you say to them, they *always* purr. If they would only purr 'yes', and mew for 'no', or any rule of that sort . . . one could keep up a conversation! But how *can* you talk with a person if they always say the same thing?'

On this occasion the kitten only purred: and it was impossible to guess whether it meant 'yes' or 'no'.

Then Alice considers confronting the normal with the mirror world – by trying to get the kitten to look at the Red Queen it had turned into through the looking-glass:

So Alice . . . put the kitten and the Queen to look at each other. 'Now, Kitty!' she cried, clapping her hands triumphantly. 'Confess that was what you turned into!'

('But it wouldn't look at it,' she said, when she was explaining the thing afterwards to her sister: 'it turned away its head, and pretended not to see it: but it looked a *little* ashamed of itself, so I think it *must* have been the Red Queen.')

How did Alice, at the end of her dream, change the Red Queen back into the white kitten? By *shaking* it: 'I'll shake you into a kitten, that I will!'

She took her off the table as she spoke and shook her backwards and forwards with all her might.

The Red Queen made no resistance whatever: only her face grew very small, and her eyes got large and green: and still, as Alice went on shaking her, she kept growing shorter – and fatter – and softer – and rounder – and – and it really *was* a kitten, after all.

If we could only pick up and shake mirror images, as we can objects, we wouldn't be nearly so bemused by reflected images.

Mirrors do, for a clear optical reason, reverse *depth*. This is entirely different from Alice's 'things go the other way', and her comment that 'words go the wrong way' in the Looking-Glass world. The optical reversal of far and near is consistent for all objects; but do all things appear depth-reversed in a mirror? Surely not. For example: you don't look hollow. But why not? Perhaps you need a bit more reflection on mirrors.

REFERENCES

Carroll, Lewis (Charles Dodgson) (1872) *Alice Through the Looking-Glass*, London.
Gardner, M. (1964) *The Ambidextrous Universe*, New York and London, Penguin.
Gregory, R.L. and Wallace, J.G. (1963) *Recovery from Early Blindness: A Case Study*, *Quart. J. Exp. Psychol.*, Monogr. Supp. 2, Cambridge, Heffers. (Reprinted in Gregory, R.L. (1974) *Concepts and Mechanisms of Perception*, London, Duckworth, pp. 65–129.)
Kant, I. (1783) *Prolegomena to any Future Metaphysics*, trans. L.W. Beck (1950), Indianapolis, Bobbs-Merrill.
Lucretius (c. 80 BC) *De Rerum Natura*, trans. C.H. Sisson (1976), Manchester, Carcanet Press.

13

WITH TWO PINS AND A LENGTH OF STRING: THE ODD PERCEPTIONS OF JOHANNES KEPLER

Surely the most interesting man in the history of perception is Johannes Kepler (1571–1630). Living at the birth of modern science, his achievements range from discovering the fundamental laws of planetary motion to discovering the optics of the eye, as well as writing the first science fiction. All this he did, and more, while serving as astronomer and astrologer to Rudolf II, King of Bohemia, and later to Wallenstein, Prince of Sagan. Kepler was indeed the magician of science.

Although astronomy is the most successful of the sciences, it shows most vividly that what appears true beyond doubt can turn out to be universally shared illusion – which is, perhaps, why many astronomers are interested in perception. Kepler's study of the eye established that the 'crystalline' of the eye accommodates to different distances, and that it is not a sentient substance but is an image-forming lens, subject to the laws of optics. This placed the first stage of vision within physics, while pushing the deep problem of perception back one anatomical step to the retina – which showed at least where the problems of perception begin, if not where they end, even though, in a way, for Kepler there was no beginning or end of perception: he saw the universe and us as one harmony rather than as causes producing effects. He sought formal structures and laws, which might be animated by occult forces; his thinking being somewhat before the impact of Galileo's conceptions of force and a generation before Newton's dynamics, which was based on Kepler's laws of planetary motion. At the time Kepler lived it was heresy to see the Earth moving among the stars, though he accepted the Copernican revolution, realizing that we spin around daily and move round the Sun yearly, even though the path by which the Earth moves, and by what powers or forces, was totally mysterious. In the *Mysterium Cosmographicum* (1596) Kepler attempted, following Plato, a geometrical theory suggesting that the motions of the five known planets obey the five types of regular polyhedra. His greatness appeared when he rejected this neat scheme because it did not fit the new and far more accurate observations of Tycho Brahe any better than the earlier available observations, which went back to Babylonian times. What Kepler did was to reject the old static models based on timeless geometry, and Ptolemy's Heath Robinson Earth-centred celestial mechanisms of epicycles (Toomer 1984), to seek simple laws relating the periods and orbital speeds of the celestial bodies. To this he devoted years of arithmetical labour – which established that the planets move in ellipses, with defined laws of motion which were entirely different from anything previously conceived. His idea of relative speeds also led, in *The Harmonies of the World* (1619), to a concept now hard to appreciate as 'science' – that pleasant musical intervals accord with the relative speeds of the planets. Isn't this, though, the most ambitious psycho-physics?

Somehow this to us bizarre notion suggested Kepler's Third Law: that the square of a planet's periodic time is proportional to the cube of its mean distance from the Sun. By his heroic arithmetic from the improved observational data, he found several new keys to the universe. To our minds, it is curious that he justified them by human aesthetics rather than by what we would call objective facts, or at least working models; but Kepler believed that music and the harmony of the universe can be appreciated equally by analytical science or evocative art; as both the laws of the world and experience are in God's mind, in which we live. Although Newton later came to separate sensation from the object world, he too accepted that the laws of nature are ideas in the mind of God – which for Newton explained why mathematics works: God is a mathematician. This notion perhaps explains why Newton was so interested in God and in biblical chronologies. However this may be, Kepler singled out, in his detailed musical account of the order of the universe, *good* chords – octave, major and minor sixths, the fifth, the fourth, the major and minor thirds – to compare with ratios of planetary speeds. He conceived the musical ratios in terms of vibrating strings bent round the sides of polygons, so that each polygon was both a geometrical basis of the deep structure of the universe and a musical conception, based on Pythagoras's discovery that pitch is inversely related to the length of a vibrating string. For Kepler, enjoyment of music is not just pleasurable stimulation of the ear, for: 'The souls of men rejoice in those very proportions that God employed (in the Creation), where ever we find them, whether by pure reflection, or by the intervention of the senses (or exercise of reason) by an occult, innate instinct.'

Thus the astronomer should learn to match the harmony of the heavens with the harmony within his mind. Kepler applied this theory to astrology, too, holding that the Earth is an animated being. How the soul of the body perceives planetary influences was for Kepler no more mysterious than how retinal images give us conscious perceptions of surrounding objects. Yet he wrote in a letter:

> My aim is to show that the heavenly machine is not a kind of divine, live being, but a kind of clockwork (and he who believes that a clock has a soul, attributes the maker's glory to the work), insofar as nearly all the manifold motions are caused by the most simple, magnetic, and material force, just as all motions of the clock are caused by a simple weight.

Kepler's First Law – that planets move in ellipses – was published in 1609, together with the Second Law – that planets describe equal areas in equal times. Kepler's vital notion, that planets move in ellipses, which took such a lot of work to be convincing, was not intuitively likely and neither was it aesthetically pleasing. The ellipse was seen as an appallingly inelegant key to the universe: it is a symmetrical figure but with only one focus filled – by the Sun – the other focus being absurdly empty. One can draw an ellipse with *two* pins and a piece of string, but not with *one* pin!

Here we may pause, to consider the string. The string is much more than a static template for drawing ellipses. With the pins, it is a subtle analogue computer, which generates elliptical functions although it is never itself elliptical. The string computes, without numbers, conic sections which are the paths of the planets. This was Kepler's vision. He could not, however, be sure that the planets revolve with constant angular velocity around the Sun-filled focus rather than around the pin less focus. There were rival claims that the empty focus was the centre. Aesthetics could not decide and neither could observation; but finally mass tipped the balance of opinion and the Sun became the king pin. Doesn't it still seem amazing, however, nearly 400 years on, that it is *sections of a cone* that is the answer to how we move in the heavens? No wonder it is so hard to get rid of magic in science! Why should elliptical shapes produced by rituals with pins and strings be acceptable science, while pentagons, and even regular polygons, are taboo magic? Kepler could hardly have said why, as he did not accept the distinction. I am not sure that we now know just where the distinction lies. Even more confusing:

although regular polygons are now taboo for astronomy, they remain objects for contemplation by chemists!

In *Somnium*, Kepler's strange dream-book, and the first science fiction, the first of whose many drafts was written in 1611, we find an allegory in which Kepler protected himself against attack for holding the Copernican notion of the Earth moving round the Sun by describing what things would look like from the Moon, which was well known to be in motion. Thus he was able to point out that the stars would seem to move from the moving base, and so to imply rather than state too explicitly that the seen movements of the stars are due to the Earth moving. Kepler thus adopted the form of fiction to protect himself from punishment, for revealing what is real and what is apparent movement.

Kepler mixed fact with fancy; both were dangerous for him. Through the Church his astronomy threatened his life, though his work was ignored by his hero Galileo. In his *Somnium* Kepler described his mother as an enchantress; this probably contributed to her being prosecuted for witchcraft, to die the year after being released from custody as a witch.

In this first science fiction Kepler describes how to get to the Moon. He suggests that the best space travellers would be 'dried up old crones who since child-hood have ridden over great stretches of the Earth at night in tattered cloaks on goats or pitchforks'. To avoid being shrivelled by the great heat of the Sun, they must travel during the four brief hours of a lunar eclipse, in the shadow of the Earth, and be pulled up to the Moon by the Sun's power that raises the tides of the sea. From prehistoric times the phases of the Moon, related to the tides, have been seen as the harmony of the universe with life on Earth – and for two pins this is how we see it now.

Kepler's range of observations was greatly extended when, around 1610, he heard of Galileo's telescopic discoveries of lunar craters, and the four bright moons of Jupiter orbiting the parent body as a tantalizing Copernican model – set to taunt us, just out of reach of unaided sight. Kepler very soon had the use of a telescope to which he added optical improvements which are used today. Upon checking Galileo's telescopic observations, he supposed that as the lunar craters are elliptical, or circular, they must have been made by intelligent Moon-dwellers. Their purpose, he supposed, was to shield the intelligent inhabitants from the heat of the Sun. The lunar mountains, on the other hand, he saw as naturally occurring and *not* constructed by intelligence as they are irregular in form. Curiously, this same criterion for extra-terrestrial intelligence was accepted by NASA in the early years of space exploration: planetary probes were launched to look for circular or straight-line structures as evidence of intelligence. This was also the basis on which the American astronomers, Percival Lowell, accepted the concept of intelligent life on Mars from his observations of ordered 'canals'; these turned out to be illusory. (Evidence of lunar life was discussed in a remarkable vignette by Alfred Russel Wallace, *Is Mars Habitable?* (1907), which includes Percival Lowell's map showing intelligently designed canals on Mars. Wallace rejected Lowell's perceptions of life on Mars – as too odd.)

Surely there is something of a paradox in Kepler's (as indeed in present) acceptance of lawful order as evidence of intelligence. For it was Kepler's established laws of order of planetary and lunar orbits that convinced everyone that the heavenly bodies are *not* intelligent; yet the similar circular patterns of lunar craters were Kepler's evidence *for* intelligent lunar beings. We still accept both order and freedom of *choice* as evidence of intelligence: yet they are exactly opposed criteria! So, we may question whether organisms can be both lawful and intelligent. From which we might ask: 'Is a science of psychology possible?'

Are we constrained, like the pencil by pins and string to describe predetermined figures, or are we free to draw our own conclusions?

REFERENCES

Caspar, M. (1959) *Johannes Kepler*, trans. C. Doris Hellman, London and New York, Abelard-Schuman.

Kepler, Johannes (1619) *The Harmonies of the World*, in *Great Books of the Western World*, ed. R.M. Hutchins (1939), Chicago, Encylopaedia Britannica, pp. 1007–85.

Kepler, Johannes (1634) *Somnium: The Dream, or Posthumous Work on Lunar Astronomy*, trans. E. Rosen (1967), Madison and London, University of Wisconsin Press.

Toomer, G.J. (1984) *Ptolemy's Almagest* (c. 150 AD), London, Duckworth.

14

FRENCH WITHOUT FEARS: DENIS DIDEROT AND JULIAN OFFRAY DE LA METTRIE

Denis Diderot (1713–84) died just two hundred years ago. Yet he lives on – through the *Encyclopédie* which set the stage for the French Revolution and the Industrial Revolution, and through his brilliant *Conversations*, in which we hear his ideas now as spoken; for like the very best conversation they are both truly profound and immensely amusing.

Diderot was the son of a master cutler, and after he wrote a book lampooning Louis XV and Madame de Pompadour, and his *Philosophic Thoughts* which placed the individual above the state, the knives were out for him. His *Thoughts* (1746) were publicly burned, and he was imprisoned for writing what everyone knew of the king and his favoured lady. He married a seamstress, Antoinette Champion; but his brilliance failed to kindle a spark in her, and they remained forever ember. Nevertheless, as is often said, Diderot lit the beacon of the Age of Reason.

In the various *Conversations* we hear discussed all manner of questions relating to sensation and perception. Take the conversation between Diderot and his friend d'Alembert, who worked with him, assisted by Voltaire, Rousseau and others, to compile and write the *Encyclopédie* whose thirty-three volumes took more than twenty years of Diderot's life:

D'ALEMBERT: I'd like you to tell me what difference there is, according to you, between a man and a statue, between marble and flesh.

DIDEROT: Not much. Flesh can be made from marble, and marble from flesh.

D'ALEMBERT: But one is not the other.

DIDEROT: In the same way that what you call animate force is not the same as inanimate force.

D'ALEMBERT: I don't follow you.

DIDEROT: I'll explain. The transference of a body from one place to another is not itself motion, it is the consequence of motion. Motion exists equally in the body that remains stationary.

D'ALEMBERT: That's a new way of looking at things. . . . But what relation is there between motion and the faculty of sensation? Do you, by any chance, distinguish between an active and an inactive sensitiveness, as between animate and inanimate force? . . . The chisel of the cleverest sculptor cannot make even an epidermis. But there is a very simple way of transforming an inanimate force into an animate one – the experiment is repeated a hundred times a day before your very eyes; whereas I don't quite see how a body can be made to pass from the state of inactive to that of active sensitiveness.

DIDEROT: Because you don't want to see it. It is just as common a phenomenon.

D'ALEMBERT: What is this. . . ?

DIDEROT: I'll tell you, since you want to be put to shame; it occurs every time you eat.

D'ALEMBERT: Every time I eat!

DIDEROT: Yes, for what do you do when you eat? You remove obstacles that prevented the food possessing active sensitiveness. You assimilate it, you turn it into flesh, you make it animal, you give it the faculty of sensation; and what you do to this foodstuff, I can do, when I please, to marble.

D'ALEMBERT: Make marble edible? That doesn't seem easy to me.

Diderot grinds up a valuable statue, mixes it with leaf-mould, feeds plants with it, and then eats the plants.

DIDEROT: So, then, I make flesh, or soul as my daughter said, an actively sensitive substance. . . . You will admit that a piece of marble is much further removed from a being that can feel, than a being that feels is from a being that can think.

D'ALEMBERT: I agree. But nevertheless the feeling being is not yet the thinking being. . . .

DIDEROT: If you're worried about the question 'which came first, the hen or the egg' it's because you suppose that animals were originally the same as they are now. What madness! We can no more tell what they were originally than what they will become.

Can you tell me what constitutes the existence of a perceiving being, for that being itself?

D'ALEMBERT: The consciousness of continued identity from the first moment of reflection to the present.

DIDEROT: And on what is this consciousness based?

D'ALEMBERT: On the memory of its actions.

DIDEROT: Very good. And what is memory? Whence does it spring?

D'ALEMBERT: From a certain organization, which develops, grows weaker, and is sometimes lost entirely.

DIDEROT: Then, if a being that can feel, and that possesses this organization that gives rise to memory, connects up the impressions it receives, forms through this connection a story which is its life, and so acquires consciousness of its identity, it can then deny, affirm, conclude and think. . . . I . . . sometimes compare the fibres of our organs to sensitive vibrating strings which vibrate and resound long after they have been plucked. It is this vibration, this kind of inevitable resonance which holds the object present, while the mind is busied about the quality that belongs to that object. But vibrating strings have another property, that of making other strings vibrate; and this is how the first idea recalls the second, the two of them the third, these three a fourth and so on, so that there is no limit to the ideas awakened and interconnected in the mind of the philosopher, as he meditates and harkens to himself amid silence and darkness. This instrument makes surprising leaps, and an idea once aroused may sometimes set vibrating an harmonic at an inconceivable distance. . . .

D'ALEMBERT: I understand. So then, if this harpsichord were not only sensitive and animate but were further endowed with the faculty of feeding and reproducing itself, it would live and breed of itself, or with its female, little harpsichords, also living and vibrating.

DIDEROT: Undoubtedly. . . . With this you can overthrow all the schools of theology, all the churches of the earth. . . .

There is only one substance in the universe, in man and in the animal. The bird-organ is made of wood, man of flesh. The bird is of flesh, the musician of flesh differently organized; but both have the same origin, the same formation, the same functions and the same end.

Then, in *d'Alembert's Dream*, where Mademoiselle de l'Espinasse and Doctor Bordeu talk with animation while D'Alembert is asleep behind a curtain, we hear philosophy criticized, though later defended by Bordeu against Mlle de l'Espinasse's comment that 'There's no difference between a waking doctor and a dreaming philosopher.'

MLLE DE L'ESPINASSE: What do you call a serious subject?

DR. BORDEU: Why, the general sensitivity of matter, the formation of the sentient being, its unity, the origin of animals, their duration, and all the questions concerned with these.

MLLE DE L'ESPINASSE: Well, I call those crazy questions, about which one may dream when one is asleep, but which no man of sense will trouble about in his waking hours.

DR. BORDEU: And why so, if you please?

MLLE DE L'ESPINASSE: Because some are so obvious that it's useless to seek their explanation, others so obscure that they can't possibly be understood, and all are completely useless.

More interested in evidence than disputation, she describes a psychophysical experiment – on the unity of the self:

MLLE DE L'ESPINASSE: It seems to me that contact, in itself, is enough. Here's an experiment I've made a hundred times . . . but wait, I must go and see what's happening behind those curtains . . . he's asleep. . . . When I lay my hand on my thigh, but some time after, when both are equally warm, I can no longer distinguish between them; the limits of the two parts of my body become blended and make one.

DR. BORDEU: Yes, until one or the other receives a prick; then a distinction reappears. So, then, there is something in you that knows whether it is your hand or your thigh that has been pricked, and that something is not your foot, nor even your pricked hand – the hand suffers but the other thing knows and does not suffer.

MLLE DE L'ESPINASSE: Why, I think it's in my head.

And so it goes on. One hears now, as though one were in that room the high-pitched voices tuned to wit, as ever more wonderful inventions – some, hints of what we now try to capture with experiments – are tossed between them, to echo in our ears.

Diderot is concerned with relations of mind and matter – and with how some matter can have sensations and perceive. He rejects dualism and he sees, as in the harpsichord analogy, that mind may be a functional characteristic of matter – and so need not be a substance of its own. This is a step towards a mechanistic (rather than 'materialistic') account of mind. Diderot actually considers phenomena of physics, such as resonance, as possible bases for memory and intelligence; so his thinking is not so very far from present neurological accounts. It is interesting, surely, to contrast this with current accounts of cognitive processes in terms of formal systems having no particular references (which may mislead) to how they might be implemented.

Another remarkable Frenchman, Julian Offray de la Mettrie

(1709–51), was also a pioneer in mechanistic accounts of mind and he suffered personally and professionally for his, for the time, extremely daring views. His *L'Homme machine* (1748) is as interesting in its way as Diderot, though presented very differently. Both Diderot and la Mettrie moved away from saying that matter is mindful, to saying that certain mechanical processes that can be carried out by matter create, or *are* mind. They are both inspired by the contemporary considerations in physics of movement; for movement was not seen as being inherently in objects, though it is objects that move and movement is inconceivable without moving objects. So, they saw mind as the interrelated movements of fibres, or tuned strings or whatever, of the brain. Similarly, matter does not normally keep time though a watch made of matter keeps time, and may (like mind) be in error.

When they produced specific examples of mechanical models for mind, they were concerned not so much with attempting to design possible mind-machines as, less ambitiously, with showing by familiar analogies that mind may be thought about in the kinds of ways we understand processes of the physical world. This did not commit them to saying that physical and mental laws need be the same, or even be at all similar. If brain-based mind is surprisingly different from familiar matter, even to the extent of having sensations, this was no initial objection for, as the rapid growth of inventions at that time showed, matter is capable of many surprises. And they knew that it was possible for machines to count and calculate and that at least some inference can be described by mechanical steps. Why has it taken so long to travel further along this road? Perhaps it is that we lack Julian Offray de la Mettrie's courage and Denis Diderot's wit.

REFERENCES

Mettrie, J.O. de la (1748) *Man a Machine*, trans. G.C. Bussey, La Salle, Illinois, 1953.
Stewart, J. and Kemp, J. (1937) (trans.) *Diderot, Interpreter of Nature: Selected Writings*, London, Lawrence & Wishart.

15

SAMUEL BUTLER: NOWHERE IN A MIRROR

Samuel Butler (1835–1902) was an interesting character, though now somewhat out of fashion. Author, painter, musician and eccentric philosopher, he was the great-great-great-grandson of Samuel Butler (1612–80), author of the satirical poem *Hudibras* (1663), which appealed to Charles II because it lampooned Puritanism. Dr Johnson, in his 'Life of Butler' says of him:

> If inexhaustible wit could give perpetual pleasure, no eye would ever leave half-read the work of Butler; for what poet has brought so many remote images together? It is scarcely possible to peruse a page without finding some association of images that was never found before.

Our Samuel Butler was the grandson of Samuel Butler (1774–1839) who was for thirty-eight years Headmaster of Shrewsbury and later Bishop of Lichfield and Coventry. His own father, who was also a clergyman, was distinguished only for antagonizing his son so effectively that Samuel went as far away as he possibly could: to New Zealand, to combine sheep farming with giant killing – the giant being Charles Darwin.

In *Erewhon*, published anonymously in 1872, and to a lesser extent in the fascinating *Notebooks* edited after his death by his close friend Festing Jones (1912), and also in *Luck or Cunning* (1886), he expressed a particularly interesting Victorian reaction to Darwinism: accepting the evolution of species, but supporting vitalism against natural selection. He waged a sustained and savage war against Darwinism and, it must be said, against Darwin himself, though he was a guest at Darwin's house.

His late novel, *The Way of All Flesh* (published posthumously in 1903), explores family strife, and is largely autobiographical. Supposedly it influenced Bernard Shaw and played a significant part in establishing the twentieth-century view of the human predicament. It is not this, however, but part of the early novel *Erewhon* that interests us here. Chapters XXIII–XXV of *Erewhon* – which of course is 'Nowhere' backwards (almost) – contain an intriguing discussion of the effects of future machines on people, and also on consciousness and intelligence considered in terms of present and potential future machines.

There are also thoughts on animals and plants:

> When a fly settles upon a blossom, the petals close upon it . . . but they will close on nothing but is good to eat; of a drop of rain or a piece of stick they will take no notice. Curious that a thing should have such a keen eye to its own interests! If this is unconsciousness, where is the use of consciousness? Shall we say that the plant does not know what it is doing merely because it has no eyes, or ears, or brains? If we say that it acts mechanically only, shall we not be forced to admit that sundry other and apparently very deliberate actions are also mechanical? If it seems to us that the plant kills and eats a fly mechanically, may it not seem to the plant that a man must kill and eat a sheep mechanically?

Turning to the possible intelligence of machines, Samuel Butler has things to say that are more daring and original than anything at that time written by English or American psychologists, who in spite of their countries' leading role in technology evidently suffered philosophical machine-blindness. Butler wrote:

> There is no security against the ultimate development of mechanical consciousness, in the fact of machines possessing little consciousness now . . . who can say that the vapour engine is not a kind of consciousness? Where does consciousness begin and where end? The shell of a hen's egg is made of a delicate white ware and is a machine as an egg-cup is; the shell is a device for holding the egg as much as the egg-cup for holding the shell!

This becomes a prophetic account of artificial intelligence, as Samuel Butler moves from the previous development of machines to the then conceivable future:

> There was a time when it must have seemed highly improbable that machines should learn to make their wants known by sound,

even through the ears of man; may we not conceive, then, that a day will come when those ears will be no longer needed, and the hearing will be done by the delicacy of the machine's own construction – when its language shall have developed from the cry of animals to a speech as intricate as our own?

Then, considering the effects on us of future machines, he looks at the moral issues with disquiet – through our inadequacies, as much as theirs:

We cannot calculate on any corresponding advance in man's intellectual or physical powers which shall be set-off against the far greater development which seems in store for the machines. Some people may say that man's moral influence will suffice to rule them; but I cannot think it will ever be safe to repose much trust in the moral sense of any machine.

Machines are outlawed in *Erewhon*, as being too dangerous for man to live with.

The Victorians combined confidence with fear, in strange ways. Most of all, they seem to have been afraid of hidden motives. Beneath unconscious behaviour there might lurk motives out of reach of blame or guilt. So (dare I say it?) the Victorians were afraid of seeing themselves as more or less intelligent machines.

Perhaps no one has expressed such musings better in the century since Samuel Butler's reflections on machine mind, though we are starting to make extra-biological intelligences. Yet, in spite of his reflections reaching somewhat beyond our reality in this direction, his view of Darwinism seems to us merely cranky – while his prescient reflections on intelligence and consciousness seemed cranky to his contemporaries!

This confirms my view that the only truly objective belief is that all beliefs are subjective.

16

ON FIRST READING A BOOK BY EINSTEIN

I first read Einstein's wonderful book on relativity in the library of the ocean-liner, the *Queen Elizabeth*. This was in the middle of the war, in 1943, when she was a troop ship, a vital lifeline linking England with America. This particular crossing to New York, in mid-winter, was not entirely uneventful. There was a violent storm: several of the ship's boats were smashed by the waves breaking over her decks and some of our chaps were injured on the companionways, for the bow and stern of the ship moved up and down sickeningly over some 50 feet, so that one was alternately immensely heavy and then almost weightless. The ship carried a large gun on her stern, which may have had some effect; but she was driving through the massive waves of the gale at her full speed, which she would never do in peacetime, and she zig-zagged with violent turns to make attack more difficult. Too fast for convoy protection, she was alone and unprotected on the Atlantic run.

Through this gale-torn night, we zig-zagged through a German ambush of six submarines. We stayed up fully dressed, and throughout the night there was a running commentary from the tannoy system letting us know what was happening – like a radio play, except that it was real. It was while this was going on that I slipped into the *Queen Elizabeth*'s library and discovered Einstein.

Through the pitching and rolling, with the unnatural listing to port, then a few minutes later to starboard, as we made yet another torpedo-defeating turn, and with the wild noise of wind and wave, orchestrated by running feet and occasional shouted orders, as a background to the world torn apart by war; here, in this little book of a hundred pages, was distilled intense imagination controlled with a perfect precision of art, which made the drama of the ship at war fade away, as if almost irrelevant. Starting from 'The noble building of Euclid's geometry [is] founded exclusively on rather incomplete experience', I was transported by observations of moving railway carriages and ascending lifts to considerations of space and time beyond experience. The storm and the threatening submarines faded away, till the dawn broke on a troubled sea.

Although each sentence in Einstein's book is crystal clear, it is extremely *difficult*. It is difficult because to understand it requires deep perceptual re learning. One has to come to see and experience differently the forces in familiar moving carriages and lifts and ships. One has also to journey impossibly, as when Einstein travels through space at the speed of light looking for his face in his shaving mirror. Will he see his own face? Will light allow this? Wonderful that the speed of light turns out to be an ultimate limitation. I still feel dizzy when I think of this.

As children we discover the world hands-on (and not just hands-on, for we bite things too and learn from others' responses), and so how we see is no doubt very largely set by what it has been possible to explore. This is in part why we see many things quite wrongly – such as the Sun and stars moving to the west, though it is we that are carried to the east by the rotating Earth. It is amusing that Aristotle thought that the Earth must be stationary because when he jumped straight up he landed where he took off – which of course couldn't happen if the Earth was rushing under his feet while he left it. This was 'of course' for Aristotle (and I assume also for today's children) because he did not have our concept of inertia. Aristotle saw the continuing movement of a missile as due to air moving in to push it along from behind. Now that we understand inertia we reverse the 'obviously', to: 'Of course one keeps moving with the Earth when one jumps, because of our momentum, which is the inertia of moving things – so, what's the problem?' For us now 300 or so years after Galileo and Newton, the inertia concept is a reference, a kind of context for seeing motion and understanding the forces on ourselves as we are accelerated in pitching ships, or whatever.

Then one reads Einstein's little book – and bang goes this reference in one's mind. For the comfortable concept of inertia turns out to be related to the mean mass of the universe; as in a way Newton found with his lovely water-in-a-spinning-bucket experiment. Newton saw that when a bucket of water suspended on a rope spins round, at first the water remains flat. Then as it takes up the spin of the bucket its surface becomes curved. If the bucket's spin is suddenly stopped the water's surface remains curved, until it comes to rest with respect to the bucket, and the room – or rather the universe. When the bucket is set to spin, before the water catches up with it the water remains flat, so its motion with reference to the bucket is irrelevant. All that matters is its motion against the rest of the universe. But what if the bucket weighed as much, or more than, the universe of stars? Would the bucket experiment then give the same result? Following Ernst Mach and Einstein we can pretty well see that it would turn out quite differently. Although this step is beyond observation or experiment we can imagine it and we see the result, given these changed concepts of inertia. Or is this 'seeing'?

Then, Einstein worried why inertial mass is *exactly related* to gravitational force. Could this be just an incredible coincidence? Or are they ultimately the *same*? All of a sudden inertia does not look at all simple, yet it might be a key to finding deep simple accounts of how things are.

Pendulums are beautiful. It is wonderful that a free pendulum's swing keeps in the same direction in space, so that we can see the Earth rotating under it. But the other day I was playing with pendulums to make an experiment for the Exploratory hands-on science centre we are starting in Bristol (see essay 26). A school experiment (but much better to try it later!) is to compare what happens when the *length* of the string, or the *weight* of the bob, are changed. The shorter the string, the faster the pendulum swings. But if the bob is made *heavier*, or *lighter*, there is *no* change in the rate of swing. This is remarkable because a heavier bob is attracted more strongly to the centre of the Earth, and so the restoring force is greater – and it should swing faster. It does swing faster in a stronger gravitational field; and slower in a weaker gravity, as on a mountain, or on the Moon. Indeed – and this was the point of the Exploratory experiment – if the bob is a magnet, attracted to a long strip magnet beneath it (which is really only possible with recently available magnets), the pendulum swings faster, though it is in a fixed place on Earth. And a repelling strip magnet placed beneath it slows the swing, as though it is on the Moon. So, one can do a kind of space travelling with pendulums. But as a pendulum swings faster with stronger gravitational (or magnetic) pull, why doesn't a *heavier* bob swing faster than a light bob? The reason is that the increased *inertia* of the heavier bob requires more force to accelerate it, and this extra force required is *exactly* the increased gravitational attraction. This means that inertia and gravity are precisely related. For Newton this exact relationship was a total mystery. It was too much of a coincidence and yet there was no visible or conceptual link between inertia and gravity to explain it.

This was one of the questions that led Einstein to suppose that inertia and gravity are ultimately the same. But to say this he had to re-describe and re-see the universe, and then persuade his fellow physicists to follow him, which they did. So, much hangs on a pendulum.

We have to be switched into an exploratory mode by such questions to move away from our infant learning and childish view to seeing the universe as it is described by physics. But then everything looks very odd. It is odd not only because so much of it lies outside our 'immediate' experience, whatever this is, but also because familiar things become related in different ways. Given significant questions, playing with pendulums and other quite simple toys and phenomena allows us to re-live our original perceptual-conceptual learning, to open our eyes and understanding to new perceptions. Given good questions, playing with a pendulum can be more effective than the most expensive and powerful tools for knowledge-gaining. This, at least, is the hope of hands-on science.

This is part of what I learned, that wartime stormy night, at peace with Albert Einstein.

Some of the best questions look trivial while some profound-looking questions turn out to be trivial. One of my favourites is why one sees oneself (or a book, or whatever) left-right reversed in a mirror, but not up-down reversed (see essay 12). It is amusing that many extremely bright people – Plato, Kant, Martin Gardner, and more immediately some of my cleverest colleagues and students – have got this absolutely wrong, in various ways, by getting on a wrong track. The difficulty is to see what sort of a question one is considering – and this can generally only become apparent when one finds the answer! Thus, in the mirror problem, it is very easy to forget that one has turned oneself, or the book or whatever, round to face the mirror. And when the turn makes the object upside down, it looks upside down and not 'mirror-reversed'. The difficulty is to see where the answer is; for it is not in the mirror, or in optics, or in one's perceptual system. Once one sees *where* the answer lies there is no difficulty seeing it. In this case it looks and is trivial, as it does not generalize to other questions and answers.

Nevertheless this is worth thinking about if only to learn one's own inadequacies at thinking. So, we have made a series of hands-on mirror experiments for the Exploratory. One is a mirror which rotates in its own plane – nothing happens. This shows how possibilities can be ruled out not only by 'thought' experiments but also by actually trying it out as a game against nature. Then there is a pair of rotatable mirrors, fixed at right angles to form a corner – which removes the usual left-right reversal when the corner is vertical. But does this help explain the original mirror reversal? No! So cancelling, or nulling, does not always serve to show what is significant. Then, lastly, there is a mirror with a figure that slides away or towards it – with a corresponding identical figure beside it but sliding in the opposite direction. This moves exactly as the *image* moves in and out in the mirror. This is the only true reversal from a plane mirror. Does this explain the original reversal? No! So the answer does not lie in mirrors or optics. Presumably one goes through tests like these while thinking, with experiments keeping one on the rails. But normally we don't have enough experiments, simple as they can often be, as guides and checks and for suggesting new possibilities. Was Einstein actually looking in his shaving mirror when he wondered what would happen at the speed of light?

Why are mirror reversal and so many 'simple' questions puzzling? It is perhaps because we do not know *where to look* for answers. How one does this I don't know. Perhaps there are no general rules or guides. But, somehow, this is what Einstein succeeded in doing for the deepest questions of the Universe and how we perceive it. If he had done this only once or even a couple of times it might be put down to chance or a lucky streak; but given that just a few people have discovered answers of several kinds, surely it must be that some people are really good at it. They have some special skill or insight into where to look.

Presumably this comes from skill in framing questions, and trying out all sorts of possibilities which are far removed from conventional wisdom. The amazing thing about Einstein is that he was wise as well!

REFERENCE

Einstein, Albert (1916) *Relativity: The Special and General Theory. A Popular Exposition*, trans. Robert W. Lawson (1920), London, Methuen.

17

KENNETH CRAIK'S *THE NATURE OF EXPLANATION:* FORTY YEARS ON

K.J.W. Craik's *The Nature of Explanation* (1943) opened the door to a new way of thinking. Its author, like so many brilliant Cambridge men (Rupert Brooke, for example, or Frank Ramsey), ensured his immortality by dying young. He was knocked off his bicycle outside his college by a passing car. It is impossible to re-read his book now without wondering what its successors would have been, if only its author had been able to continue.

Kenneth William Craik (1914–45) was an outstanding visual physiologist, especially on mechanisms of dark adaptation, and he was far more than a scene-setter, for he anticipated the scripts of later computer-based accounts of perception and intelligence. His early training in philosophy at Edinburgh was useful, as *The Nature of Explanation* demonstrates. It shows the power of explicit analogies from technological principles, as its central concepts are drawn with brilliant imagination and cogent arguments from the then newly invented analogue predictor mechanisms of the Second World War. As the first Director of the Medical Research Council's Applied Psychology Unit, in Sir Frederic Bartlett's department at Cambridge, Craik was concerned with visual problems such as glare and adaptation to dark or light, and also with matching new kinds of machines to men and comparing their performances. The Craik Laboratory at Cambridge is appropriately named after him.

Although Craik was a hero figure in England, his ideas were hardly known in the United States until several years after his death and so they were not directly influential in the American development of post-war cybernetics; but Warren McCulloch learned of Craik's work and arranged for his papers to be collected by Stephen Sherwood, and published under the title *The Nature of Psychology* (1966). Craik's only completed book, *The Nature of Explanation*, introduced the notion of 'internal models' as physical representations which for him constitute mind. It was written just before the impact of digital computers, so Craik based his ideas on the analogue computing devices of his day. He described the brain's internal models thus:

> My hypothesis then is that thought models, or parallels reality – that its essential feature is not 'the mind', 'the self', 'sense data', nor propositions but symbolism, and that this symbolism is largely of the same kind as that which is familiar to us in mechanical devices which aid thought and calculation. (p. 57)

First he asked why explanations of any kind are sought – describing an explanation as: 'a kind of distance-receptor in time, which enables organisms to adapt themselves to situations which are about to arise'. He broadens this to extricate us from the biological straightjacket, by suggesting:

> Apart from this utilitarian value it is likely that our thought processes are frustrated by the unique, the unexplained and the contradictory and that we have an impulse to resolve intellectual frustrations, whether or not there is a practical problem that needs a solution.

This plea for physical explanations of cognition does not, however, mean that:

> it is useless or incorrect to give apparently non-physical clinical explanations of psychological phenomena – for instance, to say that an unpleasant experience or shock may *cause* amnesia or suppression. This is a correct statement of the phenomena as far as it goes; but we are entitled to go further if we can. If we then find a more ultimate physical and physiological train of events to be invoked 'in between' the shock and the suppression, we should regard this as a more ultimate part of the mechanism, just as it is correct to say that the pressure of one's finger on the self-starter causes the engine to go, but more fundamental to say that the pressure of one's finger causes current to flow in the windings of the starting motor and still more fundamental to give an account of the flow of current and torque exerted by the motor in terms of electronic and electro-magnetic theory.

Here we see clearly what he is getting at, and why he disagreed with Sir Frederic Bartlett for suggesting that a mechanistic physical explanation, particularly in psychology, may merely be more complicated. For Craik, a mechanistic explanation 'covers the most facts by the fewest numbers of postulates and leaves the fewest anomalies outstanding'. He adds the interesting thought that:

This adequacy of and freedom from anomalies is also the credential of the particles as being ultimate, remote as they may seem from everyday life. For, once rigid causality is admitted, whether it be thought to be mechanistic or not, anomalies must be regarded as cases where explanatory concepts are wrong.

So he begins to separate internal models, physically causal though they are, from the external physical world. This leads to the body of the book, Chapter V: 'The Hypothesis on the Nature of Thought'. Reminding us of the importance for survival of predicting events, Craik considers the use of physical models (which for him can serve as symbols) and of words and numbers for prediction and reasoning – with three essential processes:

1. 'Translation' of external process into words, numbers or other symbols.
2. Arrival at other symbols by a process of 'reasoning', deductive inference, etc.
3. 'Retranslation' of these symbols into external processes (as in building a bridge design) or at least recognition of the correspondence between these symbols and external events (as in realizing that a prediction is fulfilled).

Then comes the critical step (p. 51):

this process of reasoning has produced a final result similar to that which might have been reached by causing the actual physical process to occur (e.g. building the bridge haphazard and measuring its strength, or compounding certain chemicals and seeing what happened); but it is also clear that this is not what has happened; the man's mind does not contain a material bridge or the required chemical.

Then:

this process of prediction is not unique to minds. . . . A calculating machine, an anti-aircraft 'predictor', and Kelvin's tidal predictor all show the same ability. . . . The physical which it is desired to predict is *imitated* by some mechanical device or model which ever is cheaper, or quicker, or more convenient in operation.

This, Craik says, is very similar to the three stages of reasoning, as the external processes are 'translated' into positions of gears, etc., in the model; the arrival at other positions of gears, etc., by mechanical processes; and 'finally the translation of these into physical processes of the original type'. Here we reach the nub of Craik's account of how internal models are mindful:

> By a model we thus mean any physical or chemical system which has a similar relation-structure to that of the process it imitates. By 'relation-structure' I do not mean some obscure non-physical entity which attends the model, but the fact that it is a working physical model which works in the same way as the process it parallels, in the aspects under consideration at the moment.

The model does not have to resemble the object or situation pictorially: 'since the physical object is "translated" into a working model which gives a prediction . . . we cannot say that the model invariably preceeds or succeeds the external object it models'. In the case of the nervous system, models 'permit trial of alternatives'.

He does not commit himself to any physiological account of how brain models are realized physically; the concern is only with underlying similarities of function, though there may be very large surface differences. So one could not see how they function from anatomy, however detailed. Like any other analogy, the brain model's use is 'bound somewhere to break down' – hence a rich bunch of thinking errors and perceptual illusions, which are endemic to any cognition.

The account is in terms of the analogue devices of his time which did not have the flexible symbol-handling powers of the electronic digital computers, which soon followed. So it is interesting to see how Craik treats numbers and words with his analogue account of brain function. (Imagine an analogue word processor!) Craik denies that numbers have 'real existence', and he puts much more weight than we would now on restraints of the mechanics of the device. Thus Craik does not think that the great range of applications, without leading to inconsistencies, is a proof of the 'real existence' of numbers; but that it may, rather, suggest that the neural model, or the machine, may have extreme flexibility. (This he attributes tentatively to there being only a small number of functional units, by range and lawfulness, of objects composed of only a few kinds of atomic particles.) In any case, rather than asking 'what kind of thing a number is', he considers instead 'what kind of mechanisms could represent so many physically possible or impossible, and yet self-consistent, processes as number does'. Implication is also described in these terms, as being (p. 63): 'a kind of artificial causation in which symbols connected by rules represent events connected by causal interaction'.

It was almost impossible to see at that time how a machine could generalize. Craik points out that recognizing objects from different positions, or from stimulation of different retinal regions, is easy for an organism but difficult for a machine; and that this may indicate a fundamental difference between 'recognition in its physical and psychological senses; on the other hand, they may only show that a different form of mechanism is involved in psychological recognition'. Craik reminds us here of Lashley's warning that lack of discrimination in the response of an animal may give its behaviour a false appearance of generality and abstraction; but Craik urges that properties of objects can be 'really recognized as the same because, acting on the brain mechanisms of the animal, they produce the same effect, just as a pound of butter and a pound of bacon both produce the same deflection on a balance'. He is clearly worried, however, as to how generalizing power could be achieved by a conceivable machine, for example to recognize objects over various distances and orientations – for here he is tempted to invoke consciousness as a super-mechanical causal principle for perception: 'This may be one of the functions of consciousness – to permit greater "elasticity" and flexibility and unity of response than the known properties of co-ordinations of mechanisms will accomplish' (p. 68).

He tries to resist this postulate of active powers of consciousness taking over where mechanisms seem inadequate, by looking at characteristics of some selected mechanisms: 'Sometimes a simple mechanical device will show this power in high degree. Thus, an inclined plane will "recognise" spheres, of whatever size, material and colour, and "distinguish" them from cubes, since the former will roll down it while the latter will not.' He concludes that recognition in man and animals is too flexible and adaptable to be accounted for by 'a few specific and special mechanisms of this kind' (p. 71).

So consciousness as an active principle is not entirely rejected. But, however this may be, Craik sees that the internal-model brain mechanisms must work causally in physical terms though they *represent* reality, rather than being linked in the usual causal way to the events of the external world:

> Language must evolve rules of implication governing the use of words, in such a way that a line of thought can run parallel to, and predict, causally determined events in the external world. The ability of a particular 'line of thought' to do this is the test of its correctness as an explanation. (p. 81)

Then he raises a likely criticism – or doubt – that internal models (or cognition) are needed:

Some may object that this reduces thought to a mere 'copy' of reality and that we ought not to want such an internal 'copy'; are not electrons, causally interacting, good enough? Why do we want our minds to play the same sort of game, with laws of implication instead of causal laws to determine the next step?

Craik's reply is surely an essential part of the deep answer to why we have cognitive processes. His answer is in two parts:

1. That an internal model can predict events that have not yet occurred.
2. That the interactions of electrons do not tell us what we want to know – for though the 'machine' (nature) works equally well whether we are ignorant of steps in it or not, scientific thought does not work equally well if there is a gap in the chain.

There is uncertainty, however, over the status of symbols, and how mechanisms can represent. Craik explains the so-to-say un-natural precision of geometry, which is far greater than any perception or measurement allows, by analogy with administrative law – that, for example, conscription age is fixed by a precise date of birth, rather than by physique, or whatever. So the brain's internal models are seen to legislate and impose their legislation upon how we see – as well as to free us from causal nature though they function by physically causal mechanisms. We can hardly accept Craik's account of geometry, however. Why should such 'legislation' turn out to be causally predictive for what objects turn out to be like on independent grounds? The account does not look right at this point.

Undoubtedly these ideas were triggered largely by the new technology of the Second World War, to which Craik's own contribution was considerable and of which his understanding was profound. He was writing when gun predictors acting from minimal received signals were new and had striking conceptual significance. Craik was surely right to accept the principles by which they worked, not merely as analogies but as *examples* of what he conceived for the brain. The same is so for concepts of servo-control for limb movements, for these are actual biological servo-systems, not mere analogies of what are realized in man-made machines. Likewise, Craik supposes that, hundreds of millions of years ago, brains incorporated technologies that we have invented over the last few centuries.

So, forty years ago, Kenneth Craik transformed the technology of his day into the image of man; as, long before, Homer's Hephaestus created Pandora from fire and Pygmalion breathed life into the ivory statue of Galatea. But the technology of Craik's time, though so recent, was not the same as ours. There is indeed a smaller jump from Homer (who would have known the calculating abacus) in the eighth century BC to the computing of the 1940s than from the analogue computing devices familiar to Craik to our computers today.

It has only recently become clear that computers can be extremely flexible and adaptable, and the difficulties Craik raised for generalization have now been largely solved by AI algorithms. So we are less tempted to fall back on supposed powers of consciousness to explain mental abilities, such as perceptual generalization of the shapes and sizes of things. Paradoxically, though, this makes consciousness even *more* mysterious – for what does it do?

Many people now see mind as patterns and powers of symbols, as handled by software digital brain-processing; so now Craik's account of symbols in relation to mechanisms without software hardly looks right. Software confers infinitely flexible restraints; but Craik had to rely on hardware characteristics, which would not at all necessarily be appropriate for the 'relation-structures' of his internal models. How would appropriate relation-structures be selected according to need? We see digital programming as conferring the necessary flexibility, and appropriateness as the machine changes according to needs, while at the same time it serves the symbols in the symbiosis that allows such machines to be intelligent.

Is this how it will end? Or will we come to see as merely a quaint idea, digital brains going through the precise tortuous *man-made* steps of elaborate mathematics – even to waggle a finger, or see? Will something less analytically digital, and perhaps more crudely analogue, return for accounts of brain function? Or will some new technology arise so that we come to see perception in a quite new light? Or, after all, will the brain turn out to be millions of interacting special-purpose analogue computing units, functioning without the analytical steps of software, much as Craik supposed?

However this may be, in just over a hundred pages Kenneth Craik distilled a great amount of thought on these fundamental questions that is still fermenting and inspiring us now – forty years on.

REFERENCES

Bartlett, F.C. (1946) 'Obituary notice: K.J.W. Craik', *Brit. J. Psychol.* 36, 109–16.
Craik, K.J.W. (1943) *The Nature of Explanation*, Cambridge, Cambridge University Press.
Craik, K.J.W. (1966) *The Nature of Psychology: a collection of papers and other writings by the late Kenneth J.W. Craik*, ed. Stephen Sherwood, Cambridge, Cambridge University Press.
Zangwill, O.L. (1980) 'Kenneth Craik: the man and his work', *Brit. J. Psychol.* 21, 1–6.

18

THE GENIUS OF ALAN TURING

Alan Turing (1912–54) was one of the two key figures in the creation of electronic digital computers and artificial intelligence, the other being the Hungarian-American mathematician John von Neumann (1903–57). Working almost entirely independently, these remarkable men not only set the stage but built the scenery and wrote the script for the computer revolution and also for descriptions of mind in terms of computing procedures.

Alan Turing made his fundamental contribution shortly after graduating in mathematics from King's College, Cambridge, with papers on computable numbers (1936–7) in which he showed that there are classes of mathematical problems that cannot be proved by any fixed, definite process or procedures. He did this by thinking of proof in terms of *mechanical operations*. For this, he invented the machine which is the starting-point of electronic digital computing and of artificial intelligence. The Turing Machine was described in physical terms; but it was abstract, in the sense that although its description defines all possible operations, not all of these may be realizable in practice. For example, it may be too slow. The Turing Machine can be visualized as an infinitely long tape of squares, each of which may either bear a number or be blank. The machine reads one square at a time and it can move the tape to read other squares, forwards or backwards. It can print new symbols or erase symbols. Turing showed that his very simple machine can specify the steps required for the solution of any problem that can be solved by following instructions, or explicit rules or procedures. Turing acknowledged its ancestor – the grandfather of all electronic computers – Charles Babbage's Analytical Engine of the 1830s.

Turing considered whether a human being, or rather the human mind, could be described by analogy with such a machine, by emphasizing that what the machine is *made of* is essentially *unimportant*. For example, as he pointed out, Babbage's nineteenth-century computer was mechanical, while in the twentieth century electricity would be used as it is faster and more reliable; but there is nothing essential in whether a computer is mechanical or electrical or whatever, provided only it can carry out the necessary instructions. The same, he thought, is true of *brains*, so there should not be a basic distinction between us and conceivably realizable machines. This short but crucial step depends on two assumptions: that mind is produced by physical brain and other body processes, and that the particular biological *protoplasm* material of the brain is not specially important for human intelligence or other aspects of mind. Thus, if we were constructed of different materials we would in several ways be different but we could still be intelligent perceiving beings. This step of saying that the brain's substance, and also origin, is essentially unimportant remains controversial. Curiously, both theology and neurophysiology combine to oppose it, though for very different reasons: it makes the physical brain too important for theologians and not important enough for physiologists.

In his pioneering paper 'Computing machinery and intelligence' (1950), Turing suggested how we could judge the success of a computer-simulation of the human mind. Although 'Turing's test' for assessing simulations of human minds has been criticized on various grounds, it is probably the best available way of deciding whether there is human-like intelligence in a man-made machine. This is the *Imitation Game*. Turing describes it in this way:

> It is played with three people, a man (A), a woman (B), and an interrogator (C) who may be of either sex. The interrogator stays in a room apart from the other two. The object of the game for the interrogator is to determine which of the other two is the man and which the woman.

The interrogator is allowed to put questions to A and B – though not of physical characteristics, such as length of hair – and he is not allowed to hear their voices. Thus he is only allowed to experience or question *mental* attributes. The next step is to substitute one of the humans for a machine. The machine communicates with a teletype. The question is whether the interrogator could distinguish the remaining human from the computer. Turing points out that for some questions, such as problems in arithmetic, the humans would show up revealingly poorly, and that this is perhaps an objection to the test. Nevertheless, it seems as good as any test so far suggested for distinguishing between man and intelligent machines. The test is behaviouristic; but, as Turing says, we cannot 'get inside' another human being to know by direct experience whether he or she has conscious experiences, such as sensations of colours and emotional states. He leaves it open to us to decide whether we should assume that the machine which passes the test of the Imitation Game is like us conscious, or has no awareness.

Alan Turing was the master code-breaker of the Second World War, leading the team which succeeded in reading the highest-level German secret codes, especially Enigma. This was not revealed until thirty years later, when his true importance as the originator of the first practical programmed computer, the Colossus – which was used for the code breaking – became known. The secret was remarkably well kept, so the early history of computers and of Turing's role has had to be rewritten.

While a student at Cambridge I went with the mathematical statistician Violet Cane on a not-to-be-forgotten pilgrimage to meet Alan Turing. Nowadays, however significant the journey, one would not think twice about motoring from Cambridge to Manchester. But this trip was rather different. My car was a 30-year-old open tourer Austin Seven, which I had bought for £20 from a farmer who for the past few years had used it as a chicken coop. My proud possession was painted British Racing Green and it had huge black-painted headlamps. Then, one memorable day following a slight mishap with a brick wall, I discovered a sliver of bright brass under the thick black paint. Burnishing what turned out to be solid brass lamps, they became rich-gleaming moons, so the Alan Turing Pilgrimage was undertaken with due pomp and ceremony – for this was a journey to meet a hero. There was no question of missing the scenic wonders of the Peak District on the way, for our greatest speed was 28 miles an hour, the average being nearer 10 on the winding mountain roads, a slow progress which enhanced both the view and our expectations. There was one episode of farce. Returning to the car parked outside the (then primitive) Inn on Snake Pass, we discovered inside it a sleeping sheep!

We found Alan Turing in the Manchester Computer Laboratory, which was one of the first in the world. He devoted half a day to his two entirely unknown visitors, giving his ideas on randomness and structure. He agreed to give a lecture to the Cambridge Socratic Society (of which I was Secretary, Michael Argyle, later the Oxford social psychologist, being its President). On the occasion he spoke memorably on the structure of fir cones and how such simply defined structures could be coded with minimum genetic information. This was just before the great DNA discoveries of Francis Crick and James Watson. Turing was developing Schrödinger's insight, expressed in *What is Life?* (1943), that genetic information must be stored on the molecular scale, and that the quantum theory showed how the information could be stored at this level for millions of years and be occasionally modified by chance events to give mutations. Turing's account was abstract, but it generated useful numbers and showed the importance of redundant forms for nature. Also, it was an important step from earlier vitalistic accounts, which though not usefully explanatory were still prevalent at that time for lack of anything better.

Not along after, Alan Turing died – by following the Greek ideal of love and provoking the inhumanity of man, which can be more frightening than any machine. God help us if machines get built which, on the Turing test, match us for inhumanity. He died at the height of his powers as mathematician, code-breaker and above all as a principal originator of digital computers and computational accounts of intelligence. Alan Turing's genius lives on forever in mindful machines.

REFERENCES

For a technical historical appraisal, which discusses Turing's ideas in relation with von Neumann's, see: Randell, B.R. (1972) 'On Alan Turing and the origins of computers', *Machine Intelligence* 7 (Edinburgh).

Von Neumann's final thoughts are: von Neumann, J. (1958) *The Computer and the Brain*, Cambridge, Mass., MIT Press.

There is a poignant memoir of Turing by his mother: Turing, S. (1959) *Alan M. Turing*, Cambridge, Heffers.

The outstanding biography, with a superb technical account of the whole range of Turing's ideas and achievements, is: Hodges, A. (1983) *Alan Turing: The Enigma*, London, Burnett-Hutchinson.

Schrödinger, E. (1943) *What is Life?* Cambridge, Cambridge University Press.

Turing, A.M. (1937) 'On computable numbers, with an application to the *Entscheidungsproblem*', *Proc. London Math. Soc.* (ser. 2) 42, 240–65; 43, 544.

Turing, A.M. (1950) 'Computing machinery and intelligence', *Mind* 59 (n.s. 236), 433–60.

19

PREMATURE REDUCTIONS AND MYTHICAL PRODUCTIONS: GAINS AND LOSSES OF EXPLANATION

Through the centuries, the progress of science could be described as *exorcising* myths by *exercising* powers of observation and experiment. Thus, the mutual attraction of lode stones was at first given a mythological, or magical, explanation – as occurring in these strange stones by a psychological, or more specifically sexual, attraction. The darker, stronger lodestones were supposed male, the paler and weaker, female. Although this looks like magic when applied to stones, however strange, the notion of psychological attraction (and repulsion) is still applied to people. Just why should one kind of attraction be appropriate for lodestones, and steel magnets – the other only for living organisms, especially people?

The psychological-attraction account of magnetism, which was discussed in these terms with some sympathy by Aristotle, is altogether passed over in the far more detailed contemporary studies of stones by Theophrastus, in his *De Lapidibus*. Theophrastus knew Aristotle and he was also a pupil of Plato. He became head of the Lyceum following Aristotle's death in 321 BC. The specialist Theophrastus did not attempt any explanation of lodestone attraction; though, evidently, somehow he realized that it is not psychological, but physical. And yet, even long after William Gilbert's great and first truly scientific book, *De Magnete* of 1600, psychological terminology continued to be applied to the attraction of magnets. Gilbert realized that the Earth is a vast magnet, and that this is why compass needles point systematically North–South – and yet magnetic interactions continued to be called 'sympathetic'. This in spite of the celebrated physician Thomas Browne, who in *Pseudoxia Epidemica* (1646) calls it a 'conceit' that pieces of iron touched to the same lodestone acquire affinity for each other, such that however far separated they maintain their orientation to each other. He challenged the 'sympathy' notion by experiment, placing one prepared needle on one circle, while rotating the other around a series of letters arranged around another circle. Nothing happened. But this suggested to an early Fellow of the Royal Society, Joseph Glanvill (the author of *Philosophical Considerations Touching Witchcraft* (1666)), in his *The Vanity of Dogmatising* (1665), the essential principle of Sir Charles Wheatstone's first successful electric telegraph! There is indeed a long list of sixteenth-, seventeenth- and eighteenth-century writers, given in J.J. Fahie's *History of Electric Telegraphy to the Year 1837* (1884), referring to 'sympathetic' communication of magnets – which occult notion led to human communication by what we now see as the purely physical, even though mysterious, properties of magnets.

This is just one example of physical science and technology overcoming mentalistic explanations, which in physics we now generally see as myth. But are mentalistic explanations myths in psychology? A natural progression is to assume that computer science will come to exorcise myths of mind for brain function, and perception. But something very strange is happening to the physical sciences – they are going mental!

In a recent book, *Mind and the New Physics* (1985), written by a quantum physicist, Fred Alan Wolf, we learn (p. 152) that: 'The photons in a laser tube are bosons and so tend to "physically condense" into the same state. This "boson condensation" is the physical manifestation of a universal and very human quality – the feeling of love. In other words, light is the lover. Photons "love" to be in the same state.' This leads to: 'Our bodies, our sexuality . . . is inherent in our photons and electrons.' I am not trying to knock this book and it would be unfair to do so by such selected quotations; but this kind of writing on psychology from current physics is, surely, extraordinarily like the psychological myth–magic in which the world was seen at the dawn of physics. This is the opposite of reducing psychology to physics for it is making physics look like psychology – as physics appeared before its disciplined observations and experiments, in pre-Socratic writing.

Though the brain is a physical system, it by no means follows that it functions as its constituent fundamental particles behave. It by no means follows that, though we are intelligent, the electrons of our brains and bodies are intelligent or conscious or aware. Similarly, there is a great deal more to what holds up the arches and domes of a cathedral than the individual properties and local interactions of its stones. To understand why the building stands up we need descriptions of stress lines and so on, which may not even mention stones. Or more brain-like: the importance of quantum physics for understanding computers is limited to how the transistors or chips work. But it tells us nothing about how these components carry out computations – or, in this sense, how the computer works. This kind of distinction of 'levels' from the physics of elementary particles to how a system functions most likely also applies to the brain, whether or not it is like an existing computer.

To suppose that the characteristics of the entire system are in each of its parts (or in small working systems) inevitably gives the parts amazing powers. So, mythologies are generated. When psychological qualities, such as hate, fear, or love, are attributed to electrons, to atoms, or to molecules, these are at once given properties we try hard to explain in terms of how the system functions. Another example is purpose. On these considerations we should accept only with caution the way Richard Dawkins, in his rightly celebrated *The Selfish Gene* (1976), describes the gene molecules as protecting themselves against change. Taken literally, this suggests that individual molecules are capable of acting with purpose; though Richard Dawkins may have good literary reasons for attributing purpose to molecules.

It is virtually certain that there are vital principles of brain function which are simply not envisaged in fundamental particle, or even in *any*, physics. And this does not make neuroscience metaphysics. Quite the other way: sterile metaphysics springs from assuming that complexity is contained in simple fundamentals. Then science creates its own new myths, which can be just as confusing as the ancient myths that, over the centuries, science has exorcised. Most neuroscientists would, however, accept that it is important for brain studies and psychology to be based on currently accepted physics. So it is excellent that physicists take the trouble to show how their current concepts may apply. And we will all agree that the highly nonintuitive – indeed bizarrely paradoxical – behaviour of fundamental particles must ultimately be essential for understanding some aspects of perception and how the brain works. But very few of us would accept that physics has our answers. Specifically, we should object to saying that we love because electrons are mutually attracted, or that we perceive because the fundamental particles (or individual molecules or cells) composing us perceive. The dangers here are: *premature reduction* to an inadequate fundamental account; or, conversely, *mythological production* of seemingly magical powers to particles. What is so intriguing is that the explanation of the same phenomena does not look magical when the reduction to simpler terms is adequate; or when the fundamental particles, or whatever, themselves display the phenomena. But one does have to be careful – the best available explanation of magnets is that they are made of atomic particles which attract each other!

There is a generally held assumption that the sciences range in some kind of an objective order from those which are 'fundamental' to other lesser sciences, the latter depending upon the more basic facts and concepts of the former. It is, however, possible to question this hierarchy, which generally accords logic, and especially mathematical physics, the dignity of supporting all other sciences, of being the most fundamental. Logic may be a special case, as it is clearly so very general and is non-empirical. But does physics have its fundamental status from being similarly general, or because the world is so arranged that any observer, or discoverer, essentially needs its facts and concepts as starting points? Or has physics inherited a historical right to rule supreme – inheritance from the dramatic success of Newton's account of the dynamics of the heavens? Or, is there some deeper reason why logic, mathematics and physics are the King, Queen and Prince of the sciences?

Thomas Kuhn's idea, expressed in *The Structure of Scientific Revolutions* (1962), of changing fundamental notions, or 'paradigms', for interpreting scientific evidence is clearly relevant here; for one should expect that a sufficiently dramatic paradigm revolution could displace even physics from its special place, if Kuhn's relativistic account (and earlier Hanson's (1958) *Patterns of Discovery*) holds without overriding 'objective' restraints on how descriptions and explanations may be based (cf. also Kuhn 1977).

Related issues are discussed – though very differently – in a recent paper by the American philosopher Hans Sluga (1984), in connection with the intellectual antecedents of the founder of modern mathematical logic, Gottlob Frege (1848–1925) (cf. Dummett 1973). The point is: Frege sought the absolute basis of truth, and claimed to have found it in mathematical logic. It is important to note that he claimed this although he saw that Kant (1787) was wrong to base our perception of the world, and our confidence in empirical science, on the axioms of geometry. For, following especially Karl Gauss (1777–1855), he saw that the Euclidian axioms are not extremely general, necessary truths relating perception and measurement to the object world – as had incorrectly been assumed from classical times – but are, rather, hypotheses that can be questioned and challenged. One might indeed see the displacement of Euclidean axioms from their long-held, uniquely general foundation status as the most dramatic Kuhnian paradigm revolution that has occurred so far in the history of thought. Although Frege accepted this drastic revision, he did still see knowledge as absolutely 'layered'. And Frege followed Leibniz (1646–1716) in attempting a universal notation for representing all 'levels' of reality. In these terms, he calls the laws of logic: 'those laws upon which all knowledge rests'. And also: 'those laws of thought that transcend all particulars'.

Frege gives logic this special place because, in Hans Sluga's words:

> Logic possesses for him [Frege] the status of primacy within the body of human knowledge because we must use the laws of logic as well as those of arithmetic in order to gain knowledge from our subjective experiences. Arithmetic, in turn, he believed in those early years, rests on logic, and logic can occupy this place of primacy within our knowledge because of the generality of its laws.
> (1984, p. 346)

Frege abandoned the hope of reducing arithmetic to logic; but he continued to believe that, together, they are the basis of knowledge – because 'sense perceptions alone are of little use to us'. Sluga suggests that Frege's lack of confidence in perception has at least in part a personal-historical cause: the personal influence of the great optician-physicist Karl Abbe, the original Technical Director of the Zeiss optical company at Jena, who of course designed the optics of the modern microscope – from his diffraction-limit analysis of optical image formation. Referring to the optician Abbe, the logician Frege wrote: 'Our knowledge of refraction of light teaches us that many images produced by the microscope are thoroughly unreliable' . . . 'for the knowledge of natural laws we also need those other sources of knowledge: the logical and geometrical ones.'

Hans Sluga challenges this kind of 'foundationalism' of supposing that knowledge rests on certain basics, not only by pointing to personal influences, such as Abbe's on Frege (and, let's face it, philosophies are in local geographical and family 'schools', which precludes belief in their objectivity or historical neutrality), but he also challenges directly the special fundamental role of logic:

> Logical techniques are useful for describing relatively simple formal structures, but they seem particularly well adapted to describing synchronic or timeless structures (such as the syntax of a language or a hierarchy of sets). They are not well adapted to the description of temporal structures such as processes, activities, practices, actions, social and political developments. . . . There are human enterprises and cognitive pursuits where the considerations of logical structures are of little significance.

If this is so for logic, is physics the empirical foundation of all other sciences? The argument seems to move towards saying that there are *no* absolute foundations, and that knowledge is dependent on many sources none of which stands alone. And, after all, as Ernst Mach

only slightly overemphasized, physics is a direct development of –
and depends on – human sensory perception!

REFERENCES

Dawkins, R. (1976) *The Selfish Gene*, Oxford, Oxford University Press.

Dummett, M. (1973) *Frege: The Philosophy of Language*, London, Duckworth.

Hanson, N. R. (1958) *Patterns of Discovery*, Cambridge, Cambridge University Press.

Kant, I. (1787) *Critique of Pure Reason* (2nd edn), trans. Kemp Smith, Cambridge, Mass., MIT Press.

Kuhn, T. S. (1962) *The Structure of Scientific Revolutions*, Chicago, University of Chicago Press.

Kuhn, T.S. (1977) 'Mathematical versus experimental traditions in the development of physical science', in *The Essential Tension*, Chicago, University of Chicago Press.

Sluga, H. (1984) 'Frege: the early years', in R. Rorty, J.B. Schneewind and Q. Skinner (eds) *Philosophy in History*, Cambridge, Cambridge University Press, pp. 329–56.

Theophrastus (c. 315 BC) *De Lapidibus*, trans. D.E. Eichholz (1965), Oxford, Oxford University Press.

Wolf, Fred Alan (1985) *Mind and the New Physics*, London, Heinemann.

20

IS ESP CRYSTAL BALLS?

Are there *any* paranormal phenomena to bother about? Through the ages, the vast majority of people have believed that foretelling the future – with crystal balls, or in patterns of stars or tea leaves, or whatever – is possible, if unreliable. It has been very generally and is still widely believed that perceptions can occur without physical senses. At the present time astrology is enjoying a boom, even if educated people take it with a pinch of salt – but then salt has magical associations!

As the use of tools and technology grew, to tame nature and kill enemies, magic was found to be correspondingly powerless. So science, from its beginnings, challenged magical beliefs. But although science has grown from magic and is far more successful, it does not *follow* that magic is false, even though science has shown that very many accepted ideas are mistaken. This is so for many appearances: much of what appears obviously and certainly true turns out to be false or illusory; but it does not follow that *everything* needs correcting by science. When corrected, old notions and appearances tend not quite to die; so we live in a curious mixture of what seems to be or feels true though contradicted by intellectual understanding, which is deeply confusing. It may be sufficiently confusing and unsettling to put people off scientific understanding altogether; then the occult may become especially attractive. In any case, there is always a schism between perceiving and knowing, as indeed was clear to Plato and Aristotle. Perceptual learning is probably not adequate for us ever to see things as we may know they are.

At the beginning of science, Aristotle was sceptical of magical practices and the 'hidden' occult, though there are strong traces of animism in Aristotle's physics – hence, indeed, the word 'natural', referring to the natural tendency of objects to seek the ground as they fall, or to move in straight lines, or of the stars to move in circles. So inanimate objects had natures and natural tendencies much as we have, in Aristotle's physics and much later. Plato looked for hidden geometrical principles behind visible reality. He was quite explicit that appearance is illusion, reality being hidden from the senses. If 'occult' means 'hidden' – why is not Plato's account, and a great deal of modern science which is closely related to it, as occult as magic?

Evidently 'occult' means more than merely 'hidden'; though the word is still used in its purely optical sense in astronomy, as stars have 'occultations'. Magically, 'occult' and 'paranormal' evidently mean more than 'hidden', or 'mysterious', or 'unexplained', for there are plenty of accepted phenomena that are not explained and yet are not thought of as magically occult, or paranormal. Thus there is no adequate account in current physics of ball lightning – glowing spheres of plasma, moving apparently of their own volition, and like all the best occult phenomena associated with thunderstorms. The question is, why are seldom observed lightning balls (which are so like ghosts) *respectable* phenomena for physicists, who out of hand reject claims of paranormal phenomena? Just why are lightning balls so fundamentally different from the glass or crystal balls of ESP? The answer should tell us something about normal science, even if not about magic and the occult. So this is well worth thinking about.

Science accepts phenomena as genuine either through observations, which may be by human observers or by instruments and may be quite indirect, or through theoretical considerations. There is a strong preference for easily repeatable observations; but here the claims of mediums and psychics do not stand up well, for their reported observations or claims almost always fail to be repeated in controlled experiments. It seems that the better (in scientific terms) the experiments are designed and carried out, the less they provide evidence for paranormal phenomena such as telepathy, clairvoyance, telekinesis or spoon-bending. What usually emerges is statistical artefacts, conjuring, or more or less conscious fraud. It is, also, important to note that we are not good at assessing probabilities; so when something like a telephone call from someone we have just been thinking about occurs, it may be less unlikely than we think. The ESP experimental evidence has been critically assessed by Hansel (1966), who concludes that there is no sound evidence; but the issue remains controversial, and his and other criticisms are of course in their turn criticized.

Discoveries of undoubted lasting importance have been made from magical practices. The trouble here, though, is that once accepted by science they are no longer seen as magic. A clear example is the origin of the magnetic compass. The story begins in China, in the third century BC, with the diviner's board, which consisted of an upper part representing the Heavens, and a lower part representing the Earth. The 'Heavens' rotated on the 'Earth'. For divining the future, 'pieces' representing various objects were thrown on the board, and the diviner read the future from their positions. One of these pieces was spoon-shaped, and represented the Big Dipper. This came to replace the upper part of the divining board, and it was made to spin easily. A century or so later, the spinning 'spoon' was sometimes made of lodestone. Was this to control its position, from a secret lodestone hidden in the lower board? In any case, the diviners discovered that the pivoted lodestone always pointed south – so they had a magic device that worked! As a practical compass, it became a magnetic needle floating on water. In this form by the tenth or eleventh century it was a practical mariner's compass, at first accompanied by an astrologer; but it passed out of the occult and entered technology and science – for it worked too well. When it became reliable it no longer looked like magic – even though magnetic attraction itself remained and indeed still is mysterious.

What is this 'paranormal' that science has lived with uneasily, while generally setting out to exorcise occult magic by its superior powers? Let's consider extra-sensory perception: perceptions occurring without activity of the physiologically accepted sense organs. This is not a simple issue, for new senses such as sonar in bats, or magnetic orientation in birds, are from time to time recognized by science and they are not called 'paranormal'. Bats' sonar works on a principle that was not appreciated until quite recently. The principle was developed in technology and only then recognized in bats. Magnetic homing in birds is similar, for it is assumed to be a kind of compass that birds have, though the details are not known. But this is not quite the end of the matter as magnetism itself remains basically mysterious and yet it is not thought of as paranormal. Just why magnetism is not regarded as paranormal action-at-a-distance, while telepathy, telekinesis and spoon-bending are seen (even if largely rejected) as paranormal, is not as clear as it should be. Is magnetism free of the occult simply because magnetic phenomena are reliably repeatable?

Does it not seem odd that the first vague X-ray pictures, and the fleeting unreliable early communications of 'wireless', were not regarded as paranormal when they were first demonstrated? Is this because it had already been shown theoretically, by James Clerk-

Maxwell that radio waves ought to exist – just a few years before the experimental demonstration by Heinrich Hertz? Perhaps, but Marconi's transmission of the letter 'M' across the Atlantic in 1901 was truly amazing – for it should have been physically impossible, as it was known that radio waves travel in straight lines like visible light and so they could not possibly go far beyond the horizon. Trans-Atlantic radio was, therefore, conceptually impossible when it was successfully if unreliably demonstrated. For this was before the discovery, several years later by Oliver Heaviside, of an unsuspected reflecting layer of ionized gas in the upper atmosphere, which bends these long waves though not light, round the earth.

The question is: Why were these unbelievably dramatic realizations of ancient occult dreams, of seeing through the body without pain, and talking and later seeing round the world, immediately accepted as phenomena belonging to science – even though so much remained to be explained – rather than as evidence that the occult does happen? Why are scientists not seen as incredibly powerful magicians, discovering and successfully controlling occult forces? Experiments can look like magic – especially when unholy artificial lightning is produced by weird wire coils and spark gaps, and when metal plates separated by nothing store invisible electricity. No wonder such apparatus appears in films of the occult!

There could hardly be a simple answer to what is magic, occult or paranormal and what is science; but it does seem that science works with a repertoire of accepted kinds of concepts, which can be freely transferred across widely different situations, for explanation and invention, even though the concepts may themselves be deeply mysterious. They are, somehow, authorized 'bricks' for building science and technology. But, although from time to time new 'bricks' are added, and some old ones abandoned – paranormal bricks are not allowed to enter the structure of science. The problem is to define what it is about paranormal concepts that makes science reject them as unsound bricks of straw. Is it simply that magic does *not work*? When the magic compass worked, it worked too well for it to be magic; so it transferred to science. But not all accepted science works as well as the compass! And much in science is just as mysterious as magnetism. So how are we to separate science from magic?

Science does not claim that it can explain everything. Nor does it always reject what it does not or cannot explain or describe in its own terms. Thus, music and the visual arts are accepted as important though they lie outside science – as does most of what goes on in a kitchen. Evidently, then, claims of paranormal phenomena are not being rejected simply because they are outside science's understanding. That clearly cannot be the reason, for science's main aim is to explain the unknown, and if it simply rejected what is not understood it would not have got anywhere. Science makes discoveries just because it looks carefully and thoroughly at surprising phenomena and gaps in knowledge. So *abnormal, unusual* or *surprising* cannot be equated with 'paranormal'.

Similarly, claims of the paranormal cannot simply be *incompatible* with science – for science latches on to phenomena which counter current concepts with the greatest excitement. Einstein won the Nobel prize for appreciating that the photo-electric effect could *not* be explained by conventional physics. So physics was changed – as it was changed also by the curved space of relativity.

And yet 'paranormal' is somehow incompatible with science, for it is generally rejected by science. And the rejection is different from the throwing out of discredited hypotheses, such as phlogiston. The difference seems to be fundamental. It seems to be that ESP is rejected not as incompatible only with *present* science – but with *any conceivable future science*. This, however, is a very strong claim indeed, and strictly impossible to justify, unless some limits can be set to what science may be like in the future. How can science, or anything else, predict what future science will be – or what it will accept or reject?

The Cambridge philosopher C.D. Broad (1962) suggested that we have beliefs which are deeper and more general than scientific theories, and that when these 'basic limiting principles' are violated, we move into the paranormal. Unfortunately, Broad did not give an exhaustive list of these limiting principles or justify them. Indeed this looks strictly impossible. The corollary is that it is hard indeed to see how claims of ESP can be *essentially* incompatible with science, since science changes so often and so dramatically that prediction of its developments is futile.

What would Lord Kelvin, a century ago, have made of today's quantum mechanics? It would have seemed inconceivable to him that such notions and phenomena as the uncertainty principle, and the extraordinary behaviour of liquid helium, would be basic science for his grandchildren. So how can paranormal claims be rejected as essentially incompatible with science if science keeps changing and even the greatest scientists cannot predict, for a few years ahead, what new phenomena or concepts will transform whole areas of science – or even create new sciences?

Let us look again at the claims of ESP. The particular claim is that there can be perception without physical signals – with non-material afferent links to the brain, or even with no brain at all. And there are corresponding claims of psychic efferent links, for moving objects by mind alone, as for telekinesis and spoon-bending. More general is the claim that certain patterns occurring in nature, patterns of stars or tea leaves, are messages to be read much as books are read – as though they are written by an intelligence for our intelligence –

written by an intelligence which knows the future. And they are supposed to be symbols capable of moving minds and matter. But why is it acceptable to say that a *person* has written a book when it is not acceptable to say that *nature* provides signs in the stars or in crystal balls as messages for us to read? And why is it acceptable to say that words affect us and our friends and readers, though nature is completely dyslexic? The puzzle is how *psychology* can escape rejection as being riddled by paranormal claims!

For the notion of symbols having powers has always been central to accounts of mind. And the powers of words and music – even of science's best friend, mathematics – are hardly described adequately with concepts currently acceptable to science. How we understand these sentences now (assuming we do!) is mysterious in just this way; yet it is generally accepted that reading English is not an occult skill. (This is assumed though how we experience even simple sensations, such as black and white from the page, by 'reading' retinal signals is deeply mysterious.) And yet we reject telepathy and the rest as being too mysterious. This we do, though there are plenty of patterns (such as X-ray diffraction patterns) accepted in science for unlocking nature's most deeply mysterious secrets.

It was not so long ago (in 1911) that the highly distinguished and exceptionally widely read psychologist, William McDougall, suggested that the brain works not by physical neural signals, but rather by internal psychic links of telepathy. This was a form of monadology that has a long history in philosophy and was held by men as scientifically distinguished as Leibniz. This may sound ridiculous now, as we know more about the physiology of the brain and can record some of its activity electrically; but none of us can say, without huge gaps in the account, how physical brain activity provides intelligent behaviour, perception and consciousness. A philosophical way out, which is well worth considering, is to say that mind and brain are *identical*; but unfortunately identity theories have their problems, or at the least they are extremely difficult to formulate without obvious silliness (Borst 1970). So, we have deep conceptual gaps, and in such gaps the paranormal thrives.

Why doesn't the rejection of paranormal claims, of mind affecting matter and matter affecting mind, immediately force us to reject current theories of perception and behaviour? For it is commonly assumed that mind, in some form and in some way, affects the brain, and the brain the mind. This is clearly the assumption behind all dualistic theories, and it is hardly avoided by any account except extreme behaviourism, which rejects mind as commonly understood. Why, then, aren't mind-brain theories in the category of paranormal?

Are there any brain-mind accounts which are safe from rejection as being paranormal? Some kind of *emergence* (see essay 19) of mind

from brain function may be safe science; but this may look danger-
ously spooky when we get to consciousness. And why shouldn't
adherents of the paranormal take the same tack, and claim that *their*
phenomena are respectably emergent, as mind is supposed to be
from physical brain function?

There seems to be a general lack of convincing evidence for
paranormal phenomena. Is there strong evidence against it? There
surely is – for if telekinesis and the rest occurred, it would be virtually
impossible to do science. For how could we control against telekinesis affecting our instruments? Or against telepathy, in perceptual
experiments? The kinds of controls that are essential for science
could hardly be applied effectively if the more extreme paranormal
claims stood up. Thus it would hardly be possible to do 'double blind'
experiments if there is second sight. So, perhaps there is a kind of
limiting principle: that they do not occur – or science itself would be
threatened by occult forces beyond its control.

This thought was expressed over a century ago by the physicist,
and advocate of the paranormal, Sir William Crookes (1870):

> The spiritualist tells of bodies weighing 50 or 100 lbs. being lifted
> into the air without intervention of any known force; but the
> scientific chemist is accustomed to use a balance which will render
> sensible weight so small that it would take tens of thousand of them
> to weigh one grain; he is, therefore, justified in asking that a power
> professing to be guided by intelligence, which will toss a heavy
> body up to the ceiling, shall also cause his delicately-poised
> balance to move under test conditions. . . .
>
> The spiritualist tells of tapping sounds which are produced in
> different parts of a room when two or more persons sit quietly
> round a table. The scientific experimenter is entitled to ask that
> these taps shall be produced on a stretched membrane of his
> phonautograph.
>
> The spiritualist tells of rooms and houses being shaken, even to
> injury, by superhuman power. The man of science merely asks for
> a pendulum to be set vibrating when in a glass case and supported
> on solid masonry.

I greatly doubt whether there are disembodied intelligent forces,
or any paranormal phenomena to bother about. But, just to be sure, I
wish I had infallible crystal balls.

REFERENCES

Borst, C.V. (ed.) (1970) *The Mind/Brain Identity Theory*, London, Macmillan.
Braude, S.E. (1978) 'On the meaning of "paranormal"', in J. Ludwig (ed.)
  Philosophy and Parapsychology, New York, Prometheus Books, pp. 227–44.

Broad, C.D. (1962) *Lectures on Psychical Research*, London, Routledge & Kegan Paul.

Crookes, W. (1870) 'Spiritualism viewed in the light of modern science', *Q. J. Science* 7, 316–21, in N.G. Coley, and M.D.H. Vance (1980) *Darwin to Einstein: Primary Sources on Science and Belief*, Harlow and New York, Longman.

Hansel, C.E.M. (1966) *ESP: A Scientific Evaluation*, New York, Scribner.

Ludwig, J. (ed.) (1978) *Philosophy and Parapsychology*, New York, Prometheus Books.

Myers, F.W.H. (1903) *Human Personality and its Survival after Bodily Death*, London.

21

THIS ESTRANGED INTELLIGENCE

When Macbeth demanded of the Witches: 'Say from whence/You owe this strange intelligence' he was not referring to IQ scores. Shakespeare was using 'intelligence' in its original sense of *information* or *knowledge*; especially hot news, gossip, or secrets of war. We still find this use in 'military intelligence', which does not mean that the military are particularly bright, only that they have or seek information. The relatively new technical sense of 'intelligence', in psychology, refers to tests designed for measuring and comparing not so much actual abilities but *potential* abilities of children and adults. This potentiality is generally expressed with a single number, the IQ (Intelligence Quotient) score.

The first comparative tests of human ability were carried out a century ago by Sir Francis Galton (1822–1911) who, at his own expense, built an anthropometric laboratory in South Kensington, London, in 1884. This was a long, narrow passage (6ft by 36 ft) through which visitors to the International Health Exhibition passed. Anatomical and performance measures were taken – the visitors willingly paying threepence for the privilege. Galton emphasized the variety of human abilities. His truly fascinating ideas and studies in *Inquiries into the Human Faculty and its Development* (1883) are still thoroughly worth reading today, and *Hereditary Genius* (1869) is also interesting, though it does make one ask 'What's in a name?' Galton's achievements are well described by Forrest (1974). IQ tests are especially associated with the name of the French psychologist Alfred

Binet (1857–1911), who, with is colleague Theodore Simon (1873–1961), was asked by his government to find a way to distinguish between children who did not wish or were too lazy to learn from those who were incapable of useful learning. The aim was to save educational resources for the children who would most benefit.

In America, Robert Yerkes and David Wechler introduced the Wechler-Bellevue Intelligence Scale, and the WISC-R, WPPSI and WAIS-R (Sattler 1982). These measured a wide variety of abilities, but they were funnelled into a measure of general ability (though especially of logical relations and symbolic thinking), or general intelligence. But is there really (as argued especially by Charles Spearman, 1927) only *one kind* of intelligence? Can all our potentialities be measured on a single scale? Can this do justice to the variety of human abilities and compare us fairly? This question has been asked most forcibly by Sir Peter Mcdawar (1977).

In physics we can accept, for example, that the temperatures of the enormous variety of objects can all lie on a single scale (even though several somewhat arbitrary temperature scales are used, and for necessary technical reasons several kinds of thermometer are used for measuring temperatures of the human body, ovens, stars and so on). But although temperature is a single dimension it by no means follows that there can be a valid single dimension along which human intelligence can be ranged, from 'dim' to 'bright'. For just as we have a wide variety of abilities, so there may be many kinds of intelligence.

Intelligence testing is sometimes regarded as the major (even the only!) triumph of psychology – yet it is also frequently seen as a social disaster (Gould 1981). Intelligence tests are an emotive issue as they claim to *judge* us, yet their scientific basis is hardly secure enough to command trust. Nevertheless, intelligence tests are used to compare races (Block and Dworkin 1971) and – most dangerous of all – for weighing the mental merits of girls and boys, and men and women (Montagu 1971; Macoby 1966; Sattler 1982; Swerdloff 1976).

We generally think now of intelligence as limited to human beings and, to a lesser degree, other animals and perhaps computing machines; but this is a recent view. The wandering planets and visiting comets were seen by the Greeks as intelligent beings, deciding for themselves what journeys to take among the stars, which look down to judge and occasionally guide us. The universe as a whole was seen as an intelligent living organism, and it is only for the last three hundred years or so that intelligence has become restricted to living organisms, and also possibly some specially programmed computers.

Binet and Simon set problems which were graded along a single dimension in difficulty. By finding out which could be carried out by 50 per cent of the children in each age group, they established standardized performance scores for each age. Binet defined intelligence so that each individual child's IQ remains essentially constant as he or she grows up – even though abilities improve enormously from infancy to adolescence and beyond. In spite of the increase in abilities, the average IQ score for children of all ages was set at one value: conventionally, 100 points. This was done, effectively, by adjusting performance scores by handicapping for age, up to the age of 16. Thus IQ (Intelligence Quotient) is defined as Mental Age × 100/Chronological Age. (The MA/CA is multiplied by 100 to avoid decimals.)

It is important to note that the abilities of children of different ages are not measured directly by IQ scores. Abilities improve with increasing age, though as presented the IQ scores remain (on average) unchanged. They are thus not straightforward measures of ability but are 'corrected', for normal expected development of skills with age, by the mental age/chronological age quotient. The measured ability/age quotient notion breaks down for adults, as there is no general improvement for the kinds of abilities that are tested for IQ after adolescence – although we go on getting older! So if one had a measured IQ of 100 points when a child, if the quotient procedure were extended into adulthood it would sink to 20 points by the age of 50. If all children developed at the same rate, and in the same way, each child's IQ would of course remain constant; but there are different development rates, and the early tests are not always reliable predictors. There are frequently considerable changes of IQ scores throughout childhood, so even if one does accept IQ scores at face value as tests of basic intelligence, there can still be optimism that a poor early score will improve. If a small boy is branded as having a low intelligence, or is hailed as exceptionally bright, with an IQ of 140+, his parents and teachers are apt to see and treat him in this light. He is expected to remain dull, or to flower into genius. These expectations can have marked effects, as has been shown in experiments in which children are presented to a school as having exceptionally high IQ scores, though they have only average IQ scores. The teacher's raised expectation somehow boosts the pupils to do rather better then others with the same IQ. This is also true for animals in laboratory learning experiments; if the handlers believe some animals to be special they tend to become special. This is a major reason for 'double blind' experiments.

In order to measure intelligence, however conceived, it is necessary to test observable abilities or skills. But intelligence is not simply performance or ability. It is supposed to *underlie* abilities, from the simplest problem-solving to the works of genius. Unless it is thought of as some kind of (phlogiston-like) *substance*, that we each possess in more or less degree, in order to understand intelligence we need to know the brain's *processes*, or the internal *procedures* by which we solve problems, and understand and create. This kind of understanding is, however, the aim of cognitive psychologists rather than, at least until recently, designers of IQ tests, who are more concerned with comparing individuals than with understanding what it is to be intelligent. It may be practically impossible to compare intelligence without a theoretical understanding of how intelligence works. This is one reason why computer-based artificial intelligence is so interesting, and so potentially important in human terms. For if we cannot discover ourselves – how we think or see – by introspection, it is necessary to draw analogies from what we can learn about. In practice it is easier to understand the outside world than what makes us tick, so we now adopt the opposite of primitive animism and see our internal processes in terms of physics and the processes by which our artefacts function. Computers are only one kind of artefact in which we may see aspects of ourselves mirrored. The important notion that creative problem-solving – which is surely the heart of all intelligence – depends on drawing analogies is considered very effectively by Robert Sternberg (1977).

This is central to both meanings of 'intelligence' – information or knowledge that is *given*; and ability to *invent* solutions or discover the needed knowledge. I suspect that thinking about intelligence has been strangled through not disentangling the what-is-given from the what-needs-to-be-discovered senses of intelligence.

If the solution to a problem is already known, there is no need to solve it – for then there is no problem to solve. So problem-solving ability (which is essentially what psychologists take as 'intelligence') must be assessed in situations when the answer is not already known; and when knowledge is required to solve the problem, it is important that all the candidates have much the same knowledge available, or they effectively have very different problems to solve. So when special knowledge is required, comparisons between individuals' 'intelligence' is extremely difficult. Thus we should expect the musician and the politician to have different kinds of knowledge and so to do very differently on many tests even though they are equally 'intelligent'. The question is: How can we compare their intelligences, if they have different knowledge? This is a problem for comparing children, and a much greater problem for adults with widely different experiences.

One way of isolating the problem-solving aspect of intelligence is to devise tests which do not require special knowledge, or require only knowledge which almost anyone may be expected to have. Hence the curiously arid form of typical intelligence-test questions – such as distinguishing different and similar shapes, or completing number series – designed as far as possible to be divorced from any special knowledge. Another way is to accept that different knowledge bases will affect performance, but somehow to handicap people according to their special knowledge. This means, for example, that a history student would get fewer marks for questions on Rome or the Middle Ages than a physics student would earn, even though he comes up with the same answers. If asked: 'What date was the Magna Carta?' and also: 'What is the gravitational constant?', they would be marked differently even for identical answers. The difficulty with this second method is to know how to apply fair 'handicaps' for special knowledge. The problem over the first method (avoiding special knowledge altogether) is that one cannot be sure that special knowledge is not involved. Also, questions or tasks which do not require some special knowledge may seem trivial and so may not be performed well. It may indeed be that deploying one's pet knowledge is a most important feature of intelligence. If this is so, to try to test people apart from what they have taken the trouble to learn, and what they feel secure in, may be to miss just what the tester should be looking for – what is special about each of us. More recent intelligence tests stress the importance of drawing analogies for deriving answers; and, of course, analogies must come from available knowledge, so these tests might be on better lines and they may better reflect the nature of intelligence.

The problem of how much knowledge is involved in solving intelligence test problems is especially important for claims that different races, or the sexes, have on average different intelligences. It is quite obvious that people with different racial backgrounds tend to have different experiences, and the same applies to the sexes. So how can races, or the sexes, be fairly compared? One approach is to try to devise tests free of special knowledge, but for comparisons between races this is extremely difficult and perhaps strictly impossible. To take an extreme example: for people with some cultural backgrounds even the situation of being tested, of having to sit down and concentrate to work out problems and answer questions, is outside their experience. If the second strategy is adopted – to apply 'handicaps' – it is hardly possible to handicap fairly, because it is virtually impossible to assess the effects of cultural differences, apart from performance at skills – which makes the situation logically circular.

This whole business is indeed somewhat paradoxical. We might say that Bill, who has done *well* because of unusual knowledge, has demonstrated *less* intelligence that Jack who is less educated but succeeds equally or less well. But gaining knowledge, and learning how to use knowledge effectively, requires intelligence – which Bill, rather than Jack, has demonstrated. So – which is the more intelligent?

Let's grasp the nettle and consider, in these terms, claims that men are more intelligent than women. Or, if you prefer, that women are more intelligent than men. In either case a score suggesting one of these possibilities might be due to the testers having chosen questions, or test tasks, which are more familiar to the one sex than the other. The greater familiarity or knowledge will produce a higher score – but will this indicate greater intelligence? It could signify a lower intelligence. To justify this we would have to know the contribution made by the knowledge, which it is extremely difficult to do. (And if there is a genetic component here, it may lie outside what is taken as intelligence; for example, it might lie in physical strength, for tasks such as changing wheels on cars, which makes the task easier so that it requires less intelligence.) Even if the test does not involve physical strength, which is clearly sex-related, it may involve experience which has been more easily gained by physically stronger people; and one can think of converse examples favouring women through really giving them fewer Brownie Points, intelligence-wise.

However all this may be, there is no doubt that if one asked a sample of men and women the following questions, men would generally do better than women: 'What does the differential gear in a car do?' 'What is a tee?' 'What does a halyard have to do with blocks and cleats?' 'What is the difference between stocks and shares?' But a better score for these questions would be no particular indication of greater *intelligence*, in the sense of more powerful basic problem-solving ability. It happens that men, at least in our culture, tend to be more interested than women in golf, sailing and investments, as well as in mechanical principles – though of course there are plenty of exceptions. Similarly, if men and women were asked: 'What is a roux?' or 'What is fennel used for?' or 'What is voile, or a pommel?' then women might be expected to do better. This means that a test which included a lot of the first items would *favour* men, while the items in the second test would *favour* women. The result will largely depend on whether the tests are men-favouring or women-favouring. There are physiological differences between the sexes which make some tasks slightly easier for men or for women. Thus males have on average slightly higher visual acuity and better spatial perception; while women tend to be more deft with their fingers and better at intricate work such as sewing. If tests came out with the answer that men and women have *equal* intelligence this could be due to a successful balancing act by the test designers – to give equal men-favouring and women-favouring test questions. Then the claim that men and women have equal intelligence means merely that the test designers have got their balancing act right, to bring about this result. If, on the other hand, they claim that men are more intelligent, or that women are more intelligent, this could mean that they have presented too many men-favouring or too many women-favouring questions – they have got their balancing act wrong. In neither case do we learn about relative intelligences.

This is only the beginning of a complicated situation, which has a forest of logical and statistical traps. There is also the academic prejudice that academic abilities should be rated highly in the intelligence stakes: so a successful physicist will be rated 'higher' than a successful farmer, or mechanic, or cook. This may be little more than a reflection of academic arrogance; and of course it is academic psychologists who design the tests. A teacher may see a pupil as intelligent because he or she catches on quickly to what the teacher says, rather than for originality or creative ability.

How did the pioneers of intelligence testing think about intelligence? Binet thought that intelligence mainly involves three capacities, or abilities: to take and maintain a definite direction; to change direction for attaining a desired result; and effective self-criticism. The British psychologist Charles Spearman also emphasized three abilities as basic for intelligence: to observe one's own mental processes; to discover essential relations between items of knowledge; and to discover correlates or analogies between things or situations. (Perhaps it is no accident that this is what he spent his life doing!) However this may be, psychologists' definitions are not in terms that tell us how we solve problems, so they do not tell us about what it is to be intelligent – for they do not begin to suggest how the brain or mind works.

It has been suggested that differences of intelligence have a *physiological* basis. There is recent evidence that short reaction time to stimuli correlates highly with measured intelligence. Given that a large number of processes must take place sequentially in thinking, this is not too surprising. But interesting as it is, it does not pinpoint a physiological basis for intelligence. The trouble is of course that physiological measures, and records of brain function, do not monitor in anything like sufficient detail processes that could be responsible for 'high-level' information handling and problem solving. And it is most likely that even complete records of brain activity would not give understandable answers before we have a working theory of how thinking works in information-handling terms.

Can we think more clearly about intelligence? We started by pointing out that the word 'intelligence' has two meanings: the older being, roughly, *given* knowledge; the second, ability to *invent*, or *seek* required knowledge. There is something of a paradox here, for it might be appropriate to ascribe *more* intelligence to those who have *less* knowledge – and yet succeed. At the same time we generally associate having a *lot* of knowledge with *being intelligent*. So, we seem to be in a bit of muddle which may be worth trying to sort out. The first step, I think, is to recognize that knowledge in any form is always the result of some kind of problem-solving, perhaps from the distant past. So we may think of useful knowledge as the result of problem-solving intelligence which has become 'frozen' but may be 'thawed' for present use. The American psychologist Raymond Catell has used this kind of notion, with exactly this analogy in what he calls 'fluid' and 'crystalized' intelligence (Catell 1963).

Perhaps even more appropriate terms are those of building up energy for later use in any number of ways: thus we might think of *potential* intelligence and *kinetic* intelligence. This is by analogy with building up and storing potential energy, for example by winding up a clock, or raising water – which may be used as kinetic energy in many forms. On this account (though no analogies are perfect) potential intelligence is the *available* solutions and answers which were *created* by past kinetic problem-solving intelligence.

There is no good reason to limit the past problem-solving, giving current potential intelligence, to brain power. By far the most difficult problems of existence have been solved not by us, but in the evolution of life-forms by natural selection. Thus our eyes and ears, and all the incredible chemistry and organization of plants and animals are available potential intelligence. Together with our books and tools, and what we have learned and discovered, our potential intelligence serves us with only occasional demands on kinetic intelligence. We don't have to keep re-inventing the wheel; new achievements, based on solutions from the past, are endlessly possible.

Now I think we see essential difficulties in the business of measuring intelligence. A major difficulty is that the contribution of stored potential intelligence is overwhelmingly greater than that of the inventive steps of kinetic intelligence; but it is these that psychologists try to assess. It is still far from clear that the contribution of the tools of knowledge and skills can be separated for measuring 'pure' problem-solving.

A second difficulty is that kinetic intelligence is essentially concerned with novelty – either for understanding or creating – but *creating* implies some unpredictable surprises, which can hardly be anticipated in alternative answers for scoring intelligence tests. The more original the candidate, the more he or she may consider possibilities outside the test designer's intentions; not only are they impossible to score, but also such creative people are really processing far more information than less original people and so they suffer an unknown handicap in the test situation. (As a matter of fact I once discovered a mistake in an intelligence test I was given, on a problem of mechanical understanding involving a clock escapement-like mechanism, in which a pallet was drawn the wrong way round. One had to assume the intention of the device to see the mistake; but this of course took more processing than if one had simply accepted the obvious solution. The test was changed as a result of questioning the 'correct' solution – which was not in fact correct.)

What then *is* intelligent behaviour? It surely involves the use of knowledge – which may be in many forms from symbolically stored facts and generalizations in brains or books to, more immediately, tools. But problem-solving involves stepping outside the knowledge base, at least to combine existing items in new ways. What we are calling kinetic intelligence includes *novelty*, and the novelty must be at least *appropriate* and preferably *successful*, to be called intelligent. So, we may define 'kinetic' intelligence as 'the generation of appropriate, successful novelty'.

Having defined it, we see how difficult it is to measure: how do we measure or compare novelties, appropriatenesses, or successes? To measure intelligence effectively we must surely first measure these, but they are difficult to grasp and quantify.

Until recently, psychology has been mainly concerned with *comparing* human abilities – rating people for education, jobs and so on – rather than making any serious effort to *understand* intelligence as processes of thinking. It may help to see processes of problem-solving outside brains. Thus I see no reason against saying that organic evolution – which has solved incredibly difficult problems and uses its past successes for further achievements – is (supremely) *intelligent*. For millions of years the blind processes of evolution have solved all manner of problems we can still only dimly appreciate. It is important to note here, though, that on the Darwinian account the problems were solved *without intention*; but there seems no reason to include intention in a definition of intelligence. Very likely there is survival of the fittest by ideas by a kind of natural selection in brains – which is not conscious or intentional but generates useful novelty. Keeping intention separate from intelligence allows us to consider out-of-brain problem-solving – including the inventions and developments of life-solutions by natural selection – and it allows us to include computers in the discussion. Whatever their intentions may be, computers are beginning to be intelligent since they can structure data into useful knowledge and follow heuristic rules for creating and applying knowledge – perhaps in ways we would never dream of.

However this may come to be, it is clear that just as tools have enormously extended our limbs and hands and senses, so – following language and books, and the powers of mathematical symbols for aiding problem-solving – computers multiply our kinetic intelligence. Very soon it will, surely, be absurd to be tested without one's computer aids: as absurd as being without a pen.

What is frightening is that, now that our lives are so changed by

technology, we feel restrained by our life-support biological inheritance which was designed by blind evolution for very different
conditions and is no longer appropriate. Now that we have the
beginnings of computer-based autonomous intelligences, and we can
apply kinetic intelligence in bio-technology, we may have to decide
whether to stay as we are – and live symbiotically with intelligent
machines – or apply intelligence to meet the future by re-creating
ourselves.

REFERENCES

Binet, A. and Simon, T. (1916) *The Development of Intelligence in Children*,
    trans. E.S. Kit, Baltimore, Williams & Wilkins.
Block, U.S. and Dworkin, G. (1971) 'IQ, heritability, and inequality', in U.S.
    Block and G. Dworkin (eds), *The IQ Controversy*, London, Quartet Books.
Catell, R.B. (1963) 'Theory of fluid and crystalized intelligence: a critical
    experiment', *J. Educ. Psychol.* 54, 1–22.
Forrest, D.W. (1974) *Francis Galton: The Life and Work of a Victorian Genius*,
    New York, Taplinger.
Galton, Sir Francis (1869) *Hereditary Genius*.
Galton, Sir Francis (1883) *Inquiries into the Human Faculty and its Develop-
    ment.*
Gould, S.J. (1981) *The Mismeasure of Man*, New York, Norton.
Macoby, E. (ed.) (1966) *The Development of Sex Differences*, Stanford,
    Stanford University Press.
Medawar, Sir Peter (1977) 'Unnatural science', review of Leon J. Kamin,
    The Science and Politics of IQ and N.J. Block and Gerald Dworkin (eds), *The
    IQ Controversy*, in *New York Review of Books* (3 Feb. 1977), reprinted in
    P. Medawar, (1984) *Pluto's Republic*, Oxford, Oxford University Press.
Montagu, A. (1971) *The Natural Superiority of Women*, New York,
    Macmillan.
Sattler, J.M. (1974) (2nd edn 1982) *Assessment of Children's Intelligence and
    Special Abilities*, Boston, Allyn & Bacon.
Spearman, C. (1927) *The Abilities of Man*, New York, Macmillan.
Sternberg, R.J. (1977) *Intelligence, Information Processing, and Analogical
    Reasoning: The Componential Analysis of Human Abilities*, Hillsdale, NJ,
    Lawrence Erlbaum.
Swerdloff, P. (1976) *Men and Women*, London, Time-Life International.

USING

22

INVENTING

I am a non-successful inventor. This is very different from *not* being an inventor. The difference is that I have taken out about thirty patents, and some of these remain active and may suddenly change the world. They are mainly for data recording devices and optical instruments – and for a hearing aid. Few have ever been made commercially, though not for lack of trying, for inventing has been a dominant time-consuming interest for over thirty years. It is great fun to put things and ideas together to create or find something significantly new. Whether the result will be sufficiently appealing or useful to attract commercial development is another question. In any case this trail can be a nightmare trial for your wits against others' witlessness.

Here, as examples, are some of my inventions (Gregory 1974):

1. A printing *data recorder*, 'Thoth', which I invented and built in 1952, while working in Portsmouth on escaping from submarines, following the *Affray* disaster, in which two crews were lost. At that time data recorders used continuously moving paper, with pens making a wiggly line for each kind of event being recorded. To extract the times and durations, the distance between every wiggle had to be measured – a tedious business. My recorder was called Thoth after the Egyptian scribe god who was the recorder of good and ill. It printed time from a continuously revolving counter which printed on stationary paper, which then moved on ready for the next event. The events were identified with simultaneously printed letters. Thoth was a complicated machine. After a lot of development it was manufac-

tured, and several hundred were sold by a small firm called Russell Electronics. They were then taken over by a consortium which grew too big and burst like a bubble, ruining forty inventive manufacturing firms. Some were well known and respected, and a merchant bank went down with them. Seeing all this happening, though from the side-lines, was a fascinating as well as a harrowing experience. After I was able to extract the Thoth patents, it was taken up and re-designed by the excellent Cambridge Instrument Company, who devoted a great deal of trouble at a difficult time for them. They were a delight to work with, but we never got the machine fully reliable and the project faded away. Nevertheless, it was a decisive, though not the only, move at that time away from measuring lines along miles of paper, which was generally accepted as the proper way.

2. *Little Brother* was an eye for Thoth the recorder. It was a camera, with several small photoelectric cells in place of a film. The photo-cells, which were attached with magnets, could be positioned any-where in the image plane to send pulses to Thoth so that, for example, animal movements could be recorded automatically. It worked well and it was used for several research projects, though it was never manufactured.

3. The *histogram recorder* was most amusing. It carried ball bearings over a row of vertical slots in a transparent plate. One ball at a time was carried suspended under a continuously moving belt, with a long electro-magnet which released the ball when the magnet's current was cut. Then the ball bearing dropped into the nearest slot under it, to build up to a histogram of balls. This was very entertaining to watch, and I wish it still existed. A brilliant engineer colleague turned it into a more conventional device, but frankly this was not only a lot less fun but never worked as well. This is a hazard: gadgeteers and engineers are very different, and they can cancel each other out to make a joint muddle of it. In any case, this idea is now hopelessly out of date.

4. 3-D pictures are intriguing. I invented the *'solid-image' microscope* and a *3-D drawing machine*. They are very different.

In its original version the solid-image microscope had a rapidly vibrating lens which scanned the specimen in depth. The image was projected onto a vibrating screen which gave a solid image one could walk around. But vibrating parts are a nuisance in a microscope. So, Geoff Courtney-Pratt and I designed a version with no moving parts. It turned optics upside down, to use chromatic aberration (which is normally avoided as much as possible) to produce images at different depths and present them in 3-D space. We made two of these instruments and they worked quite well; but the scanning electron microscope would almost always be much better. It was never manufactured, but the idea just might have its uses.

Although perspective and other 'monocular depth cues' allow most scenes and objects to be shown as three-dimensional on a picture plane, there are limitations. Highly unfamiliar or atypical objects may be difficult to represent – for example knots or biological structures. The 3-D drawing machine, or *Stereoscribe*, allows one to doodle in 3-D and show any structure unambiguously in depth. It works with a small moving light which is imaged twice on a pair of special electroluminescent panels to give stereo pictures of the movements, in three dimensions, of the drawing-light. It is simple and cheap to make, and it might at least be a fascinating toy. This it very nearly became; but it was dropped, though for no good reason. A version exists in my laboratory and it works. People enjoy doodling in depth.

5. Psychologists studying how we see pictures often use a 'tachistoscope' to control the exposure time. Many versions have appeared over the past hundred years, but I think I was the first to think of using what is now the common fluorescent tube as a light source, switched rapidly on and off with a controlled duration. (Actually I made it for clinical research at the National Hospital for Nervous Diseases, where it was used for years.) This is now the standard method, and my circuit for making the fluorescent tube light up fast and reliably is still used. This was patented and a version was manufactured, but I never bothered to defend the patent – life is just too short!

6. The invention which produced the most drama was the *telescope camera for minimizing effects of atmospheric turbulance*. This annoying disturbance moves the images about, so that the photographs get blurred, and, especially on large telescopes, makes the image go milky as light coming from several directions interferes so that really good, clear, stable images are only seldom formed. The situation is much better on high mountains, but even then there is room for improvement. Briefly, the method involves cancelling the ever-changing disturbed image against its average image, which is built up and stored in the camera. A photograph is then built up, from many short exposures, each occurring only when the disturbed image matches the statistically correct (though blurred) 'master' plate picture. I published the idea in *Nature*, and was then invited to a remarkable summer-long conference and working party in America. There was a problem about getting sufficiently good pictures for planning the moon landing, and there were several astronomical and defence questions that better images would help to answer. The Royal Society's Paul Instrument Fund paid for the making of the instrument, which was executed by Stephen Salter in my laboratory at Cambridge and later in Edinburgh. For the initial trials, we had the use of a small telescope in the Cambridge observatories. The weather was appalling! Then, through the generosity and give-it-a-try atti-

tude of America, we spent a winter on a mountain in New Mexico, then a summer at Gerard Kuiper's observatory on Mount Lemmon, near Tucson, working on large telescopes. Later, we tried it out at the Royal Observatory at Herstmonceux, which was equally helpful and a wonderfully beautiful place, with its superb castle.

This project became an obsession. The method worked beautifully in the laboratory, right from my very first crude lash-up on a bench with a random ripple tank to disturb the image of a model moon. Sadly, it never worked as well in practice on a telescope. This was almost certainly because the method requires very precise tracking of the moving moon, planet or stars that are being photographed. Any offset upsets the system; but this was exceedingly hard to avoid and we never quite succeeded. Still, I understand that current image-processing techniques on large telescopes do include this idea, though in a different form. Computers are now large enough and fast enough to do this job and far more. Whether our efforts actually contributed to the present sophisticated techniques I do not know. I hope they did, if indirectly (Gregory 1964).

7. The *hearing aid* notion goes back to experiments I was doing in the late 1950s, with the mathematician Violet Cane and my research colleague Jean Wallace. We devised methods for measuring increase in the random activity of the nervous system with ageing. This led to measuring (somewhat indirectly) effects of background neural masking in the cochlea of the ear and relating this to (what was then called) nerve deafness. An American, J.C.R. Licklider, discovered that speech can be understood with hardly any variations of loudness – the information lies in the time-intervals of the crossing of the speech wave around zero-energy. This suggested to several people, including us, at that time, that hearing aids should be designed to restrict the amplitude variations of the speech wave and amplify only the low-energy cross-overs which carry the information for intelligibility. This should make speech more intelligible without blasting the ear with amplified peak energies which, as Licklider (1946) had shown, do not carry much information. So, we clipped off the peaks of the wave and measured what happened. There was some but not much improvement, and it sounded awful – very distorted. This was not surprising as the amplitude peak-clipping must produce lots of harmonics which mask the speech signal. For the next twenty years I thought this was the end of the matter. Then, about ten years ago, while reading an electronics magazine on the train to London, I began to wonder whether new electronic techniques might come to the rescue of what at first sight (or rather twenty years' sight) appeared strictly impossible: to limit the amplitude of a wave without producing the harmonic distortion components which mask the signal and sound terrible.

A mathematician would almost certainly say that it is absolutely impossible, because Fourier analysis says this, and the conclusions of Fourier analysis are not to be denied. But – and this is where inventing is not quite the same as science – it turns out that although harmonic distortion must be produced by clipping (or limiting the peak amplitude of a wave), the distortion components do not absolutely have to be in the speech wave itself. The trick is to impose the speech wave onto a high-frequency 'carrier' wave (much as in a radio transmitter) and then clip the carrier. The inevitable harmonic distortion components are still produced, but they are now multiples of the carrier frequency and not of the speech wave. So they can be removed – filtered out – without losing the speech information. So, what looked impossible is in fact possible. It works well. It protects the ear from too-loud sounds and it generally improves intelligibility – by squeezing speech into the damaged ear.

This started as a research project on ageing, funded by the Medical Research Council, and ended unpredictably as a new kind of hearing aid. It could have practical importance for many of the million hard-of-hearing people in Britain, as well as the millions there must be in other countries. Why is it not available for the people it might help? It is difficult to get it manufactured because, as its circuit has many components, it cannot be made as small and inconspicuous as existing hearing aids. The dominating factor here is human vanity! In fact, although intelligibility is improved, our patients often preferred a less effective but much smaller standard device. So far we have failed to get it made as small as possible, for lack of capital resources. Also, it does not particularly help in all conditions, and some education or familiarity is necessary. (Gregory and Drysdale 1978; Troscianko and Gregory 1984.)

Why are most of my inventions not on the market? Several – the printing data recorder Thoth (though not its 'eye') and the histogram recorder – were overtaken by superior technology. Fair enough. The solid-image microscope was never manufactured; but the idea of producing solid images with vibrating screens, or their equivalent (we tried out several neater ways), is being used for 3-D computer graphics. The basic idea of the telescope image-improving system is now extensively used; but I do not know whether the present sophisticated systems owe anything to my 'steam age' solution to the problem (though they might do, for I published it in *Nature*). At least I saw what the problem was and did something about it, though this is not very surprising as my father was an astronomer, so I was brought up with telescopes and flickering images. It is odd that the 3-D drawing machine has never been developed.

A major problem of applying inventions is that it takes too much time and requires special knowledge and skills to convert a novel laboratory research tool, gadget, instrument or whatever, into a commercially acceptable product. This work was never done on the 3-D drawing machine, or on my other inventions, that might in small ways have changed the world.

It is almost impossible for a university laboratory to make an industrially acceptable product. Indeed, it is generally wrong for us to spend our time in this way for it is unlikely to produce new knowledge, or teach our students what they need or want to know.

A reason why so few inventions get taken up, and why when they do it takes so long, in this country, is the far too general lack of technical know-how and imagination among administrators and especially controllers of money who are probably much too powerful. It seems to me that they often miss good ideas and get seduced by on-the-surface attractive ones which are actually silly. This is a problem for industry.

Comparing the British with the American scene, having worked at MIT and the Bell Telephone Labs, I can confirm that it is very different in America, or at least it was a few years ago. There is (or at least was) immense enthusiasm and drive. A lot of money and effort goes into the early assessment and building of prototypes – which is the stage at which we in England are apt to pussyfoot around and let it go cold. The major American laboratories have incredible resources, such as their own microchip-making facilities – even having this facility on each floor! Above all, they are project-orientated. American careers depend on the success of projects; and when projects die or are suddenly killed off, as often happens, there is a lot of grief. But there is a lot of commitment and joy too.

Our main problem, perhaps, is not enough risk-taking. We should realize that only one in a hundred inventions will come off – and this falls to zero without enthusiasm, flexible commitment, and over-adequate financial and technical resources. I think a change of financial philosophy should be considered; to give up attempting precise predictions for inventive research, and accept that most inventions (like most biological mutations) will be short-lived – though they may be vitally important steps – and expect to lose most times. Well-endowed back-up and rapid decision-taking are most important to spot the potential winner and concentrate resources on developing it. This requires far more awareness and range of knowledge than all but a very few administrators (and I think especially controllers of finance) take the trouble to acquire.

Nationally, one sees the ebbs and flows of huge sums, with inflation and devaluation, and all that; and Canute-like attempts to stem these tides with our vulnerable but infinitely precious, sand-castles such as the universities. They may look like ivory towers, but without them we have no future; so, surely, resources for thinking and inventing should be protected at almost any cost, rather than sacrificed in the political arena.

Getting inventions taken up can drive one mad. The trick is to enjoy it, and expect to lose most of the time. It is well worth inventing for the fun of the game, which can be shared with colleagues and friends. The occasional wonderful winner surprises even its inventor. Most important, though, applied science is a great test of theoretical understanding and it feeds back into our understanding. In this regard whether an invention is successful commercially is not so important – what matters is that it is surprising and it works.

REFERENCES

Gregory, R.L. (1964) 'A technique for minimizing the effects of atmospheric disturbance on photographic telescopes', *Nature* (London) 203, 274.

Gregory, R.L. (1974) *Concepts and Mechanisms of Perception*, London, Duckworth.

Gregory, R.L. and Drysdale, A.E. (1978) 'Squeezing speech into the deaf ear', *Nature* (London) 264, 748–51.

Licklider, J.C.R. (1946) 'The effect of amplitude on the intelligibility of speech', *J. Accoustical Soc. America* 18, 429.

Troscianko, Tom, and Gregory, R.L. (1984) 'An assessment of two amplitude compression hearing aid systems, especially in high ambient noise', *Brit. J. Audiology* 18, 89–96.

23

HALF-BAKED DESIGNS

Six years ago I bought a new grand electric cooker, with two ovens, a grill with a twiddling mechanism for chickens, and four rings. The controls for the grill and the ovens are arranged horizontally along the top, while the ovens are placed vertically one above the other, with the grill at the top. The rings, which of course are horizontal, form a square, though their four controls which are to the right and above are arranged in a vertical row. How do the controls correspond with the rings? Like this:

The rings	Ring controls
A C	O(a)
	O(b)
B D	O(d)
	O(c)

Note, in this negative-transfer cooker, the vertical spatial reversal of the controls d and c for the right-hand rings C and D. During six years of use I have burned out umpteen pans, all on the right-back ring C which gets switched on in mistake for the most-used right-front ring D. These, fortunately minor, disasters have happened because the right-hand rings are spatially reversed from their corresponding controls. Isn't it ridiculous that a major manufacturer can make this perceptually fundamental design error?

One does not get used to this kind of reversal of controls-to-controlled relations. At best it slows performance; at worst it can be a direct cause of accidents which may be disastrous. Although I have now damaged so many pans on this allegedly grand and certainly expensive stove, I still sometimes get it wrong, and visitors too, to their embarrassment and mine, as often as not confuse the controls for these two rings.

It is well known to experimental psychologists that skilled behaviour, as well as informed opinion, depends on analogies derived from familiar situations, and also upon following various kinds of rules, of which we may or may not be aware. This use of knowledge from experience, including rule-formulated knowledge from the past, is known as 'transfer of training', or 'transfer of knowledge'. Spatial reversals, such as those on my cooker, are as confusing as mirrors, for they violate accepted assumptions and rules so that they have to be treated as special cases. This takes extra time and attention and is likely to lead to severe errors.

It seems from several reports that the control rooms of some nuclear power plants are designed with much the same inadequate appreciation of perceptual principles as is all too evident in my cooker. Thus, where there are two reactors, the control room may have mirror-image panels, though mirror reversals are notoriously confusing. Various confusing arrangements of controls are sometimes countered by the operators putting their own marks on knobs and switches, with sticky tape and so on; but then these may be removed by the management to make the place look neat.

In one plant, it has been stated, the switches for the primary coolant loop A are marked, as is sensible, 'A'; but for the loop B they are marked 'D', and those for loop C are marked 'B', while those for D are marked 'C'. The operators coped with this by adopting the mnemonic: '*All Dogs Bite Cats*'! We hope that this is changed by now, but of course the change will itself cause confusion, for the operators will now have to decide whether their special mnemonic still holds or is no longer appropriate to the system. Under stress, earlier learned behaviour patterns are apt to take over, which could cause further problems. A genuine design problem concerns colour-coding the states of the lamps, switches, valves, and so on. In some plants the colour red shows the open state of a valve or the closed position of a switch – red in both cases indicating flow. Green is used to indicate closed position of valves and open position of switches – no flow. But this is contrary to the very general use of red for stop and green for go, as in traffic lights. Also, in practice – it is said – yellow and blue may signal different states in the same plant, so they have ambiguous meanings. It seems that there is a lack of systematic conventions for showing when things are normal, or in some abnormal state. This must throw a severe memory load on the operators. Ships' engine rooms, evidently with success, use shapes such as in-line and crossed bars and circles, as well as colours, to show normal and current states. However this is done there are difficulties, for what is 'normal' may depend on operating conditions and these need to be appreciated. But this requires perhaps deep understanding of the system and what it is being called upon to do. Also, experiments have shown that even with skilled inspectors, when something amiss has been overlooked several times, such as a valve left open, the mistake may literally *never* be spotted.

It is generally accepted that the Three Mile Island nuclear disaster was caused in part by mechanical faults, but more by inappropriate human reactions. The unfolding situation of the nuclear plant becoming unstable has been re-enacted in a BBC 'Horizon' programme from the original transcripts of the inquiry in which the controllers on duty and other key people gave their accounts of what happened as they saw it. The evidence was taken shortly after the event and (unlike, say, a war or a major battle) this was a restricted and clear-cut situation, which one might suppose could be described precisely, while its dangers and implications made sure that it was and indeed still is studied in exceptional depth and detail.

There is much to learn from Three Mile Island. It seems clear, and well worth appreciating, that many of the instruments did not directly monitor what they displayed, so the operators had to infer from their knowledge of the system what the readings meant. When the cooling water failed, and among other things a valve opening to the atmosphere stuck open, the system was no longer its normal self. The operators had to modify, and as things got worse drastically change, their usual assumptions for reading their instruments. In fact, peculiar thuds and bangs deep in the plant due to hydrogen explosions were accepted as something amiss with the air conditioning. Instrument readings of 'impossible' pressures were misinterpreted and rejected, though they were correct and all-important. The essential cooling-water pumps were switched off when they vibrated with cavitation, since it was not realized that the supply had failed because valves had been incorrectly closed so that there was no water for them to pump. Because the operators did not understand the state of the system, the readings and symptoms became paradoxical, which froze thinking and led to blind trial and error. With a time limit of just over three hours to the total disaster of the core melting through the containment chamber, some two hours of this blind trial and error produced the nightmare uncovering of the core, and such damage and spillage of radioactive water that the plant can still only be partially examined now, several years later.

We are used to not being able to see in detail how organisms, including ourselves, function; and only experts can expect to see how complex man-made devices work. But for the operators and the plant's designers and manufacturers not to be able to read the danger signals, because they did not understand the state of the system is remarkable – and remarkably interesting for us who are concerned with perception and how and why perceptions go wrong. This is the most dramatic and revealing example of how intelligent actions depend upon assumptions, which are necessarily based on the normal and familiar. For reading the abnormal or unusual deep understanding of the system is essential, for appreciating what can happen and what to do to avoid disaster.

If deep understanding, rather than mere 'surface' operating rules, is so important for controlling advanced technology (as we have always known that it is for reading symptoms in medicine), isn't cutting down academic education, and so losing people who can see beneath the surface of things, extremely *dangerous*?

24

THE FOURTH DIMENSION
OF 3-D

It is astonishing that the use of the two eyes for perceiving the positions and forms of objects in the third dimension – depth – was not appreciated until modern times. No doubt, if the world suddenly looked flat with one eye, the importance of both working together would always have been obvious; but this does not happen. The world continues to look much the same with one eye as with two, except for rather special situations. This limited use of two eyes for seeing depth raises the question of why the elaborate neural mechanisms for combining signals from the two eyes developed through evolution to provide what is only seldom noticed as an improvement over vision by each eye alone. The answer must lie in improved precision of depth perception for specially important skills, such as for birds landing or catching fish on the wing; and primates catching branches as they leap high up in trees.

However this may be, the fact that we have stereoscopic depth vision is a recent discovery, unknown to the Greeks and indeed not at all fully appreciated until two thousand years later. Effective stereoscopic vision is restricted to quite near objects; but for near objects, closing each eye in turn gives such obviously different views that it is remarkable that the ancients did not twig the truth: that different eye views are combined into a single perception for seeing depth precisely. If artists had been able to draw the subtly different views of the eyes without too much difficulty, perhaps they would have invented stereoscopic pictures many centuries ago, but as it happened not even the simple perspective rules for a single picture were invented by artists – geometrical perspective was not discovered before it was seen in the optically projected images of the camera obscura.

This was discovered, by accident, by the tenth-century Arabian scientist Al Hazan, who reported seeing an image cast by a pinhole on the whitewashed wall of a dark room. He realized its significance but it was not appreciated, or used, for another three hundred years, when a lens was added to give much brighter images thrown on a screen, from which perfect perspective pictures could be traced. The world projected in this way on a screen cast near objects surprisingly large and (as with the usually disappointing photographs of mountains) distant objects absurdly small. Angles looked distorted, though all these changes obeyed sensible rules, which came to be known and understood as geometrical perspective. It was found that perspective pictures looked three-dimensionally real, though they were flat. And it became clear, especially to the astronomer Kepler, that an eye is a camera obscura. Why did this take so long to discover? Probably because the perspective size and shape changes of retinal images are largely cancelled by the, somewhat mysterious, perceptual processes of constancy scaling, which normally keep objects appearing much the same size over a wide range of distances, though the retinal images of near objects are far larger than those of distant objects of the same size. In fact the images in the eye, or in a camera obscura, halve in size for each doubling of the distance of the objects casting them. The perceptual correction of retinal perspective is, no doubt, why perspective is not immediately apparent all day long as we view the world from behind our retinal images. For we never see the eye's images as pictures, and it is most important to appreciate this, because there is no other eye to see them. This, indeed, would lead to another image, another eye, another image, another eye, in an endless chain leading nowhere. This is not and cannot possibly be how perception works. So we do not see the perspective of the retinal images of our eyes, for this is largely corrected, or cancelled out, by the brain's size constancy scaling mechanisms, so that we see objects much the same size whatever their distance. Thus your outstretched hand will look almost exactly the same size as your other hand at half the distance – provided they do not overlap, when your further hand will look as though it belongs to a midget. Size constancy breaks down for great distances: very distant objects look far too small; but normally this does not matter, as distant objects are beyond reach and are no threat.

Although the depth-shrinking of retinal images is largely compensated perceptually so that objects appear much the same size over a wide range of distance – so we do not normally see the world in perspective – nevertheless, the perspective shapes of the eye's images do (though not consciously) signal distances, which is why the world does not look flat with a single eye. For this, there are also other 'monocular depth cues', such as further objects being partly hidden by nearer objects; but perspective shrinking with distance is the most generally available single-eye depth cue, and it is very powerful, although we are generally unaware of it or the other cues by which we see the world in three dimensions. We are, indeed, altogether unaware of our retinal images. A retinal image is just one cross-section of the path from the world to perception, and we no more see our retinal images than we see the millions of pulses of electricity running from them down the optic nerves to the brain. And neither do we see any of the unimaginably complicated processes that go on there, in very extensive regions of the brain, for 'reading' the signals from the senses. This is a subtle business, which remains only partly understood; but it does seem odd how little of the processes of perception were appreciated until recently, considering the vast number of artists, the importance of representing scenes and objects, and the perennial philosophical interest in gaining knowledge by perception.

Since all that is needed to see perspective without the usual perceptual corrections of size constancy, which hide it, is a pin-hole projection in a dark room, or a box, it might be thought that, long ago, somebody would have appreciated perspective in this way. For surely chinks in temple walls must occasionally have given camera obscura images of the outside world, projected on an inner temple wall where it was dark. But, though Euclid wrote on the geometry of mirrors, which were set up in elaborate combinations to deceive and entertain, and though Plato wrote on shadows, there is no convincing evidence of Greek or any other ancient appreciation of perspective for *single* pictures, let alone of the brain combining the subtly different perspectives of each eye's view, for 3-D depth vision.

The first 3-D pictures were made, slightly before photography, by the English physicist Sir Charles Wheatstone (1802–75). Wheatstone thought of presenting pairs of slightly different perspective pictures, one for each eye, with the mirror stereoscope which he invented in 1832. As a matter of fact he did not publish a description of the stereoscope until 1838, in a paper which appeared that year in the *Philosophical Transactions of the Royal Society of London*: 'Contributions to the Physiology of Vision – Part the First. On some remarkable, and hitherto unobserved Phenomena of Vision'. The second part appeared in 1852. Wheatstone points out that Leonardo da Vinci came near to the concept of stereoscopic vision, in the *Trattato della Pittura* (1561), where he says that one eye may see features hidden to the other eye as they view scenes from slightly different positions, which had been appreciated long before by Euclid in his *Optics* of around 300 BC. Curiously, neither Leonardo nor Euclid considered any objects but spheres and round columns, which are incapable of providing the disparate contours or textures necessary for seeing the forms of objects by stereoscopic vision. The notion of the brain combining disparities from slightly different retinal images, together with an instrument to present stereo pairs of pictures separately to each eye, are the key concepts of Wheatstone's 1838 paper. His idea was triggered by an observation (Bowers 1975, p. 201): 'Looking at a lathe-polished metal plate (in which one sees both the surface and the reflection with a candle), which appears standing out from it . . . [o]n closing the left eye the relief disappears.' In this situation, the role of the two eyes for depth vision is clear because marks on the mirror's surface and its reflected image, lying behind it, are seen at once.

It is curious that Wheatstone's stereoscope came just before photography, which made it practical, much as holography was invented by Dennis Gabor a few years before the laser which made this a practical 3-D system. Charles Wheatstone, like Dennis Gabor, was delighted by possibilities opened up by his inventions. Thus Wheatstone wrote (in 1852):

> It was at the beginning of 1839, about six months after the appearance of my memoir in the Philosophical Transactions, that the photographic art became known, and soon after, at my request, Mr. Talbot, the inventor, and Mr. Collen (one of the cultivators of the art) obligingly prepared for me stereoscopic Talbotypes of full-sized statues, buildings, and even portraits of living persons. . . . To M. Fizeau and M. Claudet I was indebted for the first Daguerreotypes executed for the stereoscope. . . . For obtaining binocular photographic portraits, it has been found advantageous to employ, simultaneously, two cameras fixed at the proper angular positions.

3-D photography was very popular from about 1850, when Wheatstone's mirror stereoscope was replaced by the refracting instrument of Sir David Brewster (1781–1868), which is a smaller and more convenient instrument. Anaglyphs (red-green separation allowing stereo pairs to be printed overlaid) were invented by Duauron in 1891.

This account is, so far, the more or less accepted history of perspective, of stereo vision, and of 3-D pictures. Is it true? Was Wheatstone the discoverer of the principle of stereoscopic vision, and the first inventor of a stereoscopic instrument?

By the time Wheatstone described his stereoscope he was already a keen student of visual science, as we know from his papers in the *Journal of the Royal Institution* of October 1830 and May 1831,

'Contributions to the physiology of vision', though these (which were published anonymously) do not describe stereopsis. They were intended as the first papers of a series; but unfortunately, the *Journal* ceased publication at this point, and nothing further appeared until his 1838 paper in the *Philosophical Transactions of the Royal Society*. These instruments are well illustrated and described with examples of Victorian stereo pictures in John Jones's *Wonders of the Stereoscope* (1976). Wheatstone's and Brewster's papers have recently been made available in Nicholas Wade's (1983) excellent collection of their papers. The first account of stereoscopic vision is usually given (as cited by Wheatstone himself, in his 1838 paper) as the description in the 1833 edition of Herbert Mayo's *Outline of Human Physiology*. Mayo was Professor of Anatomy and Physiology at King's College, London, where Wheatstone became Professor of Experimental Philosophy a year later in 1834. Mayo refers to an unpublished paper of Wheatstone's, from which we know that he devised the stereoscope in about 1832. Mayo's is not, however, the first book to describe the basis of stereo vision. Joseph Harris's *Treatise on Opticks* in 1775 has the following passage:

> And by the parallax on account of the distance betwixt our eyes, we can distinguish besides the front, part of the two sides of a near object . . . and this gives a visible relievo to such objects, which helps greatly to raise or detach them from the plane, on which they lie: Thus, the nose on the face, is the more remarkably raised by our seeing each side of it at once!

This pushes the essential notion back nearly a century. If we look back even further, we find that there was at least one stereoscopic instrument more than a century and a half before Wheatstone's mirror stereoscope. For, a stereoscopic microscope was constructed in the seventeenth century. I came upon a reference to this in a mid-nineteenth century book on microscopy and its history, by Jabez Hogg: *The Microscope: Its History, Construction, and Applications* (1854). This has a much earlier woodcut (figure 24.1) and the following account (p. 113), though without a reference to the source:

> *The Application of Binocularity to the Microscope.* The application of this principle to microscopic purposes seems to have been tried as early as 1677, by a French philosopher – *le Père* Chérubin, of Orléans – a Capuchin friar. The following is an extract from the description given by him of his instrument: 'Some years ago I resolved to effect what I had long before premeditated, to make a microscope to see the smallest objects with the two eyes conjointly: and this project has succeeded even beyond my expectation; with

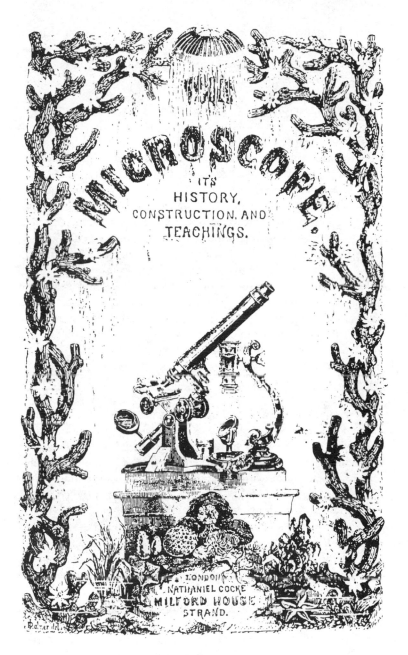

24.1   *The title page of Jabez Hogg's microscope book (1854).*

the advantages above the single instrument so extraordinary and so surprising, that every intelligent person to whom I have shown the effect has assured me that inquiring philosophers will be highly pleased with the communication.'

It seems clear, then, that a stereoscopic microscope was indeed constructed, and the power and basic principle of stereo vision appreciated, before 1677. This is over 150 years before Wheatstone's stereoscope, and less than twelve years after the first book on microscopy, Robert Hooke's *Micrographia* (1665).

Stereoscopic vision is particularly useful for microscopes because, as was shown by the great optical designer Ernst Abbe (1840–1905), the optics of microscopes does not provide perspective. The first practical stereoscopic microscope of modern times was designed in 1851 by J.L. Riddell, of New Orleans, Mississippi, described in 1854. It is based on the fact that rays from opposite edges of an objective lens give different points of view of the object space. An improved arrangement, which was very popular in Victorian microscopes, was devised by F.H. Wenham in 1860. The Wenham prism effectively splits the objective lens in two, so that rays from one half enter one eye, and from the other half the other eye, from a slightly different viewpoint, to give superb stereopsis, though at the cost of reduced resolution as the optical aperture is halved. This cost is often worthwhile. These and later developments are excellently described in the standard nineteenth-century history of microscopy: William B. Carpenter's *The Microscope and its Revelations* (8th edition, 1901). Carpenter does not refer to Jabez Hogg; but he does refer to the Capuchin friar, *le père* Chérubin. Here we find the original reference – and the original drawing of Chérubin's stereo microscope – from Chérubin's *La Vision parfaite* of 1677. Figure 24.2 is the constructional diagram, and drawing, of Chérubin's stereoscopic microscope of 1677. It consists of a pair of compound microscopes, with their objective lenses mounted very close together, with ground edges. The instrument is made of wood, in the form of a flat box, in which the eye pieces and the touching objective lenses (which would be simple, without chromatic correction) are mounted.

Wheatstone knew of this seventeenth-century stereo microscope, for he described it in *Transactions of the Microscopical Society* (1853, I, 99–102). But he did not allow that Chérubin understood stereoscopic vision, or that he appreciated the features necessary for an effective stereoscopic instrument. Chérubin's microscope must have reversed the eyes optically, giving pseudoscopic depth, but this may not have mattered. Chérubin certainly writes that his microscope gave dramatic and useful depth. In any case, it still seems to be true, 4-D-wise, that Wheatstone was the first to make drawings in 3-D –

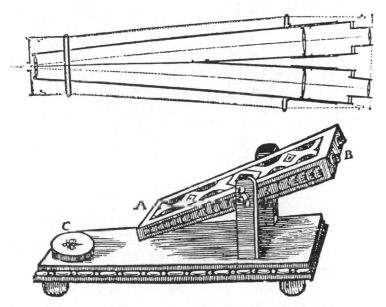

24.2   *A constructional diagram and drawing of Chérubin d'Orléans's stereo microscope (1677).*

though he was probably not the first to appreciate or to make explicit use of stereoscopic vision in an optical instrument.

Figure 24.3 is an early pair of stereo drawings made from a microscope. (They appear on page 114 of Jabez Hogg's book of 1854 – drawn by Wenham in 1853. So they are later than Wheatstone's stereo-constructed line drawings which appeared in 1838.) They are unusual in being drawn by hand. Indeed Wheatstone wrote, of using photography:

> It is evidently impossible for the most accurate and accomplished artist to delineate, by the sole aid of his eye, the two projections necessary to form the stereoscopic relief of objects as they exist in nature, with their delicate difference of outline, light and shade. But what the hand of the artist was unable to accomplish, the chemical action of light, directed by the camera, has enabled us to effect.

Jabez Hogg quotes Wenham's account (in the *Quarterly Journal of Microscopical Science*, October 1853) of how he drew this stereo pair:

> Select any object lying in an inclined position, and place it in the field of view of the microscope; then, with a card held close to the object-glass, stop off alternately the right- or the left-hand portion of the front lens; it will be seen that during each alternate change certain parts of the object will alter their relative position.

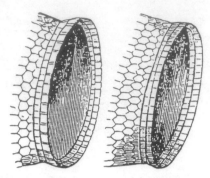

24.3   *Early hand-drawn stereo pair (of egg of bed-bug (Cimex lecticularis) by F.H. Wenham (1853). This is reproduced by Hogg (1854).*

There is a simple way, essentially similar to this, to convert a modern binocular microscope (which gives the same image to each eye and so is *not* a stereo instrument) into an effective stereoscopic microscope. As Wenham microscopes are no longer made, this is a useful trick. Place a polaroid filter over the left half of the substage condenser lens, and another polaroid rotated by 90 degrees over the right half of the condenser. Polaroids, with equivalent orientations, are placed over each eyepiece, so that the right eye receives light from the right half of the objective and the left eye from the left half. This arrangement serves the same function as Wenham's prism which also effectively divides the objective into two separate halves and routes one half to one eye, the other half to the other eye. It works well with a low-power objective; but with high powers, the small available depth of field limits its effectiveness. This is a fundamental limitation for optical stereoscopic microscopes: there is almost no depth available.

Some years ago I devised a very different kind of stereoscopic microscope, giving not a stereo pair but rather a *solid image*, with thick specimens (Gregory 1974). Instead of the limited depth of field of microscope objectives restricting the depth that can be seen, making 3-D ineffective except at low powers, this made use of the small depth of field – by moving the thin plane of sharp focus through the specimen, at a rate of fifty depth-scans a second. To reconstitute the depth-scanned image in three dimensions, it was projected onto a screen which vibrated in phase, though with a much larger amplitude than the depth scanning, which was given by vibrating the objective lens up and down fifty times a second. This arrangement gave a solid image in the volume swept by the vibrating screen. This was more than 3-D, for as one moved one's head one could see around the image, and get motion parallax as for viewing objects normally – though motion parallax is lost in the flat pictures of 3-D stereo pairs. Then, Geoff Courtney-Pratt, of the Bell Telephone Labs, and I

(Courtney-Pratt and Gregory 1973) devised a system without mechanical scanning, using the chromatic aberration of an uncorrected objective, to focus depth planes in different colours. This, again, turned optics upside down, for it *used* chromatic aberration, as the earlier version *used* the usually restricting limited depth of field of microscope lenses. Prisms in the eye pieces produced the necessary depth-related disparities to generate 3-D. But, though interesting, these did not lead to practical instruments. The scanning electron microscope does far better what we set out do, though it is not suitable for living specimens.

This is not quite all. Visiting Florence, recently, I was amazed to find in the wonderful science museum a *binocular telescope made by Chérubin*! It is not in the catalogue. But there it is, resting in a glass cabinet. It is extremely similar in construction to his stereo microscope: a series of rectangular, tooled leather-covered wooden boxes, each larger than the next, made to slide into each other, to form a draw tube over 4 feet long when extended. And in the museum's archives is Chérubin's book *La Vision parfaite*, in French (1678) and also in Latin (1681). Here there are extended discussions of stereo vision written 200 years before Wheatstone. And here there is a contemporary engraving of clearly the same stereo telescope tooled with the Borgia coat of arms. In the engraving, it is mounted horizontally, on a tall stand in a garden – it is being used as a terrestrial telescope, where stereo vision is useful.

So, we can see a stereoscopic instrument of the seventeenth century, with our own eyes today. Who said history is bunk?

REFERENCES

Bowers, B. (1975) *Sir Charles Wheatstone FRS, 1802–1875*, London.
Brewster, Sir D. (1856) *The Stereoscope: Its History, Theory, and Construction*, reprinted (1971), New York, Morgan & Morgan, London, Fountain Press.
Carpenter, W.B. (1901) *The Microscope and its Revelations*, 8th edn, revised W.H. Dallinger, London.
Courtney-Pratt, J.S. and Gregory R.L. (1973) 'Microscope with enhanced depth of field and 3-D capacity', *Applied Optics* 12, 2509.
Euclid (c. 300 BC) *Optics*, in M.R. Cohen and I.E. Drabkin, (1966) *A Source Book of Greek Science*, Cambridge, Mass., Harvard University Press, p. 257.
Gregory, R.L. (1974) *Concepts and Mechanisms of Perception*, London, Duckworth, pp. 458–74.
Hogg, J. (1854) *The Microscope: Its History, Construction, and Applications*, London.
Jones, J. (1976) *Wonders of the Stereoscope*, New York, Knopf.
Wade, N.J. (1983) *Brewster and Wheatstone on Vision*, London, Academic Press, for the Experimental Psychology Society.

25

SEE NAPLES AND LIVE: THE SCANNING EYE OF *COPILIA*

We can be faced with trying to decide whether our observations are sufficiently reliable to be the basis of publishable conclusions in science. This of course is the besetting question for claims of ESP, since what is claimed is so unlikely that we prefer to reject the 'observations' and with them the claims. But it can also be a problem in 'normal' science, especially perhaps when the observer's background knowledge is inadequate. Here is an example.

In 1963 I came across a nineteenth-century description of what seemed to be a unique eye – of a sub-tropical copepod (literally meaning 'oar-foot' from its typical oar blade, or slipper-like shape) which was found in the 1880s deep in the Bay of Naples: *Copilia quadrata*. The description was by a distinguished naturalist, Sellig Exner, who made important discoveries on the optics of compound eyes. But the *Copilia* eyes must have been extremely unusual, for although an expert Exner did not at first realize that they were eyes. He described *Copilia* as a beautiful, highly transparent, pinhead-sized creature, having a pair of lens-like structures deep in the body which, though fully visible under the microscope as *Copilia* was so transparent, hardly looked like eyes. The lens structures were 'in continuous lively motion'. What Exner did not see – and could not see, writing in 1891 – was that this might be a *scanning* eye. For the principle of image-scanning was not available to him at that time, so he was necessarily conceptually blind and therefore, in the full sense, could not see these eyes. Before they could be seen the principle by which they functioned had to be invented and appreciated. The concept of transmitting images down a single channel by scanning did not become at all familiar until the technique was introduced for television by John Logie Baird in the 1930s. It was not invented by Baird, however, but by Paul Nipkow, in 1884, in the form of a rapidly rotating disk with a spiral arrangement of holes, or lenses. It is most unlikely that Exner would have known of this or that he could have appreciated its significance before the principle was used to transmit two-dimensional pictures through a single channel. Its implications were not appreciated, considerably later, by the Chief Engineer of the BBC, who declared that transmitting pictures by radio waves would forever be impossible as radio waves are so much longer than waves of light. Image-scanning was the engineering solution.

It is also a solution for the opposite problem that an eye must solve: the conversion of patterns of light to neural signals. Each of our eyes has more than a hundred million light-sensitive receptors forming a densely packed mosaic on the retina, to transmit patterns of retinal images in parallel by the million fibres of the optic nerve. The other way of doing it, which is how television works, is to send the information spread out in time down a single channel, by scanning the scene. This, however, at least for a complex scene to be transmitted in a reasonable time, requires fast-acting components which are not found in living organisms, although they are available in electronic engineering. So a scanning eye is hardly likely. If it does occur it must have a limited performance. Perhaps, though, it might have been tried in nature and possibly still survive as an ancient experiment. It could have been tried early in evolution, leading to the thousands of optical units of the highly developed 'compound' eyes of insects; or the still greater number of channels of many of the 'simple' eyes, such as our own.

When I came across Exner's description of *Copilia* in 1962, in the department library at Cambridge it occurred to me that here might be a biological scanning eye. For, by then, scanning was a familiar principle used in television. It seemed surprising though, for an eye – and well worth investigating. At the time I was running a research group for the American Air Force on perceptual problems in space travel. My imaginative masters, in the USAF European Office in Brussels, who administered US funding of a great deal of research in Europe after the war, immediately supported a visit to the Naples marine biology laboratory to look for *Copilia*, and establish whether, millions of years before the television camera, nature had invented a scanning eye.

The 1960s were halcyon days for young scientists, for although we were personally ludicrously short of money, it was possible to get funding for almost any reasonable project. The generosity of the American Government in supporting European research, and so much else at that time, is heartening to remember. I believe the money was well spent. Of course, looking for a microscopic scanning eye is not world-saving. But it is good to know such things. They may suggest questions, and occasionally even inspire new technologies.

So, I set up an expedition to Naples, to look for *Copilia* where she had been found, a human life-time earlier; though, most curiously, since forgotten. I took my research colleague Helen Ross (who later went on to investigate perception under water with divers, and set up several experiments for micro-gravity in the space shuttle); and Neville Moray, an Oxford psychologist with a background in zoology, now in Canada. The project was made possible by the enthusiasm of Professor J.Z. (John) Young, whose celebrated work on the anatomy, learning and vision of *Octopus* was done over many summers at the Naples marine laboratory. It was a wonderful place, with its wide variety of interests and its own international mix of languages. Shutting my eyes now I can return to the bright light of the bay with its sea smell, and our dark laboratory with its jars and beakers, and our microscopes, which revealed a world of life behind the brilliant curved windows of their little lenses.

Each day, the laboratory's boat-men brought us a large glass jar, densely packed with all manner of plankton hauled from the deep water just beyond the Bay. Confronted with this daily jar, filled with an incredible variety of wriggly life, we had somehow to recognize *Copilia*. We had only the faintest idea of what to look for, as we had no picture or adequate description. Each day we searched, drop by drop, by eye and with low- and high-power microscopes. We knew, from Exner's brief description, that *Copilia* would be only a few millimetres in length and extremely transparent. After about two weeks we almost gave up. Then suddenly – there she was! Once seen, there was no doubt – we were looking at the miniature creature Exner described, though he could not at that time appreciate or fully see it.

Copilia had an odd shape for a copepod; very square, with a pair of enormous perfectly contrived anterior lenses, which looked like car headlamps. Then, deep within the transparent body, there lay another pair of lenses – pear-shaped – each attached to an orange-pigmented boomerang-shaped structure, which turned out to be a single rod photoreceptor. They were curved, not straight as in other eyes – evidently so that they could move through the body fluid. For, as Exner had said, the pair of internal lenses attached to their photoreceptors moved, oscillating laterally; moving away and to-wards each other in a 'saw-tooth' *scan*, as we now saw it, across the images from the two huge fixed anterior lenses. The optical details were confirmed later by my colleague Tony Downing, on our second expedition, when he managed to photograph the images formed by the large front lenses inside the living creature, and found that the images lay in the same plane as the moving interior lenses (Downing 1972).

The 'scanning' movements were not always present, and there might be just two or three scans and then a period of absolute inactivity. Then, often with a preparatory scan or two, she would leap into rapid darting life, sometimes for several minutes before another long death-like rest. *Copilia* has no heart (which is not unusual for copepods) so she is indistinguishable from dead in these long resting periods. (It seemed odd to us that having or not having a heart is not a defining characteristic of copepods, which are simple crustaceans; but they are catalogued and described by clearly seen features of dead specimens. As tiny lifeless hearts are hard to see, the presence or absence of a heart is not a criterion for classification of what is or is not a copepod. Could this practice of classifying from what is easily seen sometimes be misleading?) After hours of peering at her down our microscopes, we became reasonably convinced that we were looking at single-channel scanning eyes. However, there was little systematic behaviour and we never did succeed in recording from the optic nerve. The large movements and the extremely tough carapace made recording impossible, at any rate for us. Whatever her secrets, *Copilia* is so beautiful that one could spend a lifetime studying her.

Apart from learning something of *Copilia*'s eye, we found a curious perceptual effect in ourselves. Leaving the laboratory, after looking at *Copilia* all day, the little Italian cars with their eye-like headlamps turned dream-like into *Copilia*, swimming in the streets of Naples.

When thanking the American Office for making our expedition possible I sent them a large photograph of *Copilia* which, I was told, hung on the wall in Brussels for years and was much appreciated – as indeed she deserved to be.

After mulling over this for some years, we decided upon a second expedition. In 1972 we returned – to make some observations I have never dared to report. For, although we took every care and used far more sophisticated equipment this time, I cannot be sure that what we thought we saw really happened. These observations may, how-ever, alert more expert investigators to genuine discovery. So I will now, for the first time, report what I thought I saw.

Almost nothing is known of the life style of *Copilia*, except that they are found only in sub-tropical seas (not in the Atlantic Ocean) and that they are rare. We were lucky to find more than one or two a day, in our jar from the deep. Only the female has these extraordinary eyes. The male is more than twice the size of the female and is very different (which is not unusual for copepods) and has only vestigial eyes with little or no 'scanning' movement. The female does not seem to eat anything, though no doubt she ingests water, for we never saw particles of solid matter in the digestive tract, even though she is so transparent that every internal detail can be studied in the living creature. She lives for only a few days, at least in laboratory conditions. The *Copilia* we saw are probably the final briefly living adult form, following several larval stages, though these have not been identified. As she does not appear to eat, presumably she lives on stored energy and is really a mating machine seeking the relatively passive male with her scanning eyes. How does she find a male? Though she normally lives quite deep in the sea it is likely that she rises to the surface to make the search easier; for while there is an awful lot of sea, there are but very few *Copilia*.

We found that the males sometimes produce either continuous or flashing green light from specialized regions having remarkable structures. So we may guess that mating occurs at night, the female seeking the flashing lights of the extremely rare males. It was therefore a wonderful day when in our daily jar we found a rich supply of active males – with flashing lights. This was immensely surprising as we had not seen the lights before, or found many males together. We had not had such a haul before and never found the like again. When placed in a dish, the fourteen or so males formed into flashing rafts, presumably to be visible to the searching females.

There were five of us in the laboratory. Most knowledgeable was Tony Downing; but unfortunately he was heavily involved that day with his experiment on the optics of the eye, and with mending the video equipment which most annoyingly had gone wrong. (This was used for recording the scanning movements with our Lietz microscope, under various conditions including infra-red illumination in which *Copilia* is blind. We found that scanning continues in what is, for *Copilia*, darkness. We have some ten hours of Copilia behaviour and scanning recorded on tape.) Also present were my wife Freja (a Cambridge psychology graduate) and my daughter Romilly (then at school). There was also my photographic technician, Philip Clark (now a professional balloonist), and myself. So on this day of unique opportunity, 6 August 1972, we set out to study the interactive behaviour of male and female *Copilia*.

As the video system was not working on that day, I resorted to a running commentary on audio tape while observing with a high-quality dissection microscope. The male and female *Copilia* were placed in a circular glass dish 4 inches in diameter and about 1 inch deep. The lighting turned out to be extremely important – and here I do believe we made a clear-cut (though unpublished) discovery. We found, by accident, that the flashing green light of the males only occurred when there was ultraviolet (UV) available in the ambient light of the laboratory. They would glow continuously or, more often, flash only when the fluorescent strip-light was switched on, and not with tungsten illumination, either from the microscope sub-stage or from the alternative tungsten-room lighting. Also the male *Copilia*'s light ceased immediately when a UV cut-off filter was introduced to remove the UV from the strip-light. We also found that the flashes of the male would follow flashes of a (UV-rich) stroboscope light – up to about five flashes per second. Lastly, although UV was necessary, the male *Copilia* could, apparently, switch off its flashing lights of its own volition.

So far I am reporting observations made with colleagues in laboratory conditions. As we were able to repeat them several times, I suppose this is proper science and I would be surprised if the above statements are incorrect. So, we probably did find a little that was previously unknown. But now I come to attempts to discover whether the female was guided for mating by the male's lights. Here we lacked background knowledge of what to expect, which made observation extremely difficult. Although we may have discovered how mating takes place, we are not sure. The observations were so surprising that the audio tape – which still exists – sounds in places chaotic, and hardly as scientific accounts are supposed to be. But this in no way reduces its status as a record of what happened. Here is a section of the recording I made while looking down the microscope at the male and female *Copilia*. At the same time I was describing what I saw to my colleagues, who were generally busy on other tasks, but who looked from time to time at what I was reporting:

Now I have found a male with a female beside it on her side very, very close to the male, and I am going to give it room light.

They are touching each other, the female by the sixth segment; she is scanning. The other male is coming up. There are two males involved here. The female is keeling over so her underside is against the side of the male. And another female has got the other male. Hey, chaps, I've got a double mating going on here! Oh, boy! One of the males has shot off, and that female's shot off, leaving this female and this male together. There is a hell of a lot going on. Honestly, do you know, I am beginning to get the pattern of behaviour. Look, the female rocks over on her side – hang on, she is approaching the male now, coming up – she is upside down, and they always come up to the same part of the male, amidships (to use a technical term); then they approach him with their eyes, which she is doing now, in line with the tail. Tony – they always do this, and they come up with their eyes touching the male. This one is like that now. If you don't believe me come up and see it, it's exactly the same as the previous one – remember, I described it? Well, this one is doing it. Look, they go parallel with the male and put their eyes to the tail of the male.

We're looking at it by room light and a little bit of the other –

ultraviolet – light. There are four males all stacked up together there. There was another female there but that one shot off. . . . There are two males together. . . . Now the two males are tail to tail with something which is beating around but which is not actually touching the other male. It's beating around like mad. . . . It's going around in a sort of circular motion, with a long floppy thing on the end of it. The floppy bit is about as long as the animal is wide at the point of the fluorescing segment. I think it comes out of the last fluorescing segment on the left-hand side, if I have got the orientation of the animal right. Yes, I agree with that. . . . It's approaching the female now from behind, but it's still got this incredible flagellum thing on its left-hand side. I think we might be quite wrong about this. I think the flagellum is something separate. The flagellum has separated off. The flagellum is approaching the female – and has now swum back to the male. There's something extraordinary here – it's between the two, and it may have nothing to do with it of course. The flagellum approached the female, and has now swum back to the male. This flagellum is the most extraordinary structure; it's a long stalk, it's L-shaped, goes in violent motion and sort of whips along. It's still there, approaching the female and it's just past the tail of the female. There is violent activity. The female has turned on her side, the flagellum is still there. The male is still there, aimed at the female and about half a length away, this flagellum thing is still in the vicinity. Now this flagellum has a white blob at one end, and a forked tail. I don't know what on earth it can be, I suppose it must be something quite separate. There are two males now, parallel with each other, a female in front of them, the flagellum has gone off, the female is scanning and I'm just going to watch these now. There is another female coming up now from the rear, so there are now two males and two females. They are now all in a great huddle – the two males are parallel with each other facing the same way, there is a female on the end of one of the males, the anterior end, her underside next to his front eye, so to speak, and I think I might be right in saying that he may have grasped her.

Tony, I think this male has grasped this female. Do you want to look? Now there is another male coming up as well, which is glowing. Look, have a look at this – look.

Now what have we got? We have got a huddle of three males all close together, two of them pointing towards the light, the other pointing away from it, and the female is swimming around to the left of them. My God, there is another female here, they have formed a great huddle, the whole lot of them. Golly, five males all huddled together – no, six of them – one of them glowing like mad, the others not. This is absolutely incredible. I've got the female above the male and she has stuck her tail into the male.

The male is upside down, Tony.

These are the actual words in which I described my perceptions at the time. Though I was fairly sure that this was mating, I was not absolutely sure – because I did not know enough. The whirling firework object, I believe, was ejected from the male *Copilia*, and it seemed to home in on the female though it missed and was not captured. Is this how they mate?

If we had come to a firm conclusion it would have been written up as a scientific paper, in a prose lacking the original excitement and with the frankly considerable chaos filtered out. So it might have been respectable science. As it is, we are virtually sure that *Copilia* scans the world with mechanical TV camera eyes, and we are virtually sure, though it needs confirming, that the males have flashing lights as beacons for the females to find them. We are also virtually sure that the flashing lights of the male require ultraviolet light, though they can apparently switch the flashing off at will. But all this can only be written now as an essay – not as a scientific paper – because we failed to transform the chaos of perceiving into the ordered perceptions of science.

There is the possibility that *Copilia*'s scanning eye is a missing link in the evolution of compound eyes, for each eye is like a single unit (ommatidium) of a compound eye, as found in insects and right back to the first fossil eyes of trilobites. It may be that the many-faceted compound eyes of bees and dragonflies started out as a single optical probing finger, taking over the neural mechanisms of an extremely ancient active probing touch. But scanning the world with a single finger would be too slow, so perhaps the *Copilia*-like prototype eyes multiplied their optical units to become optical 'hands' with many fingers, reaching out to explore beyond the confines of touch to become the large unmoving compound eyes of present-day arthropods. On this account, our own eyes started differently; taking over regions of surface skin, already capable of signalling touch patterns, gradually becoming more sensitive to light, at first for detecting moving shadows and then for receiving images from cups with pin holes. Then, as image-forming lenses developed, to photograph the world upon millions of specialized light receptors signalling in parallel.

Once we learn how to understand we can see, conceptually to look back even into the distant past, and ahead to predict and sometimes invent the future.

REFERENCES

Downing, A.C. (1972) 'Optical scanning in the lateral eyes of the copepod *Copilia*', *Perception* 1 (3), 247–61.

Exner, S. (1891) *Die physiologie der facettirten Augen von Krebsen und Insecten*, Leipzig and Vienna.

Gregory, R.L. (1967) 'Origins of eyes and brains', *Nature* (London) 213, 369.

Gregory, R.L. (1968) 'The evolution of eyes and brains – a hen-and-egg problem', in S.J. Freedman (ed.) *The Neuro-Psychology of Spatially Oriented Behaviour*, New York, Academic Press, reprinted in R.L. Gregory (1974) *Concepts and Mechanisms of Perception*, London, Duckworth, pp. 602–13.

Gregory, R.L., Ross H.E. and Moray N. (1964) 'The curious eye of *Copilia*', *Nature* (London) 201, 1166, reprinted in R.L. Gregory (1974) *Mechanisms and Concepts of Perception*, London, Duckworth, pp. 390–584.

26

BACON'S LAST EGG: EXPLORATORY SCIENCE HANDS-ON

Francis Bacon (1561–1626) is still remembered in Popes's words as the 'wisest, brightest, meanest of mankind'. But when one thinks of Bacon's achievements in his lifetime, and how much he left to us, this seems a mean appraisal. His chief crime seems to have been that his judgements, as James I's Keeper of the Great Seal and Lord Chancellor, were not as affected by bribes as his contemporaries would have wished. The distinction between bribes and fees was certainly far less clear-cut then than now. In any case he died heavily in debt. Quite apart from his formidable legal and political careers, Francis Bacon was a considerable literary figure, as he perfected the essay form. As a philosopher he virtually invented modern scientific method, which he saw as essentially based on inductive procedures for generating knowledge from many exploratory observations and 'crucial' experiments to serve as 'finger posts' for selecting the way at cross-roads of possibilities.

Bacon set up the modern conception of science. His notion of gaining knowledge by sharing ideas and working in teams became embodied in the plan of the Royal Society of London, founded by Charles II in 1660. His *New Organum* is the basis of modern scientific method, and introduces the idea of applying science for human good. For Bacon urged the importance of devising processes and machines for the general good of mankind, based on principles of science.

Bacon's concept of co-operative work for generating knowledge was a fundamental break from Plato's authoritative notion that men are born with all knowledge but lose it more or less at birth; and to become wise we have to retrieve the lost knowledge as intuitions, to be found only through philosophy and artistic training. For Plato, truth and wisdom are intuitions available only to a very few specially trained individuals of an élite. By contrast, Bacon thought of science as knowledge built up cumulatively, piece by piece and generally by many small contributions based not so much on special intuitions as by planned experiments which, in his words, 'will level men's wits'. He made no sharp distinction between science and technology. He was a martyr to both, as he died of a cold after freezing a chicken for experimental purposes on Hampstead Heath.

It is generally thought that Bacon underestimated the importance of mathematics and that this tarnished his reputation, since the powerful Platonic tradition of his time, as well as almost all scientists of the highest standing since, revered mathematics as 'The Queen of the Sciences'. There are, however, many non-mathematical scientists – including the greatest experimenter and the greatest theoretical biologist, Michael Faraday and Charles Darwin – who show that exploration guided by hunch may bring home the bacon over mathematics.

Francis Bacon recognized the limitations of our perceptions and imagination. He says of the senses (in the *Novum Organum*, 1620, Bk 1, Section vi):

> By far the greatest hindrance and aberration of the human understanding proceeds from the dullness, incompetency, and deception of the senses. . . . Hence it is that speculation commonly ceases where sight ceases; insomuch that of things invisible there is little or no observation.

Somewhat curiously, the newly invented optical instruments were not for Bacon much help:

> For the sense by itself is a thing infirm and erring; neither can instruments for enlarging or sharpening the senses do much; but all the truer kind of interpretation of nature is effected by instances and experiments fit and apposite; wherein the sense decides touching the experiment only, and the experiment touching the point in nature and the thing itself.

He would be amazed by modern instruments and what they have shown of the universe.

The classical Greek philosophers were attacked by Bacon as mere logic-choppers, who made no real progress and so left us in the dark. But surely he was less than fair to Aristotle, who extolled observation and also (though less widely appreciated) gave considerable weight to inductive generalizations, as well as the syllogistic forms of deductive argument he invented. Nevertheless, Bacon criticized Aristotle (*Aphorisms*, 1620, Bk 1, no. 98) for: 'corrupting natural philosophy by his logic; fashioning the world out of categories'; even though Aristotle did say of inductive generalizations that (*Analytica Posteriora*, Book A, 87b): 'The universal is valuable because it shows the cause, and therefore universal knowledge is more valuable than perception or intuitive knowledge.' This is remarkably close to Bacon's own philosophy, while it is equally distant from Plato's, though Bacon criticizes them equally.

Aristotle had a stranglehold in Bacon's time, so possibly the latter's unfairness here was justified. However this may be, Bacon rejected surely too cavalierly, both in *The Advancement of Learning* of 1605 and in the *Novum Organum* of 1620, the manner of enquiry of the Greeks as too static, and so ineffective, that according to Bacon (in the preface to *De Interpretatione Naturae*): 'The knowledge that we now possess will not teach a man even what to *wish*.' Can this be justified? Bacon was reacting against his surely too simple view of Greek philosophers when he urged – and surely the pioneering Greeks would have agreed – that discovery and learning should be by active exploration, as in ship's voyages. He accepted the dangers as well as the benefits to be gained from such active exploration.

Bacon is often sadly misrepresented, though he wrote with admirable clarity. Thus, it is commonly said that he espoused induction by simple enumeration of instances as the sole way of gaining knowledge; but this does not at all match Bacon's ideas as expressed very clearly in the *Novum Organum*. It is here, in his major work, that he proposes: 'Tables of Invention'; to derive 'minor generalizations' for suggesting general or universal laws whose validity and range should be tested by experiments. Here he describes 'crucial' experiments as like cross-roads requiring choices of which road to take. These crucial decisions were more important for him than building inductions by enumeration of instances, though Bacon did criticize his contemporaries (with the notable exception of William Gilbert, whose *De Magnete* of 1600 set experimental standards which Bacon recognized) for not repeating observations or experiments adequately for gaining reliability. Though he stressed, many times, the vital importance of crucial experiments and observations, amazingly this is often ignored in recent accounts of Bacon's methods for generating knowledge and inventions.

Not nearly as well known as the *Novum Organum* of 1620 is Bacon's *New Atlantis* which appeared unfinished in 1627, the year after his death. The *New Atlantis* is an imaginary island with a civilization of pre-Socratic origin, which avoided what he saw as the stultifying effects of Greek thinking, especially of Plato and Aristotle. Prominent is the ambitious House of Salomon, in which the wonders of science and technology are presented to the people, so that they can learn by seeing and exploring the wonders of the natural world and of the creations of their civilization. This was not a museum, as it was far more than a passive collection of exhibits: it was, rather, a palace for 'hands-on' exploration of science and technology. Very likely Bacon hoped that such an interactive science centre would be founded as a result of his dreams. The imaginary House of Exploration is Bacon's last golden egg. Could it be laid in England today? This is what we are trying to find out.

Bacon's House of Exploration is certainly ambitious. It has many houses, some being caves, and towers miles high in which technologies and knowledge of all kinds are presented – including the powers and limitations of human perception:

> We have also perspective-houses, where we make demonstrations of all lights and radiations; and of all colours; and out of things uncoloured and transparent, we can represent unto you all several colours; not in rain-bows, as it is in gems and prisms, but of themselves single. We represent all multiplications of light, which we carry to great distance, and make so sharp as to discern small points and lines; also all colorations of light: all delusions and deceits of the sight, in figures, magnitudes, motions, colours: all demonstrations of shadows. We find also divers means, yet un-known to you, of producing of light originally from diverse bodies. We procure means for seeing objects afar off; as in the heaven and remoter places; and represent things near as afar off, and things afar off as near; making feigned distances. We have also helps for sight, far above spectacles and glasses in use. . . . We make artificial rainbows, haloes, and circles about light. We represent all manner of reflexions, refractions, and multiplications of visual beams of objects.
>
> We have also sound-houses, where we practise and demonstrate all sounds and their generation. We have harmonies which you have not, of quarter-sounds, and lesser slides of sounds. . . . We represent and imitate all articulate sounds and letters, and the voices of and notes of beasts and birds. We have certain helps which set to the ear do further the hearing greatly. . . . We have also means to convey sounds in trunks and pipes, in strange lines and distances.
>
> We have also perfume-houses; wherewith we join also practices of taste. We multiply smells, which may seem strange. We imitate smells, making all smells to breathe out of other mixtures than those that give them. We make divers imitations of taste likewise, so that they will deceive any man's taste. . . .
>
> We have also engine houses. . . . Also fire works for pleasure

and use. We imitate also flights of birds; we have some degrees of flying in the air; we have ships and boats for going under water, and brooking of seas; also swimming-girdles and supporters. We have divers curious clocks, and other like motions of return, and some perpetual motions. We imitate also motions of living creatures, by images of men, beasts, birds, fishes, and serpents. . . .

We have also a mathematical house, where are represented all instruments, as well of geometry as astronomy, exquisitely made.

We have also houses of deceits of the senses; where we represent all manner of feats of juggling, false apparitions, impostures, and illusions; and their fallacies. And surely you will easily believe that we have so many things truly natural which induce admiration, could in a world of particulars deceive the senses, if we would disguise those things and labour to make them seem more miraculous.

On the staff are Merchants of Light (dealers in knowledge) and Mystery-Men, as well as inventors and framers of hypotheses, including:

Three that draw the experiments . . . into titles and tables, to give the better light for the drawing of observations out of them. These we call Compilers.

We have three that bend themselves, looking into the experiments of their fellows, and cast about how to draw out of them things of use and practice for man's life, and knowledge as well for works as for plain demonstrations of causes, means of natural divinations, and the easy and clear discovery of the virtues and parts of bodies. These we call Dowry-men or Benefactors.

There is indeed a House of Salomon, across the Atlantic, the Exploratorium in San Francisco, which was founded 20 years ago by Frank Oppenheimer. He created an enchanted palace, where anyone with initiative can discover and see for themselves the world of science and how things work. This is Bacon's dream come true.

As it happened, the importance of active exploration and the inhibiting effect of glass cases in museums were impressed upon me before I had read Francis Bacon's *New Atlantis* or met with Frank Oppenheimer's extremely important ideas and great achievement, to which we will return.

The experience that deeply affected me was the case of S.B., a man who had been blind since infancy but gained his sight in middle life, by corneal grafts at the age of 52. Jean Wallace and I (Gregory and Wallace 1963) found that after the operations he was immediately able to see things he already knew from his years of exploring the world while blind, especially from touch – though for months and even years he remained effectively blind to things he had not been able to explore. Thus, he could immediately tell the time by sight, from a clock on the wall of the hospital ward, as years before he had learned to read time from his pocket watch by touching its hands. He could read single letters written or printed in upper case, though not in lower case – he had learned upper case though not lower case letters by touch, as a boy at the blind school, from letters engraved on wooden blocks for the children to explore with their fingers. Most dramatic was his response to first seeing a lathe (a tool that he had ardently wished he could use when blind) which we showed him, in a glass case, at the Science Museum in South Kensington shortly after he left hospital. As we reported (Gregory and Wallace 1963, p. 33):

> We led him to the glass case, which was closed, and asked him to tell us what was in it. He was quite unable to say anything about it, except that he thought the nearest part was a handle. (He pointed to the handle of the transverse feed.) He complained that he could not see the cutting edge, or the metal being worked, or anything else about it, and appeared rather agitated. We then asked a Museum Attendant for the case to be opened, and S.B. was allowed to touch the lathe. The result was startling; he ran his hands deftly over the machine, touching first the transverse feed handle and confidently naming it as a 'handle', and then on to the saddle, the bed and the head-stock of the lathe. He ran his hands eagerly over the lathe, with his eyes shut. Then he stood back a little and opened his eyes and said: 'Now I've felt it I can see.'

From these background ideas and experiences, we have set up the Exploratory in Bristol, which in Bacon's time was England's second city. . . . This is the first of several hands-on science and technology centres in the country. The Exploratory follows the lead of Francis Bacon and of Frank Oppenheimer: presenting science and technology without the impediment of glass cases. Here anyone may learn to see and understand by actively exploring the laws and phenomena of nature and the inventions which, created by human intelligence, have extended our eyes and hands to the stars.

The Exploratory we are building in Bristol is designed to introduce and attract children and adults to science and technology, with the primary aims of showing people how things around them work and helping to make the scientific way of approaching questions and problems more central in our culture. It should, thus, be a step towards melting the Snow dividing the two cultures: art and science.

The Exploratory is not a museum, nor is it a school; though, like museums, it should be a valuable resource for schools. It will allow anyone who is interested to discover principles of science and how things work, with hands-on interactive working models, demonstrations and simple experiments. Information and help will be provided by captions (written at various levels) and by specially trained explainers – called 'pilots', to help the explorers – who will also look after the 'plores' and generally see that everything is running properly.

As the usual museum terms, such as 'exhibit', are too passive for the Exploratory interactive models and hands-on experiments, we have coined the word 'plore': meaning a model, an experiment, or a problem or whatever to explore. So one *explores* plores. Coining some new words appropriate to the aims should help to reinforce the difference between the Exploratory and a science museum. Both, of course, have their place and there need be no competition or rivalry between them. Essentially, the Exploratory is not a custodian of historically important or valuable objects which need to be protected rather than handled, and so we can avoid glass cases, for we are concerned with principles rather than with things. We try to show how tools and toys of technology work, and how they combine, uniquely, principles of science to solve problems. Thus in technology we see past human intelligence available to us.

The working demonstrations and experiments – the plores for exploring – start with *human perception*: with how the senses provide information to perceive and understand the world, though sometimes to misperceive and misunderstand. Perceptual experiments on seeing, hearing, touching and the other senses start by looking inwards at perceptual phenomena, to give by direct experience some insight into processes for gaining knowledge – which amazingly are still hardly considered in schools, even though all our knowledge depends on perception, and exploratory interaction with the world of objects. In this light illusions are fascinating phenomena and worth serious consideration, though they may look trivial, as they are deviations from physics. From perception and learning, we move to *physiology*: recording muscle activity, heart rate, and so on, and looking non-invasively into the body with newly available techniques. Then we move to principles of *mechanics* and *physics*, and how they are combined in *technology*. This ranges from simple mechanisms, such as locks and keys and kitchen scales, to principles of electricity and computers, ending with principles of artificial intelligence. We should not, however, have too many simulations: phenomena should speak for themselves.

The main Exploratory principles are to provide opportunities to try things out hands-on (rather than the push buttons and glass cases of conventional science museums) which helps people to appreciate not only how mechanisms, or whatever, work; but also to discover when and why they do *not* work – and so the range of conditions in which phenomena occur and machines function. By active trying out and playing, optimal conditions may soon be discovered and tested, which is the basis of learning any skill. By optimizing conditions we gain the kind of understanding which, though non-verbal, underlies all skills. And we learn how carefully things need to be made or performed – and what can be left to inattention or chance. This is important for saving time and effort, by freeing the attention from a well-learned skill, and directing it to where it is most needed, perhaps to explore alternatives, even to invent new methods.

Essential for the Exploratory is good humour and tolerance, combined with an element of challenge. As it is so obvious that young animals and children learn by *play*, it is strange that so many educationalists think of play as a trivial activity. Many of our plores should be frankly fun. Many can be games: games played with friends and – as science is – games played against nature. There is a place here for some jokes, for jokes can jolt the mind into higher-energy orbits, with new potentials.

Some plores should be *surprising*. These attract particular attention, and by showing up the explorer's failure to predict correctly, they at once reveal gaps in his or her understanding. For example, blowing air between the suspended balls of a Bernoulli demonstration is surprising, in the right kind of way, as most people expect the balls to *separate* instead of, as they do, drawing together, which is counter-intuitive. By playing around with the air jet it is easy to discover the range and limits of the phenomenon. The practical importance of this effect is made clear with demonstrations of the lift of aircraft wings. Such practical demonstrations may be needed, for some people, to justify the jolt of surprise by failed prediction. In any case, the jolt of failed prediction is a most useful signal that one needs to revise one's understanding. There should not, however, be too many dramatic surprises or the Exploratory experience will be confusing. It is reassuring to get things right: so some initial hypotheses should be confirmed!

Several of the plores should be designed to reveal hidden features of the world – especially features that cannot normally be sensed. This can be done in two ways.

First, it can be done by making features that cannot normally be sensed available to the senses; for example, magnetic fields made visible with iron filings, or pressure waves of sound made visible with the gas flames of a Rubin tube. Or, more interactively, handling a spinning gyroscope wheel, which allows surprising and usually hidden forces to be experienced, literally, at first hand. These are special 'plores', and some may be familiar from school, which allows children and adults to reconsider and discover in depth. The entire point of many technologies, such as radio and television, is to make audible or visible features of the world which are normally beyond the limits of sensory experience. By starting with our perception and its limits, these technologies of communication, and how and why they work, take on an immediately human significance in which physics is closely related to physiology and psychology.

Secondly, hidden features can be revealed by careful *groupings* of plores, to show abstract conceptual relations; for example, models of conic sections and elliptical and parabolic billiards tables show wonderful properties of nature which underlie the motions of planets and the optics of telescope mirrors. While each cut cone is evocative, together they allow one to appreciate significant generalizations – and at the same time how special cases can be important. Similarly, examples of resonance show a very general principle which applies to a vast range of phenomena, and to many technologies – from clocks, through electrical phenomena and musical instruments, and the mechanisms of hearing, to the fundamental dynamics of matter as seen in chemistry. This extension of perception by interacting and playing with forces of physics is an essential aim of the Exploratory.

Not all plores need to be completely understood, to be successful. Some, indeed, should raise very difficult questions, to which perhaps no one as yet has a complete answer. Setting up interesting questions may help people to enjoy *living with questions*. Puzzling plores, especially plores that please, may help to reduce the surely too common fear of questions. It is an important point that puzzling plores may be simple and familiar. A good example is the question: Why does a book, or oneself, appear horizontally but not vertically reversed in a looking-glass? (See Essay 12.) Another example is 'Newton's bucket' (essay 16): this shows, incredibly simply, the puzzling Mach's principle which is a basic issue for relativity theory. Though we may all be familiar with what happens to the curved surface of water in a spinning bucket, how many realize that it poses fundamental questions of relative or absolute motion? In both these examples it is important to make the context, and what the problem is, clear – without being intimidating. We have a lot to learn to do this well.

Some plores should show how physical principles are combined in novel ways, in technology, to produce (generally, though unfortunately not always) desired results. Where results are undesirable, it may turn out that the new problems can be solved by applying science with further technology. These may, indeed, be spurs to invention rather than grounds for pessimism.

Although history is not the main aim of the Exploratory, time sequences are not only fascinating in their own right, but help technical understanding and express science and technology in human terms. To appreciate processes of invention it is essential to have a historical sense. We re-enact some classical experiments, such as Galileo's inclined planes and curves, for investigating how objects fall, slowed so that he could see and hear (with little bells, set to ting at equal intervals) fundamental laws of nature. We may re-perform these early experiments with the limited instruments available to past scientists, which is indeed hands-on time travelling, and again with modern instruments – which shows at first hand how technology provides tools which extend our senses and hands into new worlds; not only for Mammon, but also for seeking truth. This was Bacon's message.

REFERENCES

Bacon, F. (1620) *Novum Organum*, ed. F.H. Anderson (1960), Oxford, Oxford University Press.
Bacon, F. (1605, 1627), *The Advancement of Learning* and *New Atlantis*, ed. A. Johnston (1974), Oxford, Clarendon Press.
Gregory, R.L. (1983) 'The Bristol Exploratory – a feeling for science', *New Scientist* 100, 1984, 484–9.
Gregory, R.L. and Wallace, J.G. (1963) *Recovery from Early Blindness: A Case Study*, Experimental Psychology Monograph No. 2, Cambridge, Heffers, reprinted in R.L. Gregory (1974) *Concepts and Mechanisms of Perception*, London, Duckworth, pp. 65–1299.

27

SPELLING SPELLS

It is odd that both writing and pictures are uniquely human accomplishments. This is so though almost all animals have elaborate symbolic communications, including rich varieties of gestures and in 'higher' species facial expressions, as most brilliantly discussed by Darwin in *The Expression of the Emotions in Man and Animals* (1872).

The more one considers language the greater one's amazement that children – including oneself – succeed in learning to speak, and to read and write. How did spoken language and writing start in the first place? And why is effective structured language, and *any* writing or picture-making, unique to humans? Surely it is not coincidence that we alone of all the animals on Earth can speak, write, *and* draw pictures. Probably all written language started from simple pictures, elaborating into the wonder of the Egyptian hieroglyphics (Gardiner 1927; Katan 1980), and Chinese and Japanese scripts where complex ideas may be expressed in single ideograms. 'Hieroglyphics' means 'sacred language', and 'sacred' is related to 'secret'. There are always things hidden, only partly seen, in language and in pictures: this is their magic.

It has been said that language is man's greatest invention – more important than the wheel or even fire. It is, indeed, an open question whether we can think at all effectively without a symbolic tool-kit of language. However this may be, and it is a most important question for considering our special powers of thinking and their origin, it is truly remarkable that everything we can say can be expressed by combinations of thirty or so characters of an alphabet.

Alphabetic languages have turned out to be especially convenient for moveable-type printing, which was invented just before 1450 AD: some 3000 years after their development from picture writings, which temselves date back to the cave paintings of around 30,000 BC, perhaps much earlier. The first alphabet was developed by the Canaanites in the middle of the second millennium BC. Several scripts were later developed, especially the Phoenician and Aramaic, and later the Jewish and Greek scripts, which survive to the present day. The Latin script, which is the most common, and Cyrillic, which is used in the USSR and some other eastern countries, are both scripts developed from the Greek. In the second millennium BC there were four writing systems in the ancient world: the Hittite pictographic in the north; the Egyptian hieroglyphs in the south; the Minoan-Mycenean in the West; the fascinating Sumerian (Kramer 1963; Saggs 1962) cuneiform – wedge-shaped – writing in the east. Each of these had a very large number of signs, which took so long to learn that writing was essentially restricted to the priests and official scribes. Thus the key advantage of the early pictures, which could be understood by almost anyone, was lost as pictures became stylized and used according to special conventions – which is of course still so for modern Chinese and Japanese writing.

For the Egyptians, and no doubt for all language-speaking people, their gods were associated with the power of words for *spells* – which are perhaps closely related to how people command and persuade each other in everyday life. Thus the Egyptologist E.A. Wallis Budge (1904) says of the goddess Isis:

> Thus when she [Isis] wished to make Ra reveal to her his greatest and most secret name, she made a venomous reptile out of dust mixed with the spittle of the god, and by uttering over it certain words of power she made it to bite Ra as he passed. When she had succeeded in obtaining from the god his most hidden name, which he only revealed because he was on the point of death, she uttered words which had the effect of driving the poison out of his limbs, and Ra recovered. Now Isis not only used the words of power, but she also had knowledge of the way in which to pronounce them so that the beings or things to which they were addressed would be compelled to listen to them and, having listened, would be obliged to fulfil her behests. The Egyptians believed that if the best effect was to be produced by words of power they must be uttered in a certain tone of voice, and at a certain rate, and at a certain time of day or night, with appropriate gestures and ceremonies. In the Hymn to Osiris . . . it is said that Isis was well skilled in the use of

Some hieroglyphic symbols remain, for the 4000-year life of the language, simple pictures of what is represented:

snake   pregnant woman

Then there are symbols used for abstract concepts, such as:

motion   strength

These are obviously abstractions from particular objects – for example legs and arms associated with movement and strength. We also find symbols representing still more abstract ideas, sometimes based on mystical or magical associations, such as:

evil

Almost every Egyptian word is followed by an ideographic sign, which is either a picture of the object or a symbol representing a more general class.

For example, the word *ah*, an ox, may be written or ,

the sign being the picture of the animal and , a hide, being

the class symbol for quadrupeds. This sign is a determinative, establishing the general class to which the symbol of the ox is to belong.

Action is expressed directly in some ideographic symbols. A wall, or fort is:

. To build is represented with the wall plus the builder: . Many

human actions are represented as action postures of men and women. Here

are some examples: *to adore or to reverence* *to sing* *a defeat* *to be*

buried or embalmed . Parts of the body are used as verbs: *to see* or

to take notice of *to weep* . Animals and parts of animals

or flowers are also used as verbs, often with related though multiple mean-

ings: *to fly* or *fly away* *to stop* *joy* . A frequently

occurring symbol for 'not', is . Other logical relations are written:

if , *and* , *or* . For an example of a negation,

we may take the sentence: 'I know him not' .

27.1 *Hieroglyphic symbols.*

words of power, and it is by means of these that she restored her husband to life, and obtained from him an heir. It is not known what these words were . . . but she appears to have obtained them from Thoth, the 'lord of divine words.'

The scribe god Thoth (who became Hermes in the Greek pantheon), with his knowledge of 'divine speech', and being 'mighty of speech' and 'lord of books', was the guardian of language and learning. He judged the weighing of souls at death with a balance he watched over, so he was also the god of *equilibrium*, and of weight as well as of the heart. Thoth (who had no parentage, but was self-created) calculated the design for the heavens, and was the god of measuring. So the Ibis-headed (sometimes ape-headed) scribe Thoth was the Egyptian god of science.

The numerous picture references to the gods, with their associations with all aspects of life, no doubt served to imbue the language symbols with rich meanings. Thus the Ibis head of Thoth would evoke rich associations of writing, weighing and justice. Then there was Nut, the mother of the gods and goddess of the sky, the stars being her jewels. And there were gods of the planets, of the days of the month, of the twelve hours of the day, and other gods for the twelve hours of the night. Every aspect of life and of speculation had its gods, who very often had animal associations so that the gods and what they represented were seen living in nature. Is it because of these rich associations that the Egyptians had so many gods?

The limitation of pictures and picture writing is that they cannot at all easily express abstract ideas, or logical relations. And it is very difficult to show the *absence* of something in a picture. Even the dabbler can see quite clearly how the Egyptian picture writing struggled to extend these limits; for example, 'more important' was shown by making statues and paintings of rulers larger than those of wives, or slaves, or vanquished enemies. Most interesting, special signs – 'determinatives' – were introduced to warn where picture signs were inadequate for conveying the intended meaning. Thus the Egyptian sign for the Sun was a circle with a central dot: ⊙ ; but this same sign could also mean the abstract notion, impossible to picture directly: *time*. This was done by adding a special sign as a warning that an abstract idea was intended. This added determinative sign – a rolled papyrus scroll tied with a ribbon, to show that the meaning was hidden: ▭ – was placed next to the Sun sign. But the determinatives could be no more than warnings of ambiguity – to evoke imagination – they could not define meanings.

The use of gestures and warning determinatives were about as far as the simple picture languages could go in this direction. Speech, however, preceded writing, and although developments of writing no doubt affected speech, and also thinking, the very need to struggle out of picture writing shows that writing is a tool and not altogether our master.

But for all the evocative power of picture signs, it is important to be able to represent logical relations and numbers, which the Egyptians could do only clumsily. Their signs for logical relations were based on gestures and actions. Thus the negation – 'not' – was shown as arms outspread, like a traffic policeman: ⏝ . Later, the hands and fingers were omitted, leaving a plain horizontal line, which is our negative sign '−'. Our multiplication sign '×' is the Egyptian hieroglyph for stirring a pot.

It does seem most curious that psycholinguistic research neglects picture languages. In the psycholinguistics books I have looked at they are never even mentioned. Considering that ancient picture languages are preserved in perfect detail, and are at each stage related to events and social situations through time, one should surely see the sacred-secret hieroglyphs as a gift for understanding the development of mind: a record as rich, in its own own way, as the fossil records of evolving life. Why are picture languages – especially Egyptian hieroglyphics, with the immense scholarship that has gone into them – so neglected by psychologists? Why is psycholinguistics restricted to alphabetic languages? (But see Harris 1986.)

The origin of the invention of the alphabet is not known; but some authorities (Diringer 1968) suppose that the alphabet was invented for striking and sealing bargains, where different societies met for trade and barter, notably at Constantinople, which may have been where the alphabet was invented.

Unlike picture languages, alphabets require spelling. What is striking is how varied spelling was, until the compiling of dictionaries early in the eighteenth century, when standardized spelling became necessary to look up words, which had to be alphabetically arranged to be found. Before then, even common words and names were spelled in innumerable ways, sometimes reflecting local dialects. But given the lack of any consistent spelling, how can etymologists be so sure that spelling is a reliable guide to origins of words? For, surely, spelling has become uniform through the influence of the dictionary-makers – who invented standard spelling! So, there must surely be a great deal of dictionary-created fiction in origins of words as they are derived from how they are spelled. But none of this much matters – we are all enchanted by the spell of language.

REFERENCES

Budge, E.A. Wallis (1904) *The Gods of the Egyptians*, London, Methuen, reprinted (1969), New York, Dover, 2 vols.

Darwin, Charles (1872) *The Expression of the Emotions in Man and Animals*, London, John Murray.

Diringer, David (1968) *The Alphabet: A Key to the History of Mankind*, 3rd edn, London, Hutchinson, 2 vols.

Gardiner, Sir Alan (1927; 3rd edn 1957) *Egyptian Grammar*, Oxford, Oxford University Press.

Gregory, R. L. (1971) *The Intelligent Eye*, London, Weidenfeld & Nicolson.

Harris, Roy (1986) *The Origin of Writing*, London, Duckworth.

Katan, N.J. (1980) *Hieroglyphs: The Writing of Ancient Egypt*, London, British Museum.

Kramer, S.N. (1963) *The Sumerians: Their History, Culture, and Character*, Chicago, University of Chicago Press.

Saggs, H.W.F. (1962) *The Greatness that was Babylon: A Survey of the Ancient Civilization of the Tigris-Euphrates Valley*, London, Sidgwick & Jackson.

28

WHATEVER HAPPENED TO INFORMATION THEORY?

The notion of *information* bridges the external world of physical events and our perception and understanding, for information of events and things is separate from us in space and time. How to think about and to measure information are still controversial matters, and there are snags, or at least limitations, in all theories and methods. The lead has come from engineers, but until recently at least their concern has been with communication-transmission systems, rather than with brains or minds. With developments in artificial intelligence this is now changing, and we may look for further leads from the engineers who have to grapple with these difficult problems. The issues are technical, and we cannot altogether escape technical detail here.

Twenty or thirty years ago the great hope for quantifying perceptual decision processes, and finding out what goes on in skills, was the mathematical theory of information, which was developed for engineering communication systems and most elegantly worked out and presented by Claude Shannon and Warren Weaver of the Bell Telephone Laboratories in 1949. This promised to be able to measure amounts of information, rather as there are measures for costing energy, for estimating efficiencies and charging for messages conveyed by telegraph and telephone lines. It also promised to quantify the information-handling of the nervous system and so to give basic insights for a functional philosophy of perception and behaviour. Some of this came true, but we hardly hear of information theory now in accounts of perception – though it is extremely important for communication and control engineering. Why isn't it as useful for physiology and psychology? Has this something to do with the *subjective* nature of perception? Does this prevent *objective* measurements?

Conveying information by gestures and by speech is pre-human in origin, and indeed essential for all intelligent life. By writing, and much later by printing, information has been transmitted over space and stored in time with incalculable benefit, but attempts to transmit information very fast over distances beyond the range of speech are quite recent, and the means for costing or charging for information transmission have been devised more recently still. There is, however, a considerable history before Shannon and Weaver. Suggestions for telegraphs, using magnetism or electricity, go back to Roger Bacon's suggestion in 1267 that a 'certain sympathetic needle might be used for distant communication'. This was the lodestone, or rather a needle magnetized by rubbing with a lodestone, as used in the mariner's compass. Then there is a seventeenth-century description of a telephone working with wires by the inventive genius Robert Hooke, in the Preface to his *Micrographia* of 1664. After a discussion of optical instruments that 'must watch the irregularities of the Senses, but . . . not go before them or prevent their information', Hooke wrote:

> Tis not impossible to hear a whisper a furlong's distance, it having already been done; and perhaps the nature of the thing would not make it more impossible, though that furlong be ten times multiplied. And though some famous Authors have affirm'd it impossible to hear through the thinnest plate of Muscovy-glass; yet I know a way, by which it is easy enough to hear one speak through a wall a yard thick. It has not yet been thoroughly examin'd, how far Otocousticons may be improved, nor what other ways there may be of quickening our hearing, or conveying sound through other bodies than the Air: for that this is not the only medium, I can assure the Reader, that I have, by the help of a distended wire, propagated the sound to a very considerable distance in an instant, or with as seemingly quick a motion as that of light, at least, incomparably swifter than that, which at the same time was propagated through the Air; and this not only in a straight line, direct, but in one bended in many angles.

Just what was this seventeenth-century otocousticon telephone? Was it a 'string telephone' – a wire joining distant diaphragms? If so, how, exactly, did it work round corners? Or can it have been an electric telephone? Surely this was beyond even Hooke's ingenuity at that time. There were several suggestions for electric telegraphs a century later, following Steven Grey's discovery in 1729 that electricity could be carried on insulated wires. By the 1780s there began to appear working single-wire telegraph systems using sounders with a code. Samuel Morse (1791–1872) turned from painting to building telegraph transmitting and receiving equipment, and to inventing his code. This was clever, because it used the fewest dots and dashes for the most frequently used letters – which showed how the code must be optimized for efficient transmission of information. It was first demonstrated on Saturday 2 September 1837, at Washington Square in New York, over 1700 feet of wire. But wire was expensive and information was in demand, and rapid rates of transmission of messages soon became economically vital. This need became all too clear with the first, incredibly expensive, transatlantic cable.

This supreme triumph of Victorian engineering, as it turned out to be, was very nearly a disaster, as fundamental principles were not available or understood. It first operated in 1858, but through misuse it broke down after only a few hundred messages had been transmitted and received. The next cable was successfully laid in 1865 by Brunel's huge ship the *Great Eastern*, which also recovered and repaired the earlier cable. At first messages could only be sent at the uneconomic rate of eight words per minute – not because of the human limitations of the senders and receivers but because of the inductive inertia (or low bandwidth) of the cable. The signal strength was low, which led to the invention of relays, amplifiers and repeaters which solved the problems for the long-distance telegraph cables as they do in the nervous system; but at first the brute-force method of applying very high voltages to the cable was tried – and damaged it. Separating concepts of information from power and appreciating their statistical nature were the essential steps for the understanding and designing of information systems.

The best scientists of the time – Michael Faraday, Charles Wheatstone, William Cooke, Lord Kelvin and, as a young man whose great inventive achievements came later, Thomas Alva Edison – contributed to this extraordinarily important technical development. Apart from the practical importance of rapid international communication, it focused attention on information as a concept, and it led to notions of channels and coding and so on that generated insights into all kinds of communication, including language, which deeply influenced philosophy as well as providing suggestions for how information is handled by the nervous system.

The notion of a minimum necessary bandwidth (frequency range) for transmitting signals at a required rate was appreciated by Lord Kelvin, from his work on the transatlantic cable; but it was not formulated until 1924 by H. Nyquist in America and K. Kumpfuller in Germany, who independently stated the law that was developed to its general form by R.V.L. Hartley in 1928 – that the transmission of a 'given quantity of information' is limited by the product of bandwidth and time. Hartley went further, to define *information* as the successive selection of signs, or words, from a given list or ensemble of possibilities. For this definition he rejected *meaning* as 'subjective' (although we usually think of the meanings of messages as what matters), for it is signals, not meanings, that are transmitted. But the word 'information' remained in use though it no longer referred to meanings, which can be confusing.

Here we get more technical. Hartley showed that a message of N distinguishable signs (such as letters or dots and dashes) selected from a repertoire or ensemble of S signs, has Sn possibilities, and that the 'quantity of information' is most reasonably and usefully defined in logarithmic units, to make information measures additive. Hartley quantified information thus:

$$H = N \log_2 S$$

An essential notion for quantifying information is that the *less* likely the symbol or event, the *more* information it conveys. Information rate is not defined simply in terms of the number of symbols that can be transmitted, but also in terms of the probability (or the surprise value) of their occurrence. To modify a favourite example of Bertrand Russell's, 'Dog bites man' does not convey much information – but '"Man bites dog" is news'. The second costs more to transmit, for to be sure such an unlikely message is correct we must know with confidence that it is free of error, and this requires expensive reliability – which is difficult to achieve in engineering, or for the nervous system.

Since the simplest choice is yes or no (or on or off, for a switch) the information unit of a *bit* (binary choice) is useful. Norbert Weiner and Claude Shannon developed the Hartley approach by examining the statistical characteristics of signals, including the values of waves for analogue signals. They reinterpreted Hartley's Law, to define the average information of long sequences of n symbols as

$$H = - \sum_i^n p_i \log p_i$$

(The minus sign makes H positive, since it involves logarithms of p which is fractional.)

It is well worth playing the dictionary game of finding a word with the 'Twenty questions' technique of asking, for example, 'Is it before K?' and, if it is, 'Is it before E?', and so on. Any word in a dictionary can usually be located within twelve such binary decisions, which is quite remarkable. This is surprising because we are not used to thinking in terms of powers of two. The number of binary choices enabling selection of say a word, from a set of words, increases as follows (values rounded off):

Binary decisions required	Size of dictionary from which any word can be found (no. of headwords)	
1	2	
2	4	
4	16	(1.6×10^1)
8	256	(2.6×10^2)
16	65 000	(6.5×10^4)
32	4 300 000 000	(4.3×10^9)
64	19 000 000 000 000 000 000	(1.9×10^{19})
128	340 000 000 000 000 000 000 000 000 000 000 000 000	(3.4×10^{38})
256	160 000 000 000 000 000 000 000 000 000 000 000 000 000 000 000 000 000 000 000 000 000 000 000 000 000	(1.6×10^{77})

Surely the power of this strategy has implications for how we recall memories. It is not possible, however, to use the amazingly efficient 'Twenty questions' technique except for items which are ordered in some way, such as words arranged alphabetically in dictionaries. Memories may be filed for our almost instant recall in some orderly way that is still beyond computer technology

The greatest quantity of information that can be transmitted through a channel, with bandwidth w over time r, in the presence of disturbing random noise, was shown by Claude Shannon to be

$$w\tau \log_2 \left(1 + \frac{P}{N}\right) \text{ (bits)},$$

where P and N are mean signal and mean noise powers respectively. This represents a definite limit which no channel (including the visual channel) can exceed. If however the *coding* of the signals is non-optimal, the information rate may be very much lower, so we need to know the coding to assess physiological efficiency.

There is something odd about information as described by Shannon's theory, which is now universally accepted as the best account, for information is quite different from anything in the natural sciences. Unlike normal causes, it depends not only on what has been, and what is, but also on *alternatives* of what *might be*. It is often said that information theory can give *no* account of meaning, but the situation is not quite so bleak – because the selected alternatives may have, or be, meanings.

In order to apply information theory rigorously it is necessary to know the number of alternatives from which selections are made. Unfortunately we seldom if ever know just what these are for humans, so information theory can seldom be rigorously applied outside purely engineering situations where we have full knowledge of the system and especially its range of alternatives. A law for human response time was, however, established at Cambridge by Edmund Hick in 1952, which showed that in situations where there are clearly defined choices, such as pressing response keys to lights, the mean decision time, t, increases with the number of the possibilities, n, by

$$t = K \log (n+1)$$

The decision or choice time (the disjunctive reaction time minus the simple reaction time) is very nearly proportional to the number of bits per stimulus (where a 'bit' is a binary choice).

As a matter of history, I was the only subject apart from Edmund Hick for this experiment, which went on one hour a day for months. Hick did not complete it himself, so Hick's Law is based on my (very) nervous system.

The relation was later found by R. Hyman (1953), who showed that with each added possibility the choice time increases by just over a tenth of a second; and that this same increase in choice occurs no matter how the information is increased – by changing the relative frequencies of the alternatives, their sequential dependencies (introducing redundancy, so that some tended to follow others in predictable sequences), or by increasing the number of possibilities. The maximum rate of information (bit rate) of even the most skilled human operator looks surprisingly small: about 22 bits per second for an expert pianist; speech does not exceed about 26 bits, and silent reading may reach 44 bits per second. This seems low in engineering terms, where bit rates of thousands per second may be achieved, but we have to remember that far more is going on – with more choices to be made – in the richness of the brain's circuits. At present, information-handling computer systems are not comparable to us because they cannot do anything like as much as we can. This takes us to the Big Snag with information theory when it is applied to us.

Unlike engineering systems, organisms are not strictly limited to the set of choices allowed by the experimenter's situation or task. Thus, ideally, doing Hick's experiment I should only have been able to respond to the ten little lights, which were pinned in a random arrangement on cork mats, each lit with a particular key from the row under one's fingers. But when less than all ten were being used, to restrict the value of n possibilities, I was not, strictly speaking, blind to the others. And I could respond to a knock on the door, or to Edmund Hick asking me why I was not doing better, or saying that it was lunch time. One was not deaf or blind to all except the allowed alternative choices of the experimental condition, in spite of the long practice with each number of lights in use – so the total bit rate must have been far greater than measured. Although Hick's Law works beautifully in some conditions (interestingly when there is not *too* much practice), it cannot truly quantify the information we handle because we cannot set or assess the number of alternatives, n, we may choose from. The trouble is that, unlike a computer system, a human being's range of alternatives cannot be strictly limited by the situation he is in, or by an experimenter, or by his most concentrated attention.

In a much quoted paper, bearing the splendid title: 'The magic number seven plus or minus two', the American psychologist George Miller (1956) suggested that there is an absolute limit of around seven similar items for the immediate span of apprehension. Thus we can estimate at a glance, without counting, up to about seven dots spaced randomly. But the *effective* information in a perceptual span (the 'specious present') can be greatly increased by 'chunking' bits into larger units. This is a form of coding of data, requiring decoding of course. The most powerful coding appears to be language. Coding can set the number of bits per chunk; but the number of chunks that can be retained in immediate memory is limited to around seven. Presumably Chinese ideogram characters are efficient chunks, each conveying a lot of information. Much of learning is chunking bits of information into large units which can be stored in memory and recalled as a unit, rather like a rich ideogram. Are perceived *objects* memory-chunked bits of information?

Again, it is commonly said that information theory has nothing to say about meaning, but this is not entirely true. Donald MacKay (1960a) produced an interesting way of looking at this. He suggested that meaning was related to *conditional readiness*, as the meaning of a sentence (or of a perceived event) changes the pattern of possibilities for future action. He gave a working definition of meaning as the 'selective function on the range of the recipient's states of conditional readiness for goal-directed activity; so the meaning of a message to you is its selective function on the range of your states of conditional readiness'. Defined in this way, meaning is clearly a relationship between message and recipient, rather than a unique property of the message alone. So there is a 'subjective' side to the engineer's information. Can this be measured? It might be, if we knew the selective function of a message. Then we could apply information theory to quantify meaning, at least in some cases. MacKay went on in a later paper (1960b), 'What is a question?', to suggest that states of readiness for organisms are large numbers of conditional probabilities. Asking a question is a means of changing the conditional probabilities of the questioner's states of readiness. This notion can be expressed in computer-programming terms. If there remains a 'problem of meaning' the problem lies somewhere beyond the adequacy of this notion of selections from, or changes of, states of readiness. These can be described in computer terms, and be implemented by computers with no special problems. Surely discussions of meaning could well start at this point.

It is sometimes said that true statements have more meaning than false statements. And philosophers frequently deny meaning to logical (and even to contingent) impossibilities. Thus '2+2=5', or 'She is a dark-haired blonde', might be said to be meaningless. Such logical impossibilities are internal inconsistencies of the state of readiness, such that they are program-stoppers, preventing changes in states of readiness. It is an interesting question how general program-stoppers must be before we call them 'logical errors'. Is it possible that here lies the distinction between 'logical' and 'contingent'?

Reaction times are of continuing interest and an acknowledged source of useful data for teasing out processes of perception and decision-taking. But, given that reaction times depend on the repertoire of possibilities, which cannot be established – which is what destroyed the effective use of information theory – how can reaction-time experiments work? Why do they not suffer from the same deep trouble?

It is sad that information theory is virtually dead in current thinking on perception. Perhaps, like poor mistaken Juliet it deserves awakening from cryptic sleep: but if so – wherefore art thou Romeo?

REFERENCES

Hick, W.E. (1952) 'On the rate of gain of information', *Q. J. Psychol.* 4, 11–26.
Hyman, R. (1953) 'Stimulus information as a determinant of reaction time', *J. Experimental Psychol.* 45, 188–96.
MacKay, D.M. (1960a) 'Meaning and mechanisms', reprinted as chapter 3 in *Information, Mechanisms and Meaning* (1969), Cambridge, Mass., MIT Press.
MacKay, D.M. (1960b) 'What is a question?', reprinted as chapter 4 in *Information, Mechanisms and Meaning* (1969), Cambridge, Mass., MIT Press.
MacKay, D.M. (1969) *Information, Mechanism and Meaning*, Cambridge, Mass., MIT Press.
Miller, G.A. (1956) 'The magical number seven plus or minus two: some limits to our capacity for processing information', *Psychol. Rev.* 63, 81–97.

29

DESIGNING DESIGNERS

The sense of 'rightness' of a design can be compelling. Its converse aesthetic 'wrongness' is as powerful, for each can inspire to greatness or seduce to mislead. The question is: what guide can there be, beyond brute functional considerations, for determining design? The obvious answer is *aesthetics*. We can, indeed, only escape aesthetics in those rare situations when functional efficiency entirely dominates. Thus occasionally there may be just one best shape for the blade of a knife, or the prow of a boat, or whatever; but generally there is freedom of choice for design – and with it the danger of damaging disagreement, preventing the job getting done.

It is entirely possible to achieve agreement on functional improvements in design, and to agree that they *are* improvements, as they work better or more efficiently. Thus it may be clear to all that one knife cuts meat better than another, or that a certain hook or bait catches more fish. But where there are no clear functional advantages, agreement for co-operative work is hardly possible, unless there is shared aesthetic approval. Possibly, indeed, the survival value of tacit agreement on what is 'right' to make, protect or do, is so great that it developed in our ancestors a gene for aesthetics, by natural selection; for quarrelling communities would soon die out if they could not agree on whether their huts should be round, square or rectangular, or their pots slender or squat. If such basic yet not particularly functional decisions were matters of debate, houses, pots or boats could hardly be made.

Consistency is so great in prehistory, and often later, that aesthetics sets its seal on time and place, so that we may read for example 'Neolithic pot from Thessaly', 'Early eighteenth-century French commode', 'Mid-1930s ashtray', without words. Arguments set up and justify schools of design; but debate on non-functional features which must have *some* shape are not 'merely academic' – for such arguments, on pots or roofs or whatever, would stop production. The worst of it would be that such arguments must *keep* production stopped; for where functional efficiency does not apply, there are no logical or empirically justified answers to be found. So, from early times, without the tacit acceptance of aesthetic, and also moral decisions (which are wonderfully reflected in our sense of 'rightness' and 'wrongness' of form and behaviour) we could hardly have created, by co-operative work, axes or houses, pots or boats for us to survive by weapons and tools to learn to build effective technology. And yet it is the fun, non-functional features of things that give charm and significance to crafts, to building, and indeed to a good deal of even the most sophisticated engineering – for aesthetic styles are the personalities of things.

It is the maintained aesthetic traditions, with their generally gradual and occasionally dramatic changes, that enable archaeologists to place pottery and other artefacts in place and time. But always it is the not purely functional features that are the clue to the who, the where and the when of their origins. Rare individuals do, however, shine through even the most rigid traditions, from unnamed prehistoric potters to the archaic (late sixth century BC) Andokides figure painter on pots just as the style was changing from black-on-red to red-on-black figures, to the sculptor Phidias who in fame outshone even his master Pericles – to all the individuality within styles of the artists and their works we revere from the Greeks to our time: Wren and his churches, Rembrandt's paintings, Tompion's clocks. Such rare individuals produce changes of style which are followed, perhaps for many generations, sometimes spreading beyond the original statues, churches, paintings, clocks, or whatever. Thus there are such strange transmuted traditions as Greek temples appearing in Rolls-Royce radiators. And there are revolts and revolutions, such as from restrained flat Georgian fronts to the exuberant protuberances of Victorian buildings.

All this is fine. The troubles start when aesthetics encroaches on function so that function becomes distorted. Elaborate clocks with such tiny dials they can hardly be read; chairs too uncomfortable for use; clothes that restrict painfully. Yet, though tiny handles on tea cups may be functionally absurd no matter, for they may be charming and add out of all proportion to grand or intimate occasions. The troubles grow when the aesthetic style for one kind of artefact spreads to others where, for functional reasons, it is inappropriate. Thus a tropical flat-top style of roof is dangerous in regions of heavy snow, where roofs need to be steep-pitched to avoid consequent structural failure. Such a misplaced style, though perhaps looking 'right', can be disastrous. This has often happened, for example when domestic architecture too much affected the design of castles; and no doubt castle architecture killed many people with diseases of confinement.

Our emphasis on functional efficiency spreads beyond function. Thus a few years ago everything had to have a sleek, fast-moving, aerodynamic shape to look 'right', leading to such absurdities as high-speed ashtrays. The extreme of function-following led to the functional aridity of the Bauhaus school of design, which for us now is perhaps too fancy-free.

Here I come to a personal anathema, especially when I have become involved in commissioning a glossy catalogue or (uniquely ghastly word) brochure. The prevailing 'house style' for these publications is blocks of tiny print set between frozen seas of blank-white margins, which may occasionally sport a little drawing or inconsequential photograph. Then there are sudden pages of huge pictures, which, standing alone, are incomprehensible. This design style of our time is no doubt part of the current emphasis on the *visual*, as set by cinema and television, sadly at the cost of the printed word. Now paragraphs of print are evidently an embarrassment to the designer. The paragraphs are not indented for ready reading, but are featureless, black-and-white blocks, protecting the reader from the meanings of words. By design, this medium haunts us with ghost writing.

30

JOURNEY TO UNCONSCIOUSNESS WITH KETAMINE

Among the deep mysteries is consciousness. Why are we conscious? How is consciousness – sensations such as pleasures and pains and colours, and awareness of objects and ourselves – related to, or somehow given by, the physical processes of the brain? Why does the brain's electrical activity, or whatever, give brain-owners, and especially ourselves, consciousness although no other objects or activities in nature are conscious? At least we suppose that it does, though since consciousness is essentially private we cannot be quite sure that our friends are conscious, or quite sure that a stone does not feel a kick.

Mysteries of science are often solved by switching things on and off. That such control can give understanding should surely give technologies power to discover all manner of truths. Yes, but unfortunately the power of technologies to discover unsuspected facts, and even contribute to philosophy, has never been welcome or fully accepted in academic circles – which possibly is why they are circles. We can switch consciousness on and off with various techniques of anaesthesia. Can these techniques be used to show how consciousness is related to brain function? Can anaesthesia tell us what consciousness does? Such thoughts go back to the experiments of Humphrey Davy (1778–1829) with nitrous oxide, which he carried out with his friends the poets Robert Southey and Samuel Taylor Coleridge at the Pneumatic Institution, which had just been started by the local, somewhat too enthusiastic philosopher Dr Thomas

Beddoes. It still stands as a private house in Dowry Square, just a short walk from my laboratory in Bristol.

Humphrey Davy became Beddoes's assistant in the Pneumatic Institution after being apprenticed to a Penzance surgeon. Two or three years later he became a lecturer, and then one of the most celebrated directors, of the Royal Institution of London, his brilliant career of experimental studies in chemistry leading to the presidency of the Royal Society in 1820 and to a title. He received the highest honours also in France, though France was at war with England. Davy's career nearly ended at its beginning with his experiments on breathing gases in Dr Beddoes's Pneumatic Institution. Breathing unknown gases is of course extremely dangerous, and several times he nearly died. Davy described these experiments in his first book, published when he was 22: *Researches Chemical and Philosophical; chiefly concerning nitrous oxide, or dephlogisticated nitrous air, and its respiration* (1800). He had earlier realized that heat is motion, but returned to the theory of phlogiston, apologizing for having defended what to us now is obviously true. This is odd, for Davy's own earlier experiments on melting ice by friction provided crucial evidence against phlogiston; but he was severely criticized for the way he presented his ideas at that time. His continuing interest in gases lead to all manner of discoveries, and to the invention of the miner's safety lamp. Throughout his life, in spite of cumulative damage to his lungs, he made a practice of smelling gases during his chemical experiments; on one occasion he breathed four quarts of hydrogen, and on another knocked himself out with pure carbon dioxide. Of these first experiments with nitrous oxide at the Pneumatic Institution he wrote:

> In April 1799 I obtained nitrous oxide in a state of purity, and ascertained many of its chemical properties. Reflections upon these properties . . . made me resolve to inspire it in its pure form; for I saw no other way in which its respirability or powers could be determined.
>
> I was aware of the danger of this experiment. . . . I thought that the effects might be possibly depressing or painful; but there were many reasons which induced me to believe that a single inspiration of gas, apparently possessing no immediate action on the irritable fibre, could neither destroy, nor materially injure, the powers of life.

He tried it out on 11 April, and described one experiment:

> A thrilling, extending from the chest to the extremities, was almost immediately produced. I felt a sense of tangible extension highly pleasurable in every limb; my visible impressions were dazzling, and apparently magnified, I heard distinctly every sound in the

room, and was perfectly aware of my situation. By degrees, as the pleasurable sensations increased, I lost all concern with external things; trains of vivid images rapidly passed through my mind, and were connected with words in such a manner, as to produce perceptions perfectly novel. I existed in a world of newly connected and newly modified ideas: I theorised, I imagined that I made discoveries.

Upon returning to normality he said: 'Nothing exists but thoughts! The universe is composed of impressions, ideas, pleasures and pains!'

Davy was extremely close to discovering that nitrous oxide could be used to destroy pain for surgery. He tried it for the pain he suffered from a wisdom tooth. It stopped the pain, but afterwards the pain seemed worse. Writing in 1800, he clearly realized its medical possibilities: 'As nitrous oxide in its extensive operation appears capable of destroying physical pain, it may probably be used with advantage during surgical operations in which no great effusion of blood takes place.' It was not until 1844 that the American dentist Horace Wells used nitrous oxide for the painless extraction of one of his own teeth. Perhaps it was the levity and weird visions that the gas induced that deflected Davy from enquiring further into how it might be used for losing unwanted consciousness.

A few years ago I resolved to walk in Humphrey Davy's footsteps: to discover for myself what happens as consciousness is lost by anaesthesia. I wanted to try out perceptual experiments on the journey and record each experience; so it was important to move towards unconsciousness as slowly and steadily as possible, and to be able to speak, so that I could report what happened as it happened. Following expert advice, I decided that the anaesthetic ketamine would be best, as it is infused through a vein rather than breathed, and, most important, the muscle tone remains, so it should be possible to record what was happening throughout the experiment. Ketamine is used for plastic surgery, since the muscles remain fairly normal; but as it can have the unfortunate side-effect of producing nightmares, which may be long-standing, it is not generally used. I accepted the risk and there were no after-effects, except that I did feel under the weather for several weeks after the experiment. In case anything should go wrong, the experiment took place in an operating theatre and, to make maximum use of the situation, physiological measures were made simultaneously, though these will not be described here.

My experiences were recorded throughout the experiment on tape. The tests were designed and administered by my colleague John Harris and technician Terry Goodall. I did not know in detail what to expect.

After preliminary tests, infusion of ketamine started at 10.18 a.m. The observations, which were timed from the start of infusion, are taken from the tape and from the notes made during the experiment by John Harris:

0 min.   Infusion starts: *50 micrograms per kg per minute.*
I feel a cold sensation from saline.
1 min.   I feel slight tingling in my upper arm.
2 mins.   100% correlated Julesz random dot stereo pair is shown. The normal depth is seen.
My speech sounds slightly odd to JH. I report an 'echo' feeling; and, especially when my eyes move, I have a sense of unreality.
3 mins.   I report some loss of visual stability. When the eyes are moved: 'The wall is moving with my eyes.' [My later comment: 'This happened particularly with the first part of the eye movement.'] I report a feeling of floating, and unreality; and that my own voice does not sound right. [My later comment: 'It wasn't then hard to speak. It just didn't sound right.'] Asked if I can feel the couch: 'Almost like floating.'
4 mins.   I can describe accurately how my ankles are crossed, but say I have to think hard to describe it. I report a buzzing sensation in the head – not very pleasant. [Later comment: 'Like being in an engine room.'] I now feel pretty lousy, as though sinking down.
5 mins.   I feel that my middle has gone hollow. I have a visual image of plasticine going hollow in the middle and that's me. Just a bit like being drunk, or like a frightened child in an elevator.
6 mins.   In reply to questioning, I say: 'It's not unpleasant to look from side to side.' I have a buzzing sensation. This is loud and increasingly unpleasant.
A picture of the Zollner distortion illusion is presented. I say it looks very odd. Crazy. It moves around.
7 mins.   The Zollner figure moves irrespective of my ability to fixate it. I look at the ceiling. 'It jiggers around. It shimmers and jiggers around, especially in central vision.'
8 mins.   It is hard to describe what I'm seeing. 'The ceiling moves about, flashes about. I seem to be in a funny world, like a distorted balloon. [I comment later, when listening to the tape: 'The playback of these events sounds faster than the original events.' So time was distorted.]
10 mins.   I don't feel like mental arithmetic, but can answer that 'the square root of 9 is 3', though I now feel very odd.
11 mins.   It's as though I'm falling. I feel lousy. When asked if I want the rate of infusion to be cut, I say yes. [At this point it was extremely unpleasant.]
The diffusion rate is cut from 50 to 20 micrograms per kg per minute.

Shown her picture, I can recognize the Queen in a newspaper photo. I feel very peculiar, weird.

12 mins. The anaesthetist squeezes my Achilles tendon as hard as he can. I know my ankle is being touched, but it doesn't hurt, though my ankle is quite bruised. I can feel touch but not pain.

The Snellen cards are tried again. [My later comment: 'Reading them wasn't like ordinary reading. The type somehow intruded into another world.'] I can read odd words but omit several. The words don't make sense. Recognizing the letters, I'm one line worse than before the infusion. Speaking requires a lot of effort. At this stage I'm experiencing and knowing more of what is going on than I'm able to say.

13.75 mins. The anaesthetist asks me to try biting my tongue. I try, but report that I don't know what I'm doing. I don't know where my mouth or tongue is.

14.5 mins. Julesz random dot stereo pairs, with various 'noise' levels, so that they are graded in difficulty, are presented. 100%, 90% and 80% correlations, with uncrossed disparity all fused 'with three layers of depth'. This time there is a narrowing of attention, a kind of tunnel of awareness. It is far more difficult to do the test, though I get it right. [This was surprising as my visual world was extremely broken up and violently disturbed.]

16 mins. A picture of a Necker cube is presented. 'It jumps about, looks as though it's made of putty. Wibbly. Shimmering. Coloured. Not at all like the usual Necker cube: it moves around to left and right – but doesn't oscillate in depth. Flat.' [I later commented that 'it didn't form a proper cube – somehow the bits were separate'.]

17 mins. The ambiguous young-old woman [E.G. Boring's mistress-wife figure] is presented. I report: 'It's shimmery, in central vision. In peripheral vision it shifts about.' Asked whether it reverses, I comment that it has 'the eyelash of the young woman and the curve of the figure, it flashes about'. [I later commented that I was seeing features which could have belonged to one or other percept. These flashed in and out very fast, but the figure did not alternate as usual. I had a memory of what they belonged to but did not see the usual alternative faces.]

18 mins. The Mach figure is presented, and is recognized, though it appears to be flashing about, and with yellow edges to the lines. And: 'It doesn't move in depth, only in X and Y.' I remark: 'It's hard to describe what's happening. I don't have the proper language.' I can, however, understand what is being said around me, though with an effort. (See figure 11.3(a).)

Time is very peculiar. Not exactly faster or slower than usual, but it is hard to relate to normal, and particular events are longer in this world.

18.75 mins.   Ishihara colour-vision test-plates are shown, with almost normal responses.

I can use the words 'right' and 'left' appropriately. I can recognize JH's voice. I hear a funny (unpleasant) buzzing noise [which sounded quite different from the sound of the pump, as checked afterwards].

In a voice-recognition test, I recognize TG's voice [not spoken on tape – later I remember being confused whether TG's voice was on tape or not]. Tape recordings of four colleagues, and one unknown voice, are played. I recognize the recorded voice of Anne Griffiths (my secretary) after about 5 seconds, and Priscilla Heard (research assistant) and Philip Clark (technician), also after 5 seconds. I fail at first with Robert Williams (Ph.D. student), but get him second time round. I don't claim to recognize the unknown voice. I'm not sure whether I'm supposed to identify the voice or comment on what he is saying.

23.23 mins.   A newspaper picture of David Owen (the Foreign Secretary) is shown. I say: 'Flashing. What do you want me to do with it? It's a xerox. A person wearing a tie. Creases on it.' I don't know who it is.

25 mins.   Newspaper photo of Mohammed Ali grimacing in fun in the middle of a crowd of children, one of whom is pretending to hit him on the chin. I report a person with a glove. I don't recognize the person being hit. Children at bottom and left; glove hitting person; not sure whether person is a man or woman, white or black. 'Very strange.' I correctly report a child at the back wearing a pullover with black and white stripes. After some prompting: 'That's a boxing glove – I suppose it could be Mohammed Ali.' But I don't think it is, and don't think it's a very good photo of him. [I had to think, or concentrate, very hard at this time.]

26.75 mins.   On instruction from JH, I close my eyes. JH places a hairbrush in my right hand and asks me to say what it is: 'It has bristles. It's something like a brush.' But, most dramatically, I have a sensation of red wool, woven in squares, like a tapestry as I move my finger across the bristles [this was synaesthesia, which I have never experienced before or since] – 'purple, red images, clear like hypnogogic images. Highly saturated like Turkish tiles, orange and green and red. These come when I stroke the bristles.'

JH removes the brush and presents a comb to be touched. I describe how I'm moving my right hand and feeling the object which he is rotating. I say it has to be a comb, though I say it doesn't feel like it. I get vivid green and red sensations as the comb moves.

JH removes the comb and then touches and strokes my hand with it. I report green and red lights; also a sensation of JH stroking my hand with something hard. I feel as though I'm sinking down an infinitely long column of curtains, in red and green. A strange feeling of falling down – down – down. I report that I'm under water, and it's turbulent. A swimming-pool with turbulence. I remember JH giving me a cotton reel to feel before the infusion, so the object in my hand must be it – but it doesn't feel at all like the cotton reel felt before.

30.25 mins.   Atropine 1 mg given.

JH puts a new object (tennis ball) into my right hand. I say that I can push it with my fingers but can't identify it. I'm 'sinking down, down, as if in a strange fountain; like being in a sort of swimming pool, lots of green everywhere. Very odd.'

31.5 mins.   Physostigmine 2 mg given.

I recognize JH with his glasses on. A few Ishihara plates are shown again. My responses are as at pre-infusion.

32.5 mins.   JH asks how I'm in contact with my surroundings. I feel I'm coming back into contact, though things are swimming round and I have a restricted range of awareness. Shown the photo of David Owen again, I recall having seen the photo previously but still do not recognize the person. Shown the Zollner illusion, I cannot name it; and it looks totally unlike its normal appearance: it shimmers, looks like a shimmering staircase – very hard to describe: it's as though the Zollner is being strobed, about every 2 seconds, with a kind of wave sweeping across it. It is somewhat like the shimmering instability of binocular rivalry.

35 mins.   (Blood sample taken.) I recognize a Necker cube figure, presented by JH, who asks if it reverses in depth. 'It shimmers; keeps changing its shape. The lines look funny, wibbly, like plasticine.' JH moves his finger round one face of the cube. I say, 'It doesn't seem like a proper cube. Looks a mess.'

36.5 mins.   I recognize the Boring mistress-wife figure, but it switches rapidly in an odd way.

37 mins.   I cannot see depth in 90% Julesz figure, which looks a mess. 100% figure is presented, and fused and seen with three levels in depth. 90% figure re-presented for quite a long time, but I still cannot fuse it.

39 mins.   The Snellen chart visual acuity is about one line worse than at pre-infusion.

40 mins.   Shown a watch, I say it is 12 o'clock, though the watch (with Roman numerals) shows 11.

41 mins.   JH puts a toothbrush in my hand. 'It's got bristles.' JH asks if it's hard. No reply. 'What is it?' No reply.

42 mins.   JH holds up my hand, to show him the toothbrush. I say the touch world seems different, very different from my visual world. They are separated.

43 mins. JH asks me to close my eyes. Do I now get synaesthesia, see colours as he strokes the bristles? A long silence. I say I feel quite normal.

44 mins. I look over to the right, then back. JH asks if I'm upset. I say I now feel normal. JH asks if the ceiling is distorted. I say there's a bit of shimmering.

11.05 a.m. JH stops the tape.

WHAT DID WE FIND OUT?

During the infusion of ketamine, stereopsis for the madly disturbed random dot figures was still present, though it seemed impossible!

Colour vision remained nearly normal. (All Ishihara plates were shown before infusion. Twenty minutes into infusion plates 1–17 and plates 22–25 were shown. Of the 21 responses, 4 were different from the pre-infusion responses; but of these 1 was probably due to JH mishearing the considerably blurred speech (74 confused with 24). Not too much weight should be given to the other errors, since they involve visual confusion such as 2 with 7. The other plates having the same colour pairs for the pre- and post-infusion responses were identical. At 32 minutes (just after physostigmine) plates 1–3, 14 and 15, 26 and 27 produced the same reponses as before infusion.

Thus misperception of the Ishihara plates was minimal, if it occurred at all.

Visual acuity was measured crudely, before and during infusion, with the kind of Snellen chart which presents a continuous passage of prose in which the type size is progressively reduced in size every line or block of several lines. Before infusion the chart was placed at a distance of about 3 feet and the type size noted at which reading errors began to occur. Twelve minutes after infusion started there were difficulties and errors on a type size some 25 per cent larger. But this estimate of acuity depended on maintained ability to read aloud fluently, which was certainly impaired. So acuity did not seem to be much reduced from normal, though the visual world was highly unstable.

Visual recognition of pictures was not severely impaired. At 11 minutes after infusion I could immediately recognize a picture of the Queen. At 25 minutes I accurately described a scene of Mohammed Ali with children, but failed initially to identify Ali. And I failed to recognize a picture of David Owen, the Foreign Secretary, either during infusion or much later. In general, though, visual recognition seemed good, as I could name the people in the room and most of the visual illusion figures that were presented.

Auditory recognition remained to the very end. Four recorded voices of colleagues were recognized (at 21 minutes): three within 5 seconds, the fourth within 15 seconds. There was no evidence of impairment of auditory recognition.

Distortions and changes in pattern vision did occur. These were one of the most striking effects of the ketamine. Six minutes after infusion I said of the Zollner illusion that it was very odd and moved about. It was jazzing about so violently that I could not say whether the normal illusory distortion was present. The ceiling appeared to shimmer and jigger about alarmingly. At 16 minutes the Necker cube was presented: it looked as though made of plasticine. It was coloured and shimmery; not at all like the usual cube, as the lines and corners did not seem to belong to a single figure but were curiously separate. At 17 minutes, Boring's mistress-wife figure appeared as a sequence of features that could have belonged to one or the other percept as they flashed in and out, very fast, quite unlike the usual perceptual reversals of the entire figure, which normally appears alternately as a young or an old woman. Perception was intermittent, as though the stimulus was being turned on and off. At 18 minutes the Mach card was presented. Like the Necker cube, it did not reverse in depth. At 33 minutes (after atropine and physostigmine) the ceiling and the Zollner illusion figure appeared as before; the latter looked totally unlike its usual appearance – as though being strobed, with about two waves running along it per second. This was rather like binocular rivalry. At 35 minutes, the Necker cube appeared as before, with no reversal of depth. At 36 minutes the Boring figure appeared as before, though with more irrelevant details, such as the texture of the paper. Pattern vision was clearly abnormal, yet the violent disturbance interfered very little with visual abilities such as recognition of pictures or stereopsis.

The stability of the visual world was impaired. At 3 minutes after infusion I said that when I moved my eyes, the wall appeared to move with them, especially at the beginning of the eye movements. There was some destabilization, but this was not complete. The entire world jazzed about, though, most disconcertingly. I am amazed that I could do these tests so well (especially fusion of the Julesz random dot stereo pairs) in spite of the continuous violent movements and actual dislocations of the visual world.

There were changes in proprioception and 'body image'. At 4 minutes, I could accurately describe how my legs were crossed, but had to think hard how to do so. I had a sinking feeling, and felt that my middle had gone hollow, like plasticine. When at 12 minutes my Achilles tendon was squeezed with a lot of force, to produce bruising which lasted several days, it didn't hurt at all. So, although touch remained, pain was lost. I did, however, experience unpleasant 'distancing' from the world, and felt almost as though I was floating.

When at 14 minutes I was asked to try to bite my tongue I didn't know where my tongue or my mouth were, and was not able to do so (fortunately!).

There were auditory disturbances. I often reported a buzzing sensation in my head, which was most unpleasant. The tape reveals some hammering and banging, which was going on in a nearby room; but the loud buzzing was quite different from these noises, and different also from the infusion pump.

Time perception was odd. On one occasion (at 18 minutes) I said that events took longer in my world. On listening to the tape playback, this sounded faster than the original events had seemed. But what of playbacks of ordinary events, such as a conversation? Would this seem faster, or slower, than the original? This could make an interesting experiment on the perception of time (this needs to be done before we can interpret the change of time under anaesthesia), which seemed rather paradoxical, for though each event was drawn out I am not sure that the flow of time seemed slower than usual.

Recognition by touch was impaired. There was loss of recognition by active touch, though touch sensitivity seemed normal. I could name three objects (clothes brush, comb, cotton-reel) which were presented before as well as during infusion. However, this took much longer under the anaesthetic. And although some aspects of touch sensation were not impaired (I could feel individual bristles on a brush), somehow the object didn't feel like a unitary object. And when an object was both seen and touched there was a kind of mis-match between the visual and the tactile worlds.

There was marked synaesthesia. I experienced, and reported, that stroking the bristles of the brush, or having my hand stroked by a comb when my eyes were closed, gave brightly coloured red and green experiences. This was the most dramatic effect of all. One really did enter another world: a world of brilliant supersaturated colours and shapes, quite unrelated to what I was touching. I suppose one's inhibitory processes were failing to isolate the senses, and touch stimuli (though why only touch?) triggered dream-generating mechanisms.

What, if anything, did we find out about consciousness? Or unconsciousness? Not very much, but this was just one journey. There are many other routes to unconsciousness. Other anaesthetics have different physiological and psychological effects, and of course ordinary sleep is very different, for going to sleep is generally pleasant while this ketamine journey was unpleasant.

There is surely much of interest to be found out – especially if, with recently available scan techniques, we could record brain changes occurring during gradual loss of consciousness, through various anaesthetic journeys. But unless some such physiological experiment is involved, I will not venture into the odd perceptions of this journey into unconsciousness again.

31

ENGINEERING MIND

Much as technologies slowly developed from crafts, so attempts to understand and control mind grew from the 'folk psychology' by which we assess and explain behaviour in everyday living. Folk psychology explanations are very different from explanations of physics and technology – for they incorporate intentions, and pleasures and pains, which are not supposed to belong to the mindless, inanimate world. Only people can tell lies or seek truth, though the first is difficult to detect and the second, as we all know, is exceedingly hard to attain.

In spite of the findings of academic psychology, with its experimental data and theories, we still rely almost entirely on the quick intuitions of prehistoric folk psychology for our everyday living with friends, colleagues and lovers. This is so, even though the physical sciences and technology have utterly transformed our view of the world and how we live with inanimate objects. This great difference is odd, for it seems likely that attempts to understand and predict behaviour are far older than experiments in understanding matter. Why is there such a disparity between the physical sciences and psychology? Why is the development of physical understanding so much more successful? Let's consider some possible reasons.

Is it that the issues of psychology are far more *difficult* than those of physics? Or, very different, is it that scientific methods are too *slow* to be useful for predicting others', and controlling our own behaviour? Possibly the quick intuitions of folk psychology are more useful in 'real time' situations, much as the quickness of perception is essential for dealing with events as they happen – though the slow back-up of conceptual understanding is extremely useful when adequate decision-time is available. Is our conceptual understanding of psychology so feeble because we have to act fast in real-life situations where behaviour is concerned? Or, perhaps, is it that adequate accounts of underlying processes of behaviour require concepts that we have not yet grasped? These might be concepts emerging now in current technology: this is the claim of artificial intelligence. Only recently in the history of science has intelligence been limited to living organisms; now with AI, intelligence may indeed move into inanimate matter.

The early accounts of astronomy and chemistry were imbued with notions of mind-in-matter. As sciences, they were not at all clearly distinguished from magic astrology and magic alchemy, until just after Kepler early in the seventeenth century. Although it was his account of the planetary orbits that finally made ridiculous this free-will-in-the-sky notion, Kepler himself believed – as in early Indian (Gombrich 1975) and many other cosmologies (Blacker and Loewe 1975) – that the stars are chariots of intelligent beings. The ancient notion of mind in the sky died later in the seventeenth century, following the success of Kepler's laws of planetary motion and the mathematical physics of Newton. But Newton thought of space as God's Mind, or 'Sensorium' – such that the laws of astronomical physics are ideas in God's Mind, which we can discover and know by a kind of number-telepathy since God is a mathematician. Newton considered, though, that God might change His Mind and so change laws of physics, for large or local regions of space or time (Westfall 1971). So for Newton, although the planets were component parts of a law-abiding machine, space was imbued with mind which set the physical laws of motion of the universe. This, he decided, required that space be *absolute*, as God's Mind must be fixed, though he very carefully considered the alternative that all motion is relative. Newton described the laws of planetary motion as properties of space rather than of matter, as for him the planets and stars have no will to move as they wish and so are quite unlike intelligent living beings. Perhaps, in his work in alchemy, Newton looked for bridges between his laws of space in God's Mind and properties of matter. He also very carefully considered the relation between matter and light and our perceptions of colour and objects. He said in his *Opticks* (4th edition 1730), of our sensations of colour from light:

> For the Rays to speak properly are not coloured. In them there is nothing else than a certain Power and Disposition to stir up a

Sensation of this or that Colour. For as Sound in a Bell or musical String, or other sounding Body, is nothing but a trembling Motion . . . 'tis a Sense of that Motion under the Form of Sound; so Colours in the Object are nothing but their Dispositions to propagate this or that Motion into the Sensorium, and in the Sensorium there are Sensations.

Since the seventeenth century, the concepts and the study of mind have gradually separated from the more obviously successful natural sciences. Relations between mind and matter, which have never been free of controversies of theology, remain cloaked in mystery. The fact that we find mind so hard to conceive is not a unique puzzle – for on our present knowledge, matter is as odd as mind. Through most of the history of science, human perception has been regarded as direct knowledge of the external world. This was, however, a debating point for the Greeks and has been ever since. Thus Plato concluded that 'Knowledge is nothing but perception'; while Aristotle held that 'It is impossible to have scientific knowledge by perception.' Earlier, the soothsayer and poet Empedocles (c. 430 BC) applied explicit mechanical analogies to mind. He thought of light as physical particles, bridging the matter of the world with the mind of the observer. There were many physically causal accounts of light, especially Euclid's probing rays shooting out of the eyes to touch surrounding objects. Such more or less 'direct' accounts were challenged by Theophrastus (c. 372–286 BC) who criticized Empedocles for thinking of perceptions as *copies* of objects, by pointing out a logical regress which, though clear to Theophrastus and to Newton, is still sometimes ignored today. Theophrastus criticized Empedocles:

> It is strange of him [Empedocles] to imagine that he has really explained how creatures hear, when he has ascribed the process to internal sounds and assumed that the ear produces a sound within, like a bell. By means of this internal sound we might hear sounds without, but how should we hear the internal sound itself?

Only very gradually, and not always even now, has it become accepted that we perceive the world *indirectly*, via physiological mechanisms, which delay perception from outside events, and that perceptions are not like pictures or copies (such as wax moulded by seals, which was an ancient model for perception and memory), but rather that perceptions are *descriptions*: somewhat like descriptions in prose, which depend upon rich analogies and are never complete and are largely fictional. We now know that perception is like this – though it may *seem* to be a direct and effortless printing of the physical world on the 'wax' of the mind. The modern view, which grew from Empedocles' objection to perception as copies rather than descriptions, requires concepts of computing which are only now available to develop it into an effective theory that perceptions are 'brain descriptions', or particularly predictive hypotheses, based on sensory signals and stored data from the past. This account is, however, by no means complete – if only because the role of consciousness, or sensation, remains mysterious.

As with perception of external objects, we *seem* to see our own minds directly, by introspection through the window of a mental inner eye. This, however, has objections similar to the ancient sealing-wax-copy account of perception of the external world. Opinion has never stabilized on how adequate, or free from error, are either perceptions or introspections. It may be that, against appearances, introspection is as indirect as sensory perception is now known to be. In any case, introspection tells us very little about the vast complexity of our own internal mechanisms. This is now clear from the important finding that the artificial intelligence enterprise is extremely difficult to accomplish – far more must be going on to provide perception, language and intelligent behaviour than our introspections or traditional psychology ever conceived as necessary. This is why experiments, though difficult to design and carry out effectively, are essential for discovering processes of mind.

It may, indeed, be questioned whether we know ourselves at all apart from the reactions of other people to our actions, and by our actions and reactions to objects and events. If perceptions of these actions and reactions have to be interpreted, or 'read' according to knowledge and assumptions, in order to be perceived – then introspections are, like perceptions, questionable hypotheses. This could be useful, for it might allow us to change how we appear to ourselves – and so indeed *what we are* – if introspections are hypotheses. It is well known that Descartes tried to prove that his own self was not just a questionable hypothesis, with his famous phrase, 'I think, therefore I am'. But this is not in any case philosophically acceptable, as there is no clear reason why the 'I' is logically necessary, or even in practice always required for the 'thinking'. The point is, it may be possible to have thinking without an 'I'; we now have to consider this as a possibility given recent developments of artificial intelligence, in which machines might think without having a self, or a self-known 'I'.

Somewhat curiously, computing by machine is often thought of as a purely modern invention, even though the abacus is prehistoric and there were wheeled calculating machines as early as Pascal's machine of 1642 (the year Newton was born) and Charles Babbage invented programmable mechanisms in the 1830s. Strangely, these developments had little impact on the philosophy of mind until the cybernetic control systems of the 1950s and now the electronic digital computer of the past few decades. These have dramatically reinforced

Theophrastus' criticism of Empedocles by showing how mechanisms can, in their own workings, represent and make decisions and so be autonomously mind-like, or even mind-full.

It was clear to the Cambridge psychologist Kenneth Craik (see essay 17) in 1943, before the impact of digital computers, that mind may be described as 'internal models' of brain function, much as analogue computers can multiply, or give complex functions, without actually going through the steps of analytical calculating or reasoning. Later, with digital computer-based attempts to build intelligent robots, this analogue approach has been largely abandoned in favour of step-by-step processes as in explicit mathematical reasoning – even for the robot to waggle a finger, or walk or see. It turns out that the processes required are amazingly complicated and that quite simple actions, or seeing, require enormously elaborate internal computations. Is it possible that the current artificial intelligence approach has taken a wrong track? Is it possible that something more like Kenneth Craik's simple (though not so flexible or adaptable) cybernetic internal models are how we work, and how intelligent robots should be built? After all, it is odd that we have difficulty learning calculus at school with one part of our brain, if other parts are controlling our limbs and analysing sensory signals by using advanced mathematical procedures that few of us ever understand!

Let's look now in more detail at how mind has been seen, at various times, in terms of more or less science-based technologies.

MODELS OF MIND FROM TECHNOLOGIES

Although mind seems so different from matter – if only because matter occupies space and mind does not – accounts of mind have from the earliest times been based on currently familiar technology. Jonathan Miller pointed this out for physiology in general in his *The Body in Question* (1978), with examples such as that of Harvey who was able to see the heart as a pump because the right sort of pumps had by then been invented, and of Descartes's account of fluid transmission in nerves following the contemporary interest in hydraulics. We have only to consider later telephone-exchange, and now computer, models of mind to see how ubiquitous this principle is. And now we look to future technologies to suggest more adequate explanatory concepts. Such models are necessary because we cannot see processes of mind at all directly by introspection, or in any other way. Everyday explanations are in 'folk' terms, such as conscious intentions and emotions and 'moods'; but these are terms which do not take us at all far as explanations: they are, rather, the kinds of phenomena we want to explain. When Freud, and before him the German polymath Hermann von Helmholtz, spoke of 'unconscious inferences', they were widely attacked, for inferences were supposed to be essentially conscious. What is remarkable is that this notion of unconscious mind was generally criticized by philosophers and psychologists in spite of the well-known 'mental' rules of thinking formulated by Aristotle for syllogisms, and later by Boole and others for many kinds of logical processes – which are clearly mechanical and can quite easily be mechanized, as has been known for a long time. For psychologists today, labelling in terms of wishes (conscious or unconscious), or fears, or thoughts, is hardly explanatory because such labels do not suggest mechanisms for understanding normal mind, or failures of mechanisms by which abnormal phenomena of mind might be understood (Morton 1980).

It is worth pointing out in this connection that (as Freud (1900) clearly recognized), although matter occupies space, this is not simply so for *procedures* or *processes*, for where they take place may be widely distributed among the parts, and may not be *in* any of the parts of the mechanism. This allows physically based mind to be thought of as essentially spaceless, though the processes do proceed in time. And if there are mental mechanisms – mechanisms carrying out mind processes – we may still speak of ourselves as doing, for example, 'mental arithmetic' even though we are mechanisms, for on this kind of view mechanisms *carry out* the processes which are mind.

Going back to the earliest records, there is good evidence that from the beginnings of technology the use of tools has been crucially important for challenging belief in the magical powers of prehistoric gods. Thus, for the Assyrians of Babylon in the third millennium BC, the God of the Sky was challenged by the pickaxe, which was used with clear effect to hold back the floods and store water by building dams. The power of technology against the gods was recognized, for there was a special cuneiform symbol for the pickaxe, which was more prized than the wheel – to prise not only rocks, but man from the gods.

It seems that tools and mechanisms not only challenged magic but also set up explicit models for thinking and understanding. So much so, that we might almost say that *we* are artificial intelligences. Most dramatic is the recent evidence of elaborate Greek wheeled computing devices, especially for representing movements of the heavens. In spite of many contemporary references to such devices, as far back as the sixth century BC, it is only recently, with the full description by Derek de Solla Price (Price 1974) of the Antikythera mechanism (figure 31.1), that we have come to accept that Greek technology provided elaborate thinking tools, used to powerful effect at the dawn of organized philosophy. In the bronze of this ancient mechanism of 80 BC we can see and count the teeth of thirty-three gear wheels – which is sufficient to show that there must have been an elaborate infrastructure of technology and applied mathematics centuries earlier: back to the age of Aristotle and Plato, and even earlier, as there are references (Gregory 1981) to the mechanical globes of Thales in the sixth century, and to two constructed by Archimedes (287–212 BC). Cicero says of the second globe, which was in the Temple of Virtue:

> When Gallus began to give a very learned explanation of the device, I concluded that the famous Sicilian had been endowed with greater genius than one would imagine it possible for a human being to possess. For Gallus told us that the other kind of celestial globe, which was solid and contained no hollow space, was a very early invention, the first one of the kind having been constructed by Thales of Miletus, and later inscribed by Eudoxus of Cnidus (a disciple of Plato, it was claimed) with the constellations and stars which are fixed in the sky. . . . The invention of Archimedes deserves special admiration because he had thought out a way to represent accurately by a single device for turning the globe those various and divergent movements with their different rates of speed. And when Gallus moved the globe it was actually true that the moon was always many revolutions behind the sun on the bronze contrivance as would agree with the number of days it was behind it in the sky.

Even with the evidence of the Antikythera mechanism, saved from the sea, these references (there are several others) might be taken with a pinch of salt; but in any case there must have been centuries of development before the sophisticated Antikythera mechanism could have been designed and constructed – so they may be accepted as essentially true accounts of early mathematical devices, which most likely had deep effects as thinking tools, for example for Ptolemy's mechanism of epicycles in the sky for producing the observed motions of the Sun, Moon and planets. Plato describes the universe, in the *Timaeus*, as being created as an armillary sphere model of the heavens is constructed:

> He first marked off a section of the whole, and then another twice the size of the first; next a third, half as much again as the second and three times the first. . . . He then took the whole fabric and cut it down the middle into two strips, which he placed crosswise at their middle points to form the letter X; he then bent the ends round in a circle and fastened them to each other opposite the point at which the strips crossed, to make two circles, one inner and one outer. And he endowed them with uniform motion. . . . And when the whole structure of the soul had been finished to the liking of its Framer, he proceeded to fashion the whole corporeal

(a)

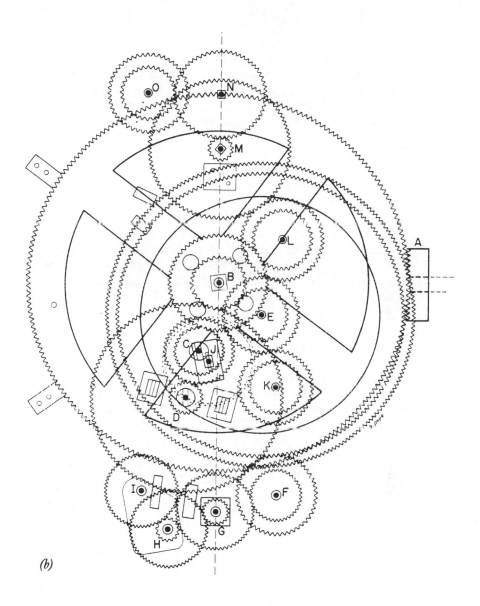

(b)

31.1 *The Greek wheeled celestial computer – the Antikythera mechanism – of 80 BC. Described by the late Derek de Solla Price, its discovery has revolutionized our ideas of Greek technology and its probable influence on early science and philosophy. (a) shows an X-ray of the bronze mass. (b) is a reconstruction of the remaining gears.*

world within it, fitting the two together centre to centre: and the soul was woven right through from the centre to the outermost heaven, which it enveloped from the outside and revolving on itself provided a divine source of unending and rational life for all time.

Plato saw the universe as an imperfect copy of an ideal design or model – much as a machine never quite behaves as it should. And Plato's distinction between the timeless reality behind appearances and the imperfections we know by the senses, may surely be the all too apparent distinction between design intention and practical performance of mechanical devices. The Ptolemaic system of the heavens of epicycles rotating upon epicycles is not only the abstract design for a machine: it is, as we now know, a machine which was not beyond the technology of the Greeks actually to make as a working model. This machine of the heavens needed a machine-minder to keep it going; but millennia later, with Newton's frictionless universe, running forever by its own inertia, the machine-minder became redundant and lost his job; so mind was exorcized from the universe. It remained, however, in *organisms* – especially in living brains, which became uniquely the ear and tongue of mind.

Greek technology contrived elaborate automata to simulate animal and human behaviour; but these failed, as thinking-tools, for gaining understanding of intelligence, and many were tricks designed to delude. Detailed designs survive, especially from the extensive writings of Heron of Alexandria (first century AD), showing that there were many kinds of mechanisms for representing animate move-ments – and also for working miracles by automated conjuring. There are complicated issues here, which are worth unravelling, though some guesswork is required. It seems clear that mechanisms were used both by the Egyptians and the Greeks, not only as useful tools for making and building things – and in various ways for controlling nature, and also of course as destructive weapons – but also as thinking tools used for clarifying ideas, and as psychological weapons for confusing and mystifying. (Even pens, mightier than the sword, seem to be two-edged.) Conjuring has a somewhat dishonourable history (see essay 10), as it was used to create spurious evidence for occult forces; but conjuring does have a surprisingly important place in the development of technology and in the use of technology for gaining understanding, as well as for deliberately misleading. Conjuring tricks are far more than mere quickness of the hand deceiving the eye: they are, rather, sequences of mechanical steps which, although they occur slowly and deliberately, the obser-ver is unable to follow. Conjuring tricks are indeed odd perceptions, as the fooled conjuree fails to follow what is happening and invents fictional processes – which may be outside conceivable mechanical principles and so appear magical. He sees not what is happening but his runaway hypotheses. At the time of the Greeks only a few people understood even simple mechanical devices; so mechanisms which would be obvious to us were seen as endowed with magical powers. But on the one hand even half-understood technology challenged magical powers – so that scientists and engineers became priests. Ancient devices included temples which, by secret mechanisms, moved of their own accord and performed rituals such as pouring libations of wine. These would have no mystery for us as we could understand their mechanical principles; but self-motivated mechanisms, which started and stopped and moved of their own accord, were beyond the understanding of all but a few, so they seemed to operate by powers of magic.

Autonomous movement was associated with a special vitalistic life force (animals were specially 'animated') essentially because there were very few ancient mechanisms capable of starting or stopping autonomously, and these were not generally familiar. There was only one convenient motor available to the Greeks: a funnel filled with sand supporting a weight which slowly sank as the sand ran through (Brumbaugh 1964). As it slowly sank, it would pull a string to work some device, such as the automata of a mechanical theatre. The Temple of Bacchus moved of its own accord with this sand-motor, changing direction and pouring a libation of wine, as though it had a mind of its own.

Perhaps Greek philosophy of mind was stuck with unnecessary mysteries, which we have inherited, of motivation and initiative and so on, as their technology was not sufficiently familiar or well formulated. As we have suggested (in essay 11, and also more fully in Gregory 1981) technology may be regarded as stored and available solutions to problems – a potential intelligence which can be tapped and used to supply instant answers. Thus, scissors are the answer to how to cut paper, or cloth – so we no longer have to think about this as a problem. We can draw upon our now vast 'potential intelligence' of solved problems by exercising usually only modest 'kinetic intelligence' for selecting and perhaps adapting what we need.

We at least seem to have purpose and intention in our intelligence; but this is not so for the incredible intelligence (there seems no other term!) of organic evolution by natural selection. For the processes of evolution provide problem-solving *par excellence* – as they have created even *us* by selections from trial and error experiments – although evolution lacks intention, conscience or consciousness. It is an interesting question how close these blind processes are to our intelligence, or to the methods of science.

The question now is whether our new technologies – especially of information processing and computing – can provide models for mind, somewhat as millennia ago mechanical tools and toys provided models for understanding the physical world. Does computer science hold similar keys for mind? It seems to promise a language and concepts for suggesting and testing theories of mind. Less certain is whether we can *create* minds – any more than the Greeks could *create* a universe with their wheeled machines for simulating hidden processes of the heavens. If we succeed we will see ourselves in new ways – by sharing the intelligent machine's even odder perceptions.

REFERENCES

Blacker, C. and Loewe, M. (eds) (1975) *Ancient Cosmologies*, London, Allen & Unwin.

Brumbaugh, R.S. (1964) *Ancient Greek Gadgets and Machines*, New York, Greenwood.

Cohen, M.R. and Drabkin, I.E. (1958) *A Source Book in Greek Science*, Cambridge, Mass., Harvard University Press.

Freud, S. (1900) *Interpretation of Dreams*, trans. James Strachey (1979), Harmondsworth, Penguin.

Gombrich, R. (1975) 'Ancient Indian cosmology', in C. Blacker and M. Loewe (eds), *Ancient Cosmologies*, London, Allen & Unwin.

Gregory, R.L. (1981) *Mind in Science*, London, Weidenfeld & Nicolson.

Miller, J. (1978) *The Body in Question*, London, BBC Publications.

Morton, Adam (1980) *Frames of Mind*, Oxford, Clarendon.

Plato, *Timaeus*, trans. Desmond Lee (1965) Harmondsworth, Penguin.

Price, Derek de Solla (1974) *Gears from the Greeks: The Antikythera Mechanism. A Calendar Computer from Ca. 80 BC*, New York, N. Watson.

Westfall, R.S. (1971) *Force in Newton's Physics*, London, Macdonald.

POST-SCRIPT

These essays have dealt mainly with questions, with occasional tentative answers or at least suggestions as to where answers might be found. I do not apologize for this emphasis as I think one can live happily with questions, which are alive with promise; while however useful or beautiful answers may be, they are fossils of past questioning and discovery. It surprises me how few question marks there are in textbooks – often none at all. And answers can be overplayed, for they rule out alternatives. When accepted as beliefs, answers shut off possibilities of new understanding, and in any case many accepted answers are just plain wrong and sometimes seriously misleading.

Just look at question marks – ? ? ? ? ? – and exclamation marks – ! ! ! ! !: they suggest an ideogram logo. Question marks are *hooks*, that catch and pull in facts and ideas. Exclamation marks, we may imagine, are straightened-out question marks – to become *weapons*, for defence or attack. For attack, they are pointing spears – especially for killing contradictory facts and new ideas. For defence, they are set up as railings – palisades – to protect beliefs. Fortunately, defensive palisades do not last forever; they get pulled down by searching question-mark hooks, or in time they crumble away, with bore-holes of boredom. But we do need at least tentative answers if only to make doubting and questioning effective. Then the exclamation-mark attacking spears can give point and direction to the searching question-mark hooks – which may reach to the stars, or approach the centre of mind.

We are absurdly small compared to the stars, and our lives may seem too short even to justify mention in the life of the universe. But whatever the answers may be, surely we can only gain dignity by questioning – as widely and deeply as possible, though with some trepidation as the spears and hooks can hurt. So, protective exclamation-mark palisades are sometimes justified, for questioning can destroy peace of mind and can maim or kill part-formed ideas. Thus, over-enthusiastic questioning can damage students at crucial stages of their thinking, when a novel idea cannot yet be justified, without further thought or evidence. Students have neither adequate defences nor powers of counter-attack, so their aim may be too easily deflected by questions, occasionally to falter and fail in what they might have gone on to do. Questions are powerful, and they can destroy, but in time most of us learn to build effective palisades to protect our part-formed thoughts from too dangerous attack. We learn to deploy spears both as offensive weapons, so that our position may not be too closely examined before we have got round to repairing inadequacies, and ranged as defensive palisades. But as we can only see ourselves from the inside we should welcome searching hooks and probing spear-thrusts – provided they are not lethal.

Some of the most important ideas in science might not have flowered had they been questioned *too* closely. For example, we now see a fatal logical weakness in the third definition in Newton's *Principia*:

> *The* vis insita, *or innate force of matter, is a power of resisting, by which every body . . . continues in its present state, whether it be of rest, or of moving uniformly forwards in a right line.*

The weakness is that rest and moving at constant speed in a straight line are not defined to prevent circular tautology. So, possibly Newton would have been perturbed from his course, and the *Principia* never written, if he had been too-much challenged, or had himself questioned his axiom as closely as it has been questioned since.

Consider a swinging pendulum (as we did in essay 16) – the simplest repeating motion in all nature. A school experiment compares what happens when the *length* of the string or the *weight* of the bob are changed. The shorter the string, the faster the pendulum swings. But if the bob is made heavier, or lighter, there is *no* change in the rate of swing. This is remarkable because a heavier bob is attracted more strongly to the centre of the Earth, and so it should swing faster. It does swing faster in a stronger gravitational field, and slower in a weaker gravity, as on a mountain or on the Moon. Indeed, if the bob is a magnet, attracted to a long strip magnet, or an iron plate beneath it, the pendulum swings faster in a fixed place on Earth. And a repelling magnet slows it, as though it is on the Moon – so one can do a kind of space-travelling with pendulums. But as a pendulum swings faster with stronger gravitational (or magnetic) pull, why doesn't a *heavier* bob swing faster than a light bob? The reason is that the increased *inertia* of the heavier bob, requiring more force to accelerate it, *exactly* counters the increased gravitational attraction. This means that inertia and gravity are exactly related. For Newton this exact relationship was a total mystery, for it was too much of a coincidence and yet there was no visible link. This was a question leading Einstein to suppose that inertia and gravity are ultimately the same. But to say this he had to re-describe and re-see the universe, and persuade his fellow physicists to follow him, which they did. So much hangs on a pendulum.

We have to be moved by questions to see the universe as it is now described by physics; for the universe looks very odd. It is odd because so much of it lies outside our experience. But given the questions, by playing with pendulums and other quite simple toys and phenomena, we may recapture our original perceptual learning, to open our eyes and understanding to new worlds. This is the hope of 'hands-on' – exploratory science.

The classical example of questioning is René Descartes's doubting everything until he came to himself. When he decided that 'I think, therefore I am' he stopped questioning, to go on to look for answers. But if Descartes had not stopped at that point but had questioned the logical validity of 'I think, therefore I am' more closely, he would have failed to find his starting-point. Then he would have been stuck in futile solipsism. Similarly, perhaps, if a physicist spent his time asking: 'What is matter?', or a psychologist: 'What is mind', they would not get anywhere. Indeed, the refusal of the behaviourists to consider consciousness had just this motive, though of course it may have been misplaced. There is a strategy problem here, for while it is often necessary to suspend questioning to get on with answer-seeking, it is always possible that the next question would have hooked an important new possibility.

With new techniques for observing and testing, questions that were rejected as meaningless – through being beyond conceivable verification, or test of truth or falsity – can, even after thousands of years, suddenly become meaningful. So what was rejected as metaphysical nonsense may become the next great discovery. This is possible in all the developing sciences, which makes one wonder where the ultimate limits of philosophical questioning and scientific discovery lie – for new technologies not only suggest new possibilities but may imbue meaning and fresh life into old dead questions.

Rather to my surprise, several of these essays touch on matters that are on the edge of or outside science: especially the *spookiness* of what goes on every day of our lives in our brains. Even odder are the claims of ESP, which we have glanced at here. Is ESP too odd to be true? Whatever the answer, this should be asked quite apart from belief or expectation either way, for it makes us question the limits of questioning. In science, limits to questioning are set by the expectation of finding answers. This may even *define* science. But, as the range of abilities to find answers keeps expanding, as new tools for discovery become available, there seem to be no absolute criteria for what is sense or nonsense – and so for what is or is not acceptable for science.

There is an advantage in writing essays over producing scientific papers: one can explore a little beyond the known without (one hopes) being written off as too fanciful or irresponsible. Having written these essays, I see there may now be a temptation towards autobiography; perhaps to show that as I can still think, I still am. This should probably be resisted, however, as it might become a tedium of anecdotes as I approach anecdotage; for the best one can hope is to become an acceptably interesting museum of oneself.

INDEX